A Narrative of The Mysterious and Dreadful Murder of Mr. W. Weare, Containing The Examination Before The Magistrates The Coroner's Inquest, The Confession of Hunt, and Other Particulars Previous to The Trial, Collected From The Best Sources of...

Anonymous

A Narrative of The Mysterious and Dreadful Murder of Mr. W. Weare, Containing The Examination Before The Magistrates The Coroner's Inquest, The Confession of Hunt, and Other Particulars Previous to The Trial, Collected From The Best Sources of Intelligenc
A narrative of the mysterious and dreadful murder of Mr. W. Weare, contaning the examination before the magistrates
HAR06223
Monograph
Harvard Law School Library
London: Printed and Published by W. Glindon, 51, Rupert Street, Haymarket; and Sold by T. Mason, 2, Great Russell Street, Bloomsbury; T. Mason, jun. 120, High Holborn, Corner of King Street; Hughes, Ludgate Hill, Corner of Stationers' Court; J. Templ

The Making of Modern Law collection of legal archives constitutes a genuine revolution in historical legal research because it opens up a wealth of rare and previously inaccessible sources in legal, constitutional, administrative, political, cultural, intellectual, and social history. This unique collection consists of three extensive archives that provide insight into more than 300 years of American and British history. These collections include:

Legal Treatises, 1800-1926: over 20,000 legal treatises provide a comprehensive collection in legal history, business and economics, politics and government.

Trials, 1600-1926: nearly 10,000 titles reveal the drama of famous, infamous, and obscure courtroom cases in America and the British Empire across three centuries.

Primary Sources, 1620-1926: includes reports, statutes and regulations in American history, including early state codes, municipal ordinances, constitutional conventions and compilations, and law dictionaries.

These archives provide a unique research tool for tracking the development of our modern legal system and how it has affected our culture, government, business – nearly every aspect of our everyday life. For the first time, these high-quality digital scans of original works are available via print-on-demand, making them readily accessible to libraries, students, independent scholars, and readers of all ages.

The BiblioLife Network

This project was made possible in part by the BiblioLife Network (BLN), a project aimed at addressing some of the huge challenges facing book preservationists around the world. The BLN includes libraries, library networks, archives, subject matter experts, online communities and library service providers. We believe every book ever published should be available as a high-quality print reproduction; printed on-demand anywhere in the world. This insures the ongoing accessibility of the content and helps generate sustainable revenue for the libraries and organizations that work to preserve these important materials.

The following book is in the "public domain" and represents an authentic reproduction of the text as printed by the original publisher. While we have attempted to accurately maintain the integrity of the original work, there are sometimes problems with the original work or the micro-film from which the books were digitized. This can result in minor errors in reproduction. Possible imperfections include missing and blurred pages, poor pictures, markings and other reproduction issues beyond our control. Because this work is culturally important, we have made it available as part of our commitment to protecting, preserving, and promoting the world's literature.

GUIDE TO FOLD-OUTS MAPS and OVERSIZED IMAGES

The book you are reading was digitized from microfilm captured over the past thirty to forty years. Years after the creation of the original microfilm, the book was converted to digital files and made available in an online database.

In an online database, page images do not need to conform to the size restrictions found in a printed book. When converting these images back into a printed bound book, the page sizes are standardized in ways that maintain the detail of the original. For large images, such as fold-out maps, the original page image is split into two or more pages

Guidelines used to determine how to split the page image follows:

- Some images are split vertically; large images require vertical and horizontal splits.
- For horizontal splits, the content is split left to right.
- For vertical splits, the content is split from top to bottom.
- For both vertical and horizontal splits, the image is processed from top left to bottom right.

Thurtell, Hunt and Probert at Supper in the Parlour of Gills Hill Cottage

A NARRATIVE

Of the Mysterious and

DREADFUL MURDER

OF

Mr. W. WEARE,

CONTAINING

THE EXAMINATION BEFORE THE MAGISTRATES

The Coroner's Inquest,

THE CONFESSION OF HUNT,

And other Particulars previous to the Trial,

COLLECTED FROM THE BEST SOURCES OF INTELLIGENCE,

WITH

ANECDOTES

OF

Weare, Thurtell, Hunt, Probert, and Others;

AND A FULL REPORT OF

THE TRIAL,

AND

SUBSEQUENT EXECUTION AT HERTFORD

Illustrated by Engravings.

"We have stretched the fiery Boaster in his Grave"
IRENE.

LONDON.

Printed and published by W. GLINDON, 51, Rupert Street, Haymarket, and sold by T MASON, 2, Great Russell Street, Bloomsbury, T MASON, jun 120, High Holborn, Corner of King Street, HUGHES, Ludgate Hill, Corner of Stationers' Court, J TEMPLEMAN, 39, Tottenham Court Road, and by all Booksellers in Town or Country.

Price 3s.

AN ACCOUNT
OF THE
MURDER
OF
MR. WEARE.

THE Murder recently committed in the neighbourhood of Watford, for cold-blooded villainy in the mode of its conception and planning, and in the cool ferocity of its perpetration, has seldom been equalled in the stained annals of human depravity. It almost stands alone in the criminal records of the country.

The whole county of Herts, and, indeed, every other county, has been for weeks past in a state of agitation on this subject; and nothing can have exceeded the anxiety evinced by all classes for the discovery of the guilty participators in the blackest crime that can stain the earth. The truth is now happily brought to light, and it affords us another striking proof that

> "——— Murder, though it hath no tongue,
> Will speak with most miraculous organ."

We approach the subject with a sensation of horror—our readers, we are sure, will soon participate with us in that feeling.

On Friday night, October the 24th, 1823, a Mr. Philip Smith, an inhabitant of Aldenham, was going from the house of a Mr. Nicholls, at Batler's Green, to his own residence in Kemp's Row, Aldenham, when he heard the report of a gun or pistol. In a minute or two afterwards he heard great groaning, apparently proceeding from the same spot, which continued for three or four minutes. He was with his wife at the time. She was in a donkey-chaise, and he was walking behind. He would have gone to the spot, but was afraid to quit his wife, who was dreadfully agitated. The noises proceeded from a lane leading from Batler's Green to the road running from Highcross to Radlet.

The same night, a man named Freeman, who was on his way to meet his wife, saw a gig, in which were two men driving towards the lane, at a very rapid pace, the horse seemingly much out of wind. He accosted them, observing that they were driving hard, to which one of them made a slight answer, which Freeman could not distinctly hear. The gig stopped just as Freeman entered the lane.

On the following morning, before it was quite daylight, two labourers, named John Hetherington and William Hunt, went to work in the lane spoken of, called Gill's Hill Lane, and while there, two men came sauntering along, and when they had passed the labourers a short distance, they stooped down, as if searching for something in the hedge. That same morning, about eight o'clock, Hetherington found a pistol and penknife by the side of the bank, the former of which was covered with blood and bits of hair on the outside, and within the barrel were several small particles, which on being shown to a medical gentleman of the name of Pidcock, at Watford, were declared by him to be a portion of the brains of a human being.

The whole of the above circumstances being communicated to the Magistrates residing at Watford, Robert Clutterbuck and John Finch Mason, Esquires, they immediately commenced an active inquiry, and, in order to have the best assistance, they wrote to Bow Street, and Ruthven, one of the principal officers, with Upson, a very active constable of the establishment, were sent down. This was on Tuesday evening, the 28th of October, and before twelve o'clock at night, with the assistance of the local constables, two men named Probert and Thomas Thurtell, were taken into custody, and committed for further examination to the Castle of St. Albans. Or rather, in justice to an active officer, we should state, that Charles Forster, of Berkhampstead, was the person who apprehended Thomas Thurtell and Probert, and not Ruthven, as erroneously stated in the papers.

Very early in the morning of Wednesday, Ruthven and Upson apprehended two men — the one named John Thurtell (brother to Thomas Thurtell), and the other Joseph Hunt — the former at the Coach and Horses, in Conduit Street, Bond Street, and the latter, at his own lodgings, No 19, King Street, Golden Square.

In the room occupied by Thurtell, Ruthven found a pistol of large dimensions, and in Thurtell's pocket another smaller one, seemingly almost new; he also found some clothes belonging to him, the sleeves and body of which were much stained, indeed in some parts, literally soaked in blood; his hat also had some marks of the same kind, and his hands, Ruthven perceived, were much cut and bruised all over. Nothing material was found at Hunt's lodgings.

The two prisoners, after being shortly examined at Bow Street, were conveyed, on Wednesday, in separate chaises, to Watford, where they arrived between five and six o'clock in the afternoon.

The Magistrates, meanwhile, had been most actively engaged in procuring evidence, and by ten o'clock on Wednesday night were prepared with a mass of testimony of a very strong nature. Probert and Thomas Thurtell were not brought from St. Albans. The other two prisoners were kept strictly watched, in separate rooms, at the Essex Arms Inn, where the investigation before the Magistrates commenced at half past ten o'clock at night. The prisoners were not brought into the room, it being thought best to keep them ignorant of the entire evidence against them, at least for a short time.

ELIZABETH FREEMAN was called, and being sworn, said, that on Friday night, the 24th of October, a little before eight o'clock, she saw two men in a gig in Gill's Hill Lane

JOHN HETHERINGTON, labourer, sworn. This witness stated, that he was at work with William Hunt, in Gill's Hill Lane, about six o'clock on the morning of Saturday last, October 25th, when two men, one of whom was tall, and wore a white hat, and the other a shorter person, with large black whiskers, passed them. When they had proceeded about ten poles they stooped down, and appeared to be "grappling," in the hedge, as if looking for something that they had lost. In about five minutes they went further up, and turned back, and as they passed again, one of them told Hunt he was capsized there in his gig, the night before. Hunt asked the man in the white hat if he hurt himself, and he replied " but little." On being asked if the horse was hurt, or the gig damaged, the tall man said, " No, the gig did not go over, nor the horse fall." The same morning, witness found a penknife on the spot where the men had been looking, and shortly afterwards, on the same spot, he found the pistol marked with blood, &c. At twelve o'clock the same day, the same two men, very neatly dressed, and both having black hats on, came again down the lane in a gig. "They looked hard' at the spot where the pistol and knife had been found. About half an hour afterwards, Mr Probert, who occupies Gill's Hill Cottage, came down the lane alone, and asked some questions. [The witness related the conversation, which, however, did not bear upon the case.]

WILLIAM HUNT was sworn, and corroborated the testimony of his partner, adding that the man in the white hat said, " This lane is a very nasty dark place, as dark as the grave—I was coming up here last evening, and was capsized out of my gig." Witness asked him if he had hurt himself? and he said, " No, but he had lost a silk handkerchief and a pen-knife, which he had since found." Witness asked him if he had hurt himself or horse, or if the gig was broken? and he said, " No, it never fell." Witness said it was a queer thing that he should be capsized out of his gig without its falling. The men went away without answering.

SUSAN ANN WOODROFFE, (servant to Mr Probert, at Gill's Hill Cottage,) stated, that her master came home about nine o'clock on Friday evening last, the 24th October, with two gentlemen. The same two left the house at ten o'clock on Saturday morning. They went out that morning about six o'clock, and returned in about half an hour. The two gentlemen did not go to bed on Friday night, neither of them came through the kitchen that night.

A gardener in the employment of Probert, proved that he saw the two men go out together towards Gill's Hill Lane on Saturday morning.

JAMES HADDIS, aged 13, was sworn, and deposed as follows. Had lived with Mr. Probert seven months, and looked after his horse and gig. Last Friday about ten o'clock at night, Mr. John Thurtell came to his master's house in a gig alone. It was a dark grey horse, and a dark green and black gig; the horse's head was leading from Batler's Green when he drove into the yard; he had a great coat on of a light colour; his outside clothes did not appear to be dirty. In half an hour Mr Probert came in with another man; their gig came in the direction from Radlet, he saw Mr. J. Thurtell's inside clothes and boots on the following morning, and they were covered with dirt—they were "nothing but dirt." On his great coat were spots of blood, " middling-sized drops." The gentleman with Thurtell had large black whiskers; he saw the other gentleman rubbing Thurtell's coat with a wet sponge; this was on Saturday morning. Saw no blood on that gentleman's coat. The gig in which Mr Thurtell came appeared very heavy, as if it had luggage in it. Thurtell never said any thing to him about an accident; Thurtell was wiping himself on Friday night with a sponge in the stable. On Sunday, as witness was coming from Mr. Nicholls's, he saw several " lumps" of blood on the dirt heaps, and two holes in the hedge in Gill's

Hill Lane. Thurtell brought a sponge with him. There was a bag in his gig, with a brass padlock, which the two persons took away with them on Saturday morning; they came again on Sunday, and witness went up to London with them and his master on Monday. He was taken to the Coach and Horses in Conduit Street, Bond Street, and left there by Mr Probert, who was to return in two hours, but did not come back at all. The grey horse and gig appeared to be hired.

The Prisoner, JOSEPH HUNT,

was then called in, and Mr NOEL, who attended as solicitor for the prosecution, told him that the Magistrates and he would feel it their duty to put some questions to him, but it was fit he should be warned that he was not bound to answer a single one unless he chose, and above all, he was not at all bound to say any thing likely to criminate himself. With this warning he of course would exercise his own judgment.

The prisoner then underwent a very long interrogation, and made the following Confession, which we give very nearly in his own words. This should be compared with his Confession before the Coroner's Inquest, given in page 38.

" One night that I was at Rexworthy's billiard-rooms, John Thurtell told me he wished to see a Mr Weare, and on entering the house, we saw Mr Weare sitting there. After some conversation between Rexworthy and John Thurtell, the latter called Mr Weare out of the room, and they were absent for about twenty minutes. I was, at that time, in conversation with Mr. Green and Mr. Rexworthy about a billiard table. During that conversation, Thurtell and Mr Weare returned, and I and Thurtell went away.

" As we were on our way up the Haymarket to the Cock, Thurtell told me that Mr. Weare had behaved extremely ill to him, for he with another man of the name of Lemon, had won 300*l* of him (Thurtell) at *blind hookey*. When he discovered that he had been robbed of his money by false cards, he challenged Mr Weare with foul play, and Weare's reply was, ' You dare not say a word about it, for you know you have defrauded your creditors of that money.' John Thurtell then observed to me that sooner or later he would be revenged. At one time in particular, he (John Thurtell) was in difficulty, and applied to Mr Weare for the loan of 5*l*. and Mr Weare's reply was, ' Go and rob for it as I do.'

" On Thursday night, which was the night before the murder took place, John Thurtell asked me to call on him on Friday morning, which I did. Said he, 'Hunt, I wish you would take a walk with me.' We walked together as far as High Street, Marylebone. When we got into High Street, we stopped at a pawnbroker's shop. After looking at some jewellery which was in the window, John Thurtell observed that those pistols (here the examinant looked at and pointed to the pair already mentioned, which were on the table marked, 'Hill,' I believe) were just the things he wanted to shoot cats with. They were marked 1*l.* 17*s.* 6*d.* and he gave 1*l.* 5*s* for them.

"We then returned to Mr Tetsall's, the Coach and Horses, in Conduit Street, and dined. After dinner, John Thurtell asked me to get him a horse and chaise immediately, as he had to meet a gentleman who was going into the country with him, on a shooting excursion. He gave me 1*l.* 10*s* to get the horse and chaise, for which I paid 1*l.* 5*s.* He desired me not to say where the horse and chaise were going. Mr Probatt, the proprietor of the horse and chaise, supposed it was going to Dartford; but it came down into Hertfordshire.

"As soon as the horse and chaise came to the door, which was at a quarter before five o'clock, John Thurtell told Mr Probert, of Gill's Hill, who was present, that in consequence of warrants being issued against him and his brother for a conspiracy to defraud the County Fire Office of 1,900*l.* he should go to his (Mr. Probert's) cottage for safety. Mr. Probert said, 'Well if that's the case, you may as well wait, and we will go together.' John Thurtell said, 'No, I can't stop, I have a gentleman to meet at Cumberland Gate,' and he immediately drove off, taking with him a great coat which he borrowed of his brother Tom. I did not see him put these pistols into his pocket when he started, but to the best of my knowledge they were about his person.

"After three quarters of an hour had elapsed, Mr. Probert of Gill's Hill Cottage, said, he did not want to travel by himself, and would be glad if I would take a seat with him in his gig, and spend a pleasant evening or two. I accepted Mr. Probert's offer. (Here the examinant described several houses at which he said they stopped and drank.) We arrived at Mr Probert's cottage, when John Thurtell came up and said, 'I have settled that b——, who robbed me of 300*l.*' Probert said, 'Who d'ye mean? What d'ye mean?' 'Why,' said John Thurtell, 'I mean to say, that I have blown his brains out, and he *lays* behind a hedge in the lane.' 'Nonsense, nonsense,' said Probert, 'you have never been guilty of a thing of that kind, John Thurtell, if you have, and near my cottage, my character and family are ruined for ever, but I cannot believe that you have been guilty of so rash an act—'here, Hunt, (to examinant) take in the loin of pork, and desire the cook to dress it immediately.' I went into the kitchen, and waited until Probert came in, which, to the best of my knowledge, was after a lapse of five minutes.

"Before we went into the parlour, I said to John Thurtell, 'You are jesting about killing a man to-night?' 'Ay, but I have,' was his reply, 'and no one else but Weare, that robbed me of my 300*l.*' Mr. Probert said, 'John you have produced such an effect on me, that unless we retire, and get some refreshment, my senses will totally leave me.' We then had a glass of brandy."

Here he described the supper which was served up, and said that John Thurtell complained of being sick, and could not eat.

"After supper, Thurtell called me and Mr. Probert out, and produced a very handsome gold watch, with a gold face, saying, 'What do you think of it now? This is something towards the 300*l* I was robbed of, and if you will go with me, I will show you where he *lays* stiff enough.' Mr. Probert and myself both declined, observing, that we would not witness such a sight for the world. Thurtell said—'You will not see him, for he is in a sack.' I and Mr Probert declined going near the spot.

"About one o'clock in the morning, Mr. Probert called me out, saying, 'Do you think Thurtell has been guilty of this murder?' My reply was—'It looks very suspicious, his having the gold watch, and in consequence of which, I would rather decline going to bed, and, if it was agreeable to him, I would sit up in the parlour with him, through the night.'

"About three o'clock in the morning, John Thurtell said—'Come, and look at him he is a b——y rogue, and I have had my revenge!' We both declined going near the spot, and walked about the garden till four o'clock. John Thurtell said, 'If you decline going to fetch him, I will go myself,' and in about ten minutes he left me and Mr Probert, for the purpose, as we supposed, to fetch the dead man, William Weare.

"While he was gone, Mr Probert said to me, 'Good God, Hunt! what shall I do if this account of Thurtell's be true?' [Examinant detailed some further conversation]

During the conversation, Thurtell returned, saying, 'He is so heavy, I cannot carry him; and if you will not assist me in moving him from behind the hedge, I shall put a bridle upon my horse and throw him across his back,' and he accordingly took out his horse with a bridle on. Mr Probert said he hoped he would not bring a dead man near his premises; 'What b———y stuff you talk,' said John Thurtell. 'I shall bring him and chuck him into your fish-pond."*

"While he was gone with the horse, I and Probert went into the parlour. Probert was much agitated, and as for myself, I had not a nerve but what was in a state of convulsion. As near as I can recollect, about a quarter or half-past five o'clock in the morning, Thurtell came into the parlour, and said, 'I have thrown him into the fish-pond.' 'Then, by G—,' said Probert, 'I insist upon your getting him immediately off my premises.' Mr. Probert and myself went to the fish-pond, where we saw the feet of a man upwards in the water. Thurtell fetched a line, which he threw across the feet, so as to sink them, at the same time saying, 'Probert, don't you be alarmed, for I would not have you get into trouble, knowing that you are a man that has a family. Let him remain here till night, and then I will get him safe away.'

"On Monday night Thomas Thurtell asked me to go to Mr Probert's, and inform him of the disappointment respecting the bail. John Thurtell said, 'If you are going down, I'll go with you, and take that man away from Probert's premises.' I said, 'If you are going upon that business, don't think I shall aid or assist you.' His reply was, 'I want no assistance; I can do it myself easy enough.'

"When we arrived at Probert's, Thurtell appeared greatly agitated. When we had been there some time, Probert and Thurtell went out, and in ten minutes Probert returned by himself. In half an hour, Thurtell came in, and asked us to put the horse in his gig, and take it round to the gate. We did so, and Thurtell brought upon his shoulder a corpse, (a male corpse,) one part in a sack, and the feet hanging out. He asked Probert to lend him a hand to put the corpse into the gig, but he refused. He then asked me, but I declined.

---

* The compunctions of Macbeth were different from those of Thurtell

" ——— I'll go no more;
I am afraid to think what I have done
Look on't again I dare not."

"He then put the corpse in the chaise himself, and tied the feet to the dashing iron. He then said there was plenty of room for me in the gig, besides him and the corpse. I declined having any thing to do with it, and said I would walk on, and he might overtake me. I walked on two miles, when Thurtell overtook me, and told me he had disposed of the corpse in a small muddy marsh about four feet deep. From thence we made the best of our way to town. And now, gentlemen, I believe you have it as clear as if you had been present yourselves."

JOHN THURTELL was next called, and received a similar caution; he underwent a long interrogation. When it had nearly closed, he was asked if he ever carried pistols, and he said he never did; being pressed, he said he found a small pistol on a bank near Probert's house, on Sunday morning last, which Ruthven found upon him when he was apprehended. Ruthven produced the pistol.

Mr. NOEL said he had already cautioned the prisoner as to his answering questions, and he was now about to put to him some of a very important nature. "Do you," said Mr. N. suddenly, "Do you know Mr. Weare?"

PRISONER (firmly)—I do.

Do you know where he is?—I do not.

When did you see him last?—On Tuesday last week was the last time.

Did you see him last Friday?—No, I did not. I did not meet him by accident on Friday, in the Edgeware Road.

Mr. NOEL.—Now, Mr. Thurtell, you have said you found this pistol near Probert's, what would you say when I tell you I can produce the fellow to it, found within a few yards of the same spot?—I know nothing about that.

The pistol, with the blood and hair still adhering to it, was then closely exposed to the view of the prisoner, from the paper in which it was wrapped, and his countenance and manner underwent a change too visible to escape the notice of the most careless observer. His complexion naturally sallow, assumed a deadly paleness, and he appeared to shudder and shrink backwards at the sight of the weapon; the state of which, however, it should be added, was such as might produce a strong effect even upon a perfectly innocent man.

The pistols were then compared. They were of the same size, each had "Hill, London," engraved on it, and they were numbered 2 and 3. In the make, ornament, and every part, they exactly resembled each other.

Mr. NOEL—I can tell you, Thurtell, Mr. Weare is not to be found.

THURTELL—I am sorry for it, but I know nothing about him

The prisoner was removed, and the labourer, HETHERINGTON, who had been in the room during Thurtell's examination, swore positively, that he was the man who wore the white hat, and who spoke to him on Saturday morning

WILLIAM REXWORTHY, (of 4, Spring Gardens, billiard-room keeper,) being sworn, stated, that on Thursday last he saw John Thurtell and Mr. Weare, of Lyon's Inn, at his house together. Mr. Weare said that he was going out of town with Thurtell the next day, for a few days shooting in Hertfordshire. On the following day Mr Weare called upon witness, about three o'clock in the afternoon, and said he was on his way to join John Thurtell, in the Edgware Road.

THURTELL was recalled, and persisted in saying that he had never seen Weare since Tuesday, or Wednesday at the latest.

HUNT was recalled, and, after some questions, was shewn the two pistols.

Mr NOEL, after acquainting him with the manner in which they were found, addressed him at some length, and desired him to retire.

In a few minutes he sent for Mr Noel, and shortly after, he was again conducted before the Magistrates, and made a very long statement to the following effect —

"He said he was a dealer and professional singer He knew Mr. Probert extremely well, but never was at his cottage in Hertfordshire until Friday evening last. He received an invitation on that day from Probert, to dine with him and John Thurtell, at the Coach and Horses in Conduit Street. After dinner Probert said to him (Hunt), 'Hunt, I have often spoke to my wife of your singing, and I should like for you to go down with me for a day or two to my cottage.' In consequence of that invitation, he agreed to accompany Mr. Probert out of town, and they went away together in the evening in a gig.

"In Oxford Street he (Hunt) purchased a loin of pork, which was to be cooked for supper. They stopped at several houses on the road, and drank brandy and water; and when they arrived at Probert's cottage, they drove into the yard, and found John Thurtell and a lad in the stable.

"Probert went into the stable, telling him (Hunt) to take

the pork into the kitchen, and get it cooked. He was quite sure he went into the kitchen, and got the pork cut into chops. In five minutes Probert and Thurtell followed, and they went into the parlour, where they found Mrs. Probert and Miss Noyes, her sister.

"John Thurtell started in a gig from Conduit Street, about a quarter of an hour before Probert and him (Hunt). No reason was given for their not starting together. He supposed they sat up about two hours after supper, singing several songs. They then all went to their repose. He did not go to bed, but slept on a sofa. He believed John Thurtell did not go to bed either, but remained in the room with him.

"It might have been about ten o'clock when they arrived at Probert's cottage. There was nothing said about disappointment at the absence of a guest, who was expected. There was no one waiting in Gill's Hill Lane for him and Probert when they arrived. John Thurtell laid down on chairs. The supper party consisted of him (Hunt), John Thurtell, Mr. and Mrs. Probert, and Miss Noyes. Thomas Thurtell was not there at all on Friday night.

"He (Hunt) got up at seven o'clock on Saturday morning. He never went out on Friday evening after he arrived at Probert's. Not one of the party went out during the evening. There were no boots or shoes brushed on Saturday morning. He was quite certain he never used a sponge for any thing on Saturday morning.

"John Thurtell had a large blue coat on that night, and Probert had a drab. He (Hunt) went out at seven o'clock on Saturday morning with Probert. They went through a field, and broke into a lane. They went over a hedge into the lane. Did not meet a 'solitary soul' in their walk. John Thurtell was with them. They never separated in their walk. He never heard of any accident to either of the Thurtells. Did hear John Thurtell say, he had scratched his hands getting through some briars. He showed him his hands after breakfast, and made that remark."

When he had finished this account, it was past nine o'clock on Friday morning, the investigation having continued without intermission throughout the night. He concluded by offering to conduct the proper persons to the spot where the body of Mr Weare would be found.

At this period a gentleman who had attended, and taken

notes of the whole proceedings for the London journals, was about to quit the room to make arrangements for following the parties in search of the body, when he was called back, and informed by Mr CLUTTERBUCK, the senior Magistrate, that he was perfectly at liberty to publish the whole of the proceedings, with the exception of "the confession," and that, the Magistrates desired, should not be published, as they considered such a publication would be exceedingly improper

The Reporter said, he was extremely sorry to be under the necessity of stating, that he must refuse a compliance with the mandate just issued from the Magistrates

Mr CLUTTERBUCK said, the confession, if published, would prejudice the persons accused before trial, and it must not be published

The Reporter said, he was unwilling to prejudice any man, especially one labouring under so heavy an accusation as the present, and if he thought that the publication of this "confession" would operate to the injury of persons accused, he certainly should lament it exceedingly; but he had a duty to perform, and must endeavour to execute it to the best of his judgment and ability. He had attended for the purpose of reporting the whole of the proceedings, and he felt himself bound to do so

Mr NOEL said, that the Magistrates had prohibited the publication of "the confession," and the Reporter, if he persisted in his determination, would be acting "in contempt of the Court of King's Bench." It had been decided long ago, and over and over again, that Magistrates had the power to order a Reporter to quit the place in which the examination was held; and if he suffered one to remain, he had the power to prohibit the publication of any part of the proceedings, if he chose

The Reporter was about to offer a remark, when Mr Noel said the Magistrate would do right in preventing him (the Reporter) from leaving the room with the notes which he had been taking of the proceedings

Mr CLUTTERBUCK said, he would cut the matter very short. The Magistrates had thought fit to prohibit the publication of this "confession," and it should not be published. He required the Reporter to give up his note book before he quitted the room

The Reporter said, that a compliance with such an order was perfectly out of the question.

Mr CLUTTERBUCK.—Then I shall order a constable to take it

The Reporter said, he should not give it up, and Mr. Clutterbuck looking towards a constable, and held up his hand, of course intending to put his threat into execution The Reporter not choosing to undergo a search by a police officer, took his note book from his pocket, and placing it on the table, begged it to be distinctly understood, that in giving it up he did so under coercion, and that he yielded only to what he must deem to be absolute force.

The note-book was then sealed, and when the proceedings of the day had terminated, it was sent to a newspaper office in London.

Mr NOEL stated subsequently, that the publication of " the confession" would obstruct the due course of justice, and prevent important discoveries.

The Magistrates immediately requested Mr Noel, Ruthven, and a number of officers, to attend Hunt to the pond, where, as he had stated, the corpse was concealed.—Hunt went in a post-chaise, accompanied by Ruthven, and on arriving near a pond, which is on the side of a lane leading from Radlet to Battledore (or Batler's) Green, in the parish of Aldenham, Hunt put his hand out of the chaise, and said, "That is the place"

A drag was provided by Mr. Field, the landlord of the Artichoke, at Elstree, and a man threw it into the water, and drew it out without finding any thing. Hunt called out of the chaise, " It is not there, but further that way" (pointing on one side of the water). The drag was again thrown in, and the body of a man, enveloped in a new sack, was drawn out, placed on a ladder, and carried to the Artichoke public house

The following is an accurate description of the corpse when it was brought out of the water. The head, and as far as the abdomen, were enveloped in the sack, the body having been thrust into it head foremost, the feet were tied together with a piece of cord, to which were appended a pocket handkerchief filled with flint stones weighing about 30 pounds. Another cord was tied over the sack, round the waist of the deceased, to which was affixed a very large flint stone, and in the end of the sack a great number of stones had been placed before the body was put into it

The Magistrates gave orders for the body not to be examined till the Jury were impanelled, and on Friday morning, when the Jury, with the Coroner, took a view of it, no one could be certain, though very little doubt could possibly exist, that the deceased was Mr. Weare

On the night when the murder was committed, (Friday Oct. 24,) Probert and Hunt arrived, about eight o'clock, at the Artichoke at Elstree, in a gig, and stopped there drinking till about a quarter before nine o'clock, they had five one-shilling glasses of brandy and water, and then left the house

When Hunt was returning from the pond, he addressed himself to Mr Field, the landlord of the Artichoke, in the following words —"I and Probert were sitting under the tree in front of your house for an hour, on the night of the murder, drinking— You know this?" Mr Field replied in the affirmative. Hunt continued ' " Probert wanted me to sing, but I was so very *muzzy* (drunk) that I could not "

After the evidence was taken before the Magistrates at the Essex Arms Tavern, Watford, on Thursday afternoon, John Thurtell was brought into the room, and the whole was recapitulated; at the conclusion, he said, " I wish to ask Hunt a question." The Magistrates told him, that he could not be permitted, at present, to confront Hunt.

Thurtell then replied, "I wish to ask Hunt where he was on last Tuesday night ' He was again informed, that at present he could not be allowed to see Hunt. He then asked leave to write to Mr Serjeant Vaughan for his professional assistance, which was instantly granted. He was placed in a small room, strongly ironed, and very narrowly watched throughout the day. His bearing on Wednesday night was exceedingly bold, and there was a great degree of levity in his manner; but after the examination he became exceedingly dejected, and sent for Ruthven, with whom he continued in conversation for a long time, in the course of which he accused Hunt of having committed the murder, but admitted that he himself was concerned in it In the afternoon the Magistrates issued an order for his being conveyed to the county gaol at Hertford, and he was taken there in a chaise by two constables of Watford, well armed On his arrival he was placed in a cell by himself, and was watched during the night. Hunt remained in custody at Watford.

The Coroner issued summonses for a Jury to assemble on Friday morning, at the Artichoke at Elstree, and the Magistrates gave orders that Hunt should be conveyed where the inquest was appointed to sit, and also Thomas Thurtell, and Probert

CORONER'S INQUEST

On Friday morning, October 31, at eleven o'clock, the Coroner for the county, Benjamin Rooke, Esq, arrived at the Artichoke, at Elstree, and in a short time afterwards, Robert Clutterbuck, Esq, J. F. Mason, Esq, and Thomas Haworth, Esq, Magistrates, Colonel Drinkwater, a great number of gentlemen, and several Clergymen of the first respectability in the county, arrived.

Between eleven and twelve o'clock, Hunt, Probert, and Thomas Thurtell, arrived at the inn in different post chaises, accompanied by police officers. Thomas Thurtell was attired in a white great coat, he is in person about five feet ten inches high, and possesses a handsome face and person. On descending from the chaise he recognised a person with whom he shook hands, and asked him how he was

Hunt and Probert appeared to feel very little; the latter is a fine looking man, with a most expressive countenance and gentlemanly demeanor

The arrival of a brother of the deceased excited a considerable sensation; his distress was so extremely great during the whole of the enquiry, as to excite the sympathy of every one present

The following persons, respectable inhabitants residing in the neighbourhood of the scene of this horrid transaction, were sworn on the Jury:—

Robert Field, Foreman

Richard Parker,	John Stacey,
Richard Brown,	John Young,
W. Marsters,	Wm. Eames,
W T Harrold,	John Morris, and
John Brown,	Josh Molineux.

The Jury being sworn, proceeded to view the body in a room up stairs It presented a spectacle truly horrible. There was a wound on the right cheek, evidently occasioned by a pistol ball, which had passed into the interior of the head On the left temple was a wound, or rather a hole, which went nearly through the head It appeared to have been caused by some blunt instrument being driven with great force into the head The aperture corresponded in size with the barrel of the pistol, in which brains were found, as before described The instrument, whatever it was, had penetrated both hemispheres of the brain. The throat of the unfortunate man was cut nearly from one ear to the other Bruises were still visible in his body

After the Jury had assembled, Probert, Thomas Thurtell and Hunt, were brought to the house, and placed in separate rooms. Probert was taken, in company with the Coroner and Jury, to the room where the corpse was lying, and was asked if he had ever seen it before?" He looked at it, and said in a tone of solemnity, "I never saw that corpse before in my life. I declare to God I never did. You may rely upon it, I never saw that unhappy man before." He betrayed no extraordinary emotion. He was conveyed back to his room, and there in a few moments he made disclosures, which will be found in pages 29 and 30.

In the course of the morning a search was made about the premises of Gill's Hill Cottage, and in a dunghill was found a shirt steeped in blood, and cut down the middle from top to bottom. This, on being compared with some shirts of the deceased, was found to be of the same size, and the work in each corresponded. A sack was also found there, and some pieces of cord.

The Jury having returned to their room,

Mr. NOEL, the solicitor for the prosecution, addressed a Reporter for a London newspaper to the following effect:—

"SIR—In consequence of what took place before the Magistrates at Watford, when a London Reporter refused to promise not to publish parts of the proceedings which the Magistrates thought might defeat the ends of Justice, and to prevent which, the Magistrate was compelled to take forcible possession of the Reporter's notes, the Magistrates now present, have deputed me to inform you, that they require of you to avoid sending forth to the public print for which you are employed, such parts of Hunt's confession, as they deem necessary to be suppressed for the present."

The Reporter said, that he certainly would not report any thing that would at all tend to defeat the ends of justice.

A Magistrate said—Then, Sir, you will not refuse to shew us your report before you send it to London.

The Reporter replied, that it was a novel thing in a Court of Justice, for a Judge to demand a sight of the notes of a Reporter; he certainly could not accede to such a proposition, but he would pledge his word that he would give no evidence which the Coroner would be kind enough to point out as improper for publication.

Mr. NOEL—We are satisfied, and the reason we request this is, that when the horrid deed was first discovered, the body could not be found, and we had strong suspicions that it had been conveyed to London and disposed of, and that evidence to convict the murderer was by that means destroyed, and in order to obtain a knowledge where the body was, the Magistrates held out to one of the parties accused, supposed to be less guilty than the rest, some favour if he would impeach his accomplices, and give information where the body was concealed, the party in consequence of these promises made to him, did make a confession, which confession, if published, may be the means of causing the guilty to evade punishment, as they will shape their defence to meet this confession. The Magistrates have no objection to certain parts, or a summary of the confession, being published."

The Reporter said, that he would give a summary merely; and the conversation terminated

Mr. WARD, Mr. SHUTE, and Mr. KENDALL, surgeons, of Watford, were then directed by the Coroner to view the body, and see if they could discover the immediate cause of death

Ruthven and Upson, the officers, and the surgeons, returned to the apartment where the body lay, and took it out of the sack. The body exhibited a spectacle which made every one who beheld it shudder. The Jury then viewed the body, and afterwards received evidence.

A Magistrate proposed to read the confession of Hunt. The Coroner said that it was unusual to receive evidence before a Coroner's Jury, that had been previously taken by a Magistrate, the most regular mode would be for him to examine Hunt, and take his statement from his own lips, as he might now detail facts different from, or in addition to his written confession.

Mr. REXWORTHY, proprietor of the billiard-rooms, Spring Gardens, sworn. Said he was a friend of the deceased, and had seen the body; he knew it to be the remains of Mr William Weare, of London, who took leave of him on Friday morning, the 24th inst and then had, to the knowledge of witness, about 24*l.* on his person. Previously the deceased possessed bank post bills and other bills to a considerable amount. Witness left London as soon as he heard that John Thurtell was charged with the murder of a man whose body was not found, as he knew that Mr Weare had been invited to accompany Thurtell on a shooting excursion.

Mr PHILLIP SMITH, an inhabitant of Aldenham, gave evidence to the same effect as we have already mentioned. In addition, he stated that he forgot to mention, that prior to his hearing the pistol fired, he heard a chaise coming in the direction from Highcross to Radlet. He afterwards heard groaning, but did not go to see the cause, as he had his wife with him, and they went home. The next morning he informed Mr. Nicholls, a neighbour, of the circumstance.

JAMES FREEMAN, sworn.—He was going on the evening of Friday, the 24th October, to meet his wife, and passed across a field leading into Gill's Hill Lane, by Probert's house; when he came into the lane it was about eight o'clock; there were two gentlemen in a gig, one of them alighted from it for a certain purpose. Witness said to the gentleman, " You have driven your horse very fast, he is much out of wind," they gave no answer. Witness then said, " This is a very dark, crooked, bad lane to go down in the evening." No answer was made to that, and witness walked on. The man who got out of the chaise had a light great coat on, buttoned with a loop; there were no lights to the gig, it was a clear starlight evening, so that he could distinguish persons very plainly; it was a bay horse in the chaise, with a light face; the men had both black hats on; he followed them for some distance, and then returned to meet his wife.

ELIZABETH FREEMAN, the wife of last witness, sworn.— She met two gentlemen on the night of the murder, travelling in a chaise, along Gill's Hill Lane; she described them similarly to her husband; they were about a quarter of a mile from Mr Probert's, of Gill's Hill Cottage, when she saw them. On Sunday last, she met Probert's boy, and having heard previously that some gentlemen had met with an accident in the lane, she asked him if his master had met with a misfortune in his gig, and the boy said that the gentleman was overturned, and came home very dirty, with spots of blood on his coat.

JOHN HETHERINGTON, a labourer, being sworn, gave evidence to the following effect:—He was at work in Gill's Hill Lane, about six o'clock on Saturday morning, the 25th October, and saw two men walking about fifty yards up the lane from Gill's Hill, towards Battledore Lane. One had a white, and the other a black hat on, the former was a tall man, with black whiskers, and the other shorter, with a white coat. They " grappled" in the hedge; witness and a fellow-labourer, named Hunt, spoke to the gentlemen, and one of them said, " I was thrown out of my chaise here, last night." Witness was sure he should know the tallest man with a white hat, if he were to see him again.

The witness, by order of the Coroner, was taken into the rooms where Probert, Thomas Thurtell, Hunt, and other persons were, but could not identify amongst them the man with black whiskers, who answers the description of John Thurtell.

Witness heard his fellow-labourer, Hunt, ask the gentlemen if they were hurt, and the tall one replied that he was capsised; but neither horse or gig were overturned. After witness had breakfasted, he walked up the lane again, supposing, if the gentleman had been overturned, that some money might have been thrown out of his pockets, and, on searching, he found a knife, which was covered with blood. The knife was produced. About ten o'clock the same morning, he found a pistol in the hedge, near the spot where he had previously seen the gentlemen "grabbling." The pistol was bloody. Witness gave the pistol to Mr Nicholls, his employer, who was in his chaise about 20 yards up the lane, and Mr N. told him that Mr. P. Smith had informed him that he had heard the report of a gun in the lane on the overnight. On the spot where the pistol was found, witness kicked up the leaves, and the more he kicked them the more blood was found: and Mr. Nicholls said, "I am afraid that something very bad has been done here." Witness told Mr Nicholls, who was at that time in his chaise, that he had seen two gentlemen "grabbling" there. Mr. Nicholls told him not to divulge any thing that he had seen. This took place about ten o'clock on Saturday morning, the 25th of October. About eleven o'clock the same morning witness saw the same two gentlemen come down Gill's Hill Lane, in a chaise; they were then neatly dressed, and both had black hats on. One of them (the same person who, about six o'clock in the morning, had a white hat on) asked witness how he did? This person was John Thurtell, whom he saw on Thursday last at Watford. These were the only two persons who came down in a chaise that day. A man came down with a large dog soon afterwards.

WILLIAM HUNT, a labourer, being sworn, deposed, That he was in Gill's Hill Lane, and saw two gentlemen on Saturday morning, October 25th, about six o'clock, as they passed him on foot, one was a short man, with a dark complexion, and wore a black coat, and a black hat;

the other was a tall swarthy man, with sandy whiskers, and appeared to have a dark coat on, with a white hat indented on both sides. Witness said "Good morning" to the tall one, and he replied, "You are going to widen the lane?" Witness said, "Yes, and where I can't widen it, I shall trim it up." The tall man said, "This is a d—d dark lane, I was capsised out of my gig here last night." Witness said, "Was you, Sir?" He said, "Yes." Witness said, "Did you hurt your horse?" He replied, "No, my gig never fell." Witness answered, "It is strange, Sir, that you should be capsised out of your gig, and your gig not be upset." The gentlemen then went towards Gill's Hill, previous to which, the short man stooped in the hedge and returned with something which he appeared to have picked up, and which he carried in a yellow handkerchief on the end of a stick when they went away. This handkerchief is supposed to have contained congealed blood, which the parties removed to prevent a discovery.

Mr NICHOLLS, a respectable farmer, corroborated the evidence of his tenant, Hetherington, as to receiving a pistol stained with blood from him, and discovering a "sprinkling" of blood in the hedge. He received the pistol on Saturday morning, and did not give it up to the Magistrates till Tuesday, witness told Hetherington that Mr. P Smith had informed him that he heard a gun or pistol fired on Friday night, did not know that the Magistrates sat at St Alban's on Saturday, or he should have given information to them, witness was in company with Probert on Sunday, Oct. 26, at his house on private business, he remembered saying on that occasion to Mr. Probert, "What the devil manœuvres were you at on Friday evening?" Probert replied, "What manœuvres do you mean? I know nothing of it." Witness replied, "I suspect some one at your house fired a pistol in Gill's Hill Lane on Friday night." Probert said, "What time was the pistol fired?" Witness said, "Eight o'clock." Probert said, "It was not me, nor any at my house, for I did not arrive at home till long after that time." Witness had this conversation with Probert before his making any communication to the Justices, and previous to this time he had received the pistol from Hetherington, which had blood upon it, had seen a bloody knife found on the spot, had seen the blood on the ground, and heard of the groans, and yet he did not suspect that a murder had been committed Did not see the brains or the hair on the pistol till Monday morning. Witness had not wilfully done wrong in not communicating these facts earlier to Mr. Mason, the Magistrate, for he thought that as there was a good deal of drinking going on at Probert's, that some of them were going to London, and that some one belonging to the family had concealed himself in the hedge, and had fired to alarm his companions as they passed.

CORONER—You have told us part of what passed between you and Probert on Sunday evening, tell the remainder

WITNESS—I was not there above half an hour with Probert

CORONER—Was not something said by Probert about dragging a pond?

WITNESS—There was. A Mr Heward was present, and Probert spoke about filling up his pond. Witness said it would be a pity to have the pond filled up Heward replied jokingly, "It shall be dragged first, and some large fish will be found in it" At the time, it appears, the body of the deceased was in this pond Witness wrote on Monday last to Mr. Mason, and informed him, that he suspected a murder had been committed The road to Probert's cottage was unfrequented by almost every one but Probert, and the persons at Probert's house.

The Coroner reprehended the conduct of this witness in not giving earlier information to the Magistrates, and expressed his surprise, that after he had received the blood-stained pistol, heard of the groans, &c that he did not instantly give information, instead of visiting Probert The consequence of this delay had been the escape of one of the murderers (Hunt) from justice, for he had been admitted a witness for the Crown, by the Magistrates, as they were afraid the body was disposed of, if Mr Nicholls had given information, the body, which was not removed from Probert's pond till Monday night, would have been found, and there would have been evidence, in all probability, to convict Hunt also, who, in the opinion of the Coroner, was equally guilty with his accomplices.

Mr. Nicholls regretted that he had delayed making the communication to the Magistrates

The Coroner said, that he acquitted him of any intentional wrong, and knew him to be a most respectable man.

SUSAN ANN WOODROFFE, servant to Probert, deposed,

that her master came home on Friday, Oct 24th, from London, about nine o'clock at night, with two other persons, viz Mr Hunt, and John Thurtell Hunt and John Thurtell had both white hats on when they arrived Mr Probert gave witness some pork chops to cook, and told her not to get them cooked till he came back, and he then went out with the other two gentlemen, with a lantern and candle—Mrs. Probert told witness that they were gone to Mr Nicholls's, on business. They left the house about ten o'clock, and returned about eleven, and when witness took the chops into the parlor, all three were there, and supped Mr Hunt and Mr John Thurtell sat up all Friday night smoking and drinking, whether they went out in the night she could not say On Saturday morning she saw John Thurtell sitting on a sofa in her master's room, with her master's white hat on, and Hunt was asleep on a chair; Hunt and John Thurtell left the house about six o'clock, and Mr. Probert followed them, they returned before Mr. Probert, and were absent about half an hour. Mr Probert has a large dog, she could not say that the dog went out with him on Saturday morning, Mrs. Probert and her sister, Miss Noyes, were at Mr. Probert's cottage on Sunday, and also the two Mr Thurtells, Mr Hunt, and Mr Noyes, Mr Probert's wife's brother,—Mrs. Probert was with the company in the parlor the greater part of the day, and on Monday morning Thomas Thurtell and James, Mr Probert's boy, went away in a chaise; witness had seen John Thurtell with a yellow handkerchief. On Monday evening the Thurtells and Hunt came again to Mr Probert's, and left soon afterwards in the chaise; Mrs. Probert let them out at the gate, she did not observe any thing particular about the fish-pond, she did not hear the report of a pistol on Friday night, Thos. Thurtell did not arrive at Probert's till Sunday last

JAMES HADDIS sworn Is the servant boy of Mr. Probert, he recapitulated his evidence given before the Magistrates, as inserted in a preceding page. In addition, he said that Mr. Probert, Hunt, and John Thurtell, went out on Friday night, about ten o'clock, and were absent about three-quarters of an hour, with a candle and lantern, they all returned together. It was a little before ten o'clock, when he saw John Thurtell sponging his coat Was not aware if Probert, Hunt, and John Thurtell went towards the pond on Friday night, at ten o'clock.

(A mahogany box, a double-barrelled gun, and a carpet bag used for travelling, the property of the deceased, were shewn to witness); witness saw the gun and the mahogany case at Mr. Probert's, on last Saturday morning; he also saw a bag resembling the one produced. Saw John Thurtell on Saturday morning, when he went away with Hunt, about seven o'clock; he then wore Wellington boots, very dirty all over, his trowsers were very dirty about the legs, his coat was dirty on the back and arms, and he appeared to have been on the ground. The same morning, John Thurtell had his blue dress coat off, and Hunt was sponging it as it hung on the door in the kitchen, there was no blood on the blue coat, but there were spots of blood on his light great coat.

A coat found by Ruthven in Hunt's lodgings was produced.

Witness could not identify it; a large piece of sponge produced was identified by him to be that used by John Thurtell and Hunt, in sponging the bloody clothes. On Sunday, John Thurtell, Thos Thurtell, Hunt, Probert, Mr Noyes, Mr Heward, and Mr. Nicholls, were at Probert's. Mr. Noyes came alone in a chaise, and Mr. Heward and Mr. Nicholls came about business. On Monday morning, Probert told him to clean himself to go to town with Mr Hunt and Thomas Thurtell, he did so, and accompanied them to London, Hunt drove them to St, Clement's Church, and then got out, and went into a house, but did not take any thing out of the chaise, from there they went to the Coach and Horses, Conduit Street; witness was left there, and told that Mr Probert would come to him in two hours, Mr. J Thurtell got out of the chaise, and Hunt drove away, he did not see Mr Probert on the Monday or Tuesday, a Police Officer took him away on Wednesday, witness had never before been taken to town.

CORONER—The boy was removed out of the way by the parties to avoid accidents

THOMAS ABEL WARD, of Watford, surgeon, being sworn, delivered the following evidence.—I was present at the examination of the body of the deceased person, Mr Wm Weare, this evening. I believe the immediate cause of the death was a wound on the anterior angle of the parietal bone, given by some instrument, which, from the marks, I am inclined to believe was the barrel of a pistol. Part of the skull was beat into the brains. There was another wound under the protuberance of the right cheek bone, which had the appearance of a common gun or pistol-shot wound, and the ball repelled by the cheek bone. I am of opinion that the wound on the right cheek was not of a nature to cause death, but that the deceased died from the beating on the skull with the pistol barrel. The injury was of that nature, that I conceive the pistol barrel must have been " punched" with desperate violence into the skull of the unfortunate man.

Witness here produced a piece of deceased's skull bone, which he had extracted from the brains of the deceased on opening the head.

" I also observed a wound cut by a sharp instrument on each side of the throat, the jugular on the left side was divided, and the wound was sufficient to occasion death; the wound on the right side of the throat did not injure any parts of vitality, but merely severed the flesh under the ear."

CORONER.—It seems that after the deceased was shot, he was able to struggle with his murderer, and that he received the blows on his head when resisting, and to make sure, as "dead men tell us no tales," his murderers completed their horrid work by cutting his throat.

THOS. JOSEPH RUTHVEN, an officer of Bow-street, being sworn, said, On Wednesday morning I apprehended John Thurtell, in consequence of some information which caused me to suspect he was concerned in the murder of Mr Weare. I secured him at Mr Tetsall's, the Coach and Horses, Conduit Street, and found a pistol on his person, which I produce. It is the fellow to the one produced by Mr Nicholls, found in the lane near Probert's house. In his waistcoat I found ten swan-shot, a pen-knife, and a pistol key. When I entered his apartment, he knew me, and began to talk about the bill found against him and his brother for a conspiracy to defraud the Fire Office, and I did not undeceive him as to the nature of my errand, till I had put the handcuffs on him. He offered no resistance.

Mr REXWORTHY recalled—Identified the knife produced as the property of the deceased; witness had it in his hand on the Friday the deceased left London, and knew it by a mark on the handle.

MR WARD, the surgeon, of Watford, re-examined.—Was of opinion that such an instrument as the knife produced had been used to inflict the wounds in the deceased's throat.

RUTHVEN re-examined.—I found a muslin neckerchief also in John Thurtell's lodgings (he produced it), it is bloody, and is marked "T Thurtell" He told me that he sometimes wore his brother's clothes. I also produce a shirt, with no marks on it, and a black waistcoat, which I took off his back, it is bloody, particularly about one of the pockets, as if a bloody hand had been thrust into it. I also produce a coat, which I took off his back, which is very bloody in several places. [These articles were exhibited to the jury] I also produce a horse pistol, which I found at Mr Tetsall's, and Mr Tetsall told me, that he had lost the fellow to it.

CORONER.—Perhaps the fellow pistol may be found not far from hence.

Witness continued.—On searching Hunt's house, at No. 19, King Street, Golden Square, London, on Thursday night, I found a double barrelled gun, maker's name "Manton," and a mahogany backgammon-board, containing two dice boxes and a pair of dice, also a large sponge, and a shooting jacket, with a call or whistle; I also found a travelling bag, containing shirts marked "W W." the initials of the deceased, also a variety of shooting implements, with shooting boots and shoes, maker's name, "Dow, York Street, Covent Garden."

Mr. RIXWORTHY was again called, and identified a neckerchief, and other property found in Hunt's lodging by Ruthven, to be that of the deceased.

A JUROR.—The deceased brought all his shooting tackle with him, intending, no doubt, to sport in this neighbourhood for some time.

RUTHVEN continued.—I also found a piece of cord, which I produce (the cord being compared with that by which the legs of the deceased were tied, corresponded.)

CORONER.—There can be little doubt but all this property belonged to the deceased.

RUTHVEN.—Mr. Coroner, I am requested by Mr Probert, to say that he wishes to make some communication to you; he says "that he will not die with lies in his mouth."

Mr NOEL.—He has applied to me to make a disclosure

CORONER.—If he has any thing to say I can have no objection to hear him, but he must be warned that he does it at his own peril, without any promise or request on the part of the Magistrate

THOMAS BATE, a boy in the employ of Mr. James Wardel, (the owner of Gill's Hill Cottage, which was let by him to Probert, and who has taken possession of the same since Probert's apprehension), deposed, That he was clearing out Probert's stable on Thursday afternoon, and under a heap of dung found a torn and bloody shirt, and a sack tied in a bundle. The shirt found in John Thurtell's lodgings by Ruthven, on being compared with the bloody shirt, was of the same make, and marked with the deceased's initials The sack was soaked with wet

A MAGISTRATE observed, that it was in evidence that the clothes of the deceased were cut off his body with a knife before he was thrust into the sack.

JAMES HADDIS, Probert's boy, was again called to identify the sack, but could not

Mr NOEL —We have proof that the body of the deceased was first concealed in Probert's pond, and afterwards removed to the pond where it was found, and probably it was first put into this sack with the clothes on and deposited in Probert's pond, and subsequently removed, after being stripped of the clothes, into the new sack in which it was found.

[The pond in which the corpse was discovered is above two miles distant from Probert's cottage, and the body was removed thither on Monday night, the 27th of October, in the chaise, by the murderers]

RUTHVEN entered the Jury room, and stated to the Coroner, that he had been with Probert again, and had told him that he understood that he (Probert) wished to make some communication Probert replied, " I have no objection to see the Coroner and Magistrates ;" he (Ruthven) told him that he might have no objection, but the question was, did he wish to see them or not ?

Probert said, "What had I better do—can't you advise me ?" He answered that he could not advise, for he must know his own situation best. Probert then expressed a wish to see the Magistrates, and they went to him, when he made an ample confession, from which it appeared, that his was not the hand that committed the murder, and after it was perpetrated, John Thurtell threatened to murder him if he opened his lips on the subject, and told him that he had picked out seventeen persons of substance that he intended to rob and murder, and that the deceased was one of them

The evidence was then read over to the different witnesses, and most of them were bound over to appear at the next Hertford Assizes, to give evidence against Thurtell, Probert, and Hunt, for the murder of Mr. Weare.

The Coroner then said, that it was impossible to go through the whole of the evidence on Friday night, as it was then getting late, and he therefore adjourned the inquest to the next day

Ruthven was dispatched to London, to bring down a witness whose evidence was expected to be of great importance.

ADJOURNED INQUEST
Elstree, Saturday, November 1.

This morning, at 12 o'clock, the Coroner and Jury reassembled at the Artichoke Tavern. The Magistrates of Watford, Robert Clutterbuck, Thomas Haworth, J. F. Mason, and George Watlington, Esquires, were in early attendance, and many gentlemen of respectablity in the county.

Before the Jury were impanelled, or the Coroner arrived, the prisoners, Probert, Hunt, and Thomas Thurtell, who had been confined during the preceding night in St Alban's gaol, arrived in three chaises, attended by the local police A considerable crowd was collected in front of the inn, whose expressions evinced the strong indignation which this foul murder had excited The prisoners were conducted into separate rooms, under the care of the officers. They were relieved from their irons, and from all unnecessary coercion. Soon after the Magistrates had taken their seats, Mr Noel, the Solicitor, entered the room, and addressing them, said, that Thomas Thurtell had expressed a wish, before the examination proceeded, to have some communication with him (Mr Noel) and the Coroner

Mr. CLUTTERBUCK asked if the Coroner was come?

Mr NOEL said, not yet, but he was expected every moment

The Magistrates said they saw no objection to this course if the prisoner wished it.

Mr. NOEL then quitted the room.

The new sack in which the body was found was then produced before the Jury, and laid on the table It was split from top to bottom, and at the bottom there was a large stain of blood—this was where the head had rested

Information was also given to the Magistrates, that Hunt and Probert, on their way down to the house of the latter on Friday night, purchased half-a-bushel of corn from a baker of the name of White, at Edgware, and took an old sack with them. They also stopped at the house of a publican of the name of Clarke, at Edgware, with whom they were acquainted. Hunt entered into conversation with Clarke on the subject of the bill of indictment which had been preferred against the Thurtells for conspiring to set their house in Watling Street on fire. Clarke, who knew the Thurtells, said it was a bad business, on which Hunt took out a newspaper, containing a contradiction to the statement that the bill had been found.

Probert now seemed very impatient to be off, and Clarke, while they stood in the house, heard another chaise and horse drive by. They at last set off towards Elstree, at great speed.

On the Sunday morning, John Thurtell called at Clarke's as he was going down to Probert's to dine; he asked if Mrs. C. had any lemons, (Clarke being out) and took some with him, as he said to make punch. He afterwards met Clarke in Edgware, and shook hands with him; Clarke remarked he looked very ill, and he assigned the pressure of his own private affairs as the cause of his agitated appearance: he then drove on.

Clarke saw Hunt on Friday at Elstree, and in consequence of some suspicion that he (Clarke) had been conveying information from one prisoner to the other, he was called before the Magistrates, but upon being questioned, he stated that he had been merely speaking to Hunt of the atrocity of his conduct.

The Magistrate asked Clarke, what he had said to Probert? Clarke replied, that the words he used were these — "Good God, how could you call, and drink and joke, in the way you did at my house, when you had concerted, and were about to commit, such a horrid murder?"

The Magistrate asked if that was all he had said?

Clarke replied, that he believed he said to Probert, "that it was a horrid and brutal piece of business, and he believed they were all in it." He declared that he had not spoken to the other prisoners.

The Magistrate then dismissed him, expressing satisfaction at his explanation.

On Friday, Hunt was spoken to by a person who had been an acquaintance of the deceased, who asked him, how he could join in such a horrible transaction? Hunt replied, "I did not do the act, I certainly knew of its being concerted, for some time before it took place, and a fortnight before, I went to Mr Rexworthy's, to inform him of the intention to rob and murder his friend Weare, but when I was about to communicate the fact to him, I had not the heart to do it."

The Coroner gave orders that no person whatever should be admitted to the prisoners, as it was important to prevent conversations taking place, which might be conveyed from one of the accused to another.

CONTINUATION OF THE EXAMINATION

The inquiry then proceeded, by the examination of the following witnesses —

CHARLES LEWIN, of Watford, wine merchant, was called, and stated, That in consequence of information he received, he went with Mr Johnson to search for the body. They arrived at a pond called Hill Slough, on the road to St Alban's, in the parish of Elstree, on the right road as you go to St. Alban's. After searching for five minutes, a ladder was got, and the body was found. A sack was over the upper part of the body, and the legs were naked. the mouth of the sack was tied round with a cord, at the end of which was tied a piece of stone, and a handkerchief filled with stones to prevent the body from floating. There were stones also in the sack.

Mr GEORGE JONES, of Stanmore, being sworn, deposed, That he was present when the sack, containing the body of the deceased, was cut open. The hands were crossed on the chest—under each arm-pit was a large flint stone. The legs were also crossed and confined with a cord, which secured the sack round the body. There was a red shawl handkerchief round the neck of the deceased.

Mr. HEWARD was then called in —He stated, That he was the proprietor of the cottage occupied by Probert at Gill's Hill —it was a leasehold, and he let it furnished—witness lives at 58, Hatton Garden—knew Probert for four years— on Wednesday last, 29th October, had Probert's goods seized for rent. He had heard something of this affair and therefore he had made the seizure. Witness saw a carriage in the yard of the cottage on Tuesday morning before he had the seizure made, and understood Probert was going to move. Witness was in the house on the Sunday after the murder. He saw a person at the kitchen door on that day—he believed, from the description, that it was Hunt—he was brushing his coat. Witness, on the same day, went with Probert to Mr. Nicholls's. They were in conversation about the house, when Mr. Nicholls said, "By-the-bye, Probert, do you know anything of a gun going off, down your lane, the other night? I suppose it was some of your friends got groggy, and fired a pistol to alarm some one going by. I have done the same thing myself in my younger days." Probert said, he did not know any thing about such a circumstance.

On recollection, witness remembered something was said about filling up the pond in the garden—and he said they ought to drag it first, as there was a good stock of fish there. There were some large fish there; for he had put some in, weighing a pound, three years ago. After they talked about the fish, Philip Smith said, that on Friday night, about half-past eight, as he was going along the lane, with his wife and a Mr. Osmond, he heard a gun go off, and afterwards groans, and would have gone to see what it was, but his wife would not let him. He described the groans as violent, and said he stopped and listened till he heard the last of them. Three or four minutes might have elapsed before he heard the last groan. When the conversation finished, Mr. Nicholls said, "I thought it was a joke, but now I think it was something more serious." Probert was present the whole of this time, but said nothing particular, he denied all knowledge of the affair. Witness afterwards returned to Probert's house, and he said to him, as they walked along the road, "What is this all about?" and Probert said, "I don't know." On the same day, he saw John Thurtell and two other persons come towards Probert's house, one of them was Mr. Noyes, and the other he supposed to be Mr. Thomas Thurtell, as he had heard he was expected. John Thurtell and Noyes were in a gig, the other was walking. Supposed they all came together.

The witness was then directed to retire, for the purpose of viewing Hunt. On his return, he said—"I don't know that I ever saw that man before. Perhaps I might."

Mr Noel.—Can you say whether there is any difference in his person?—I am not aware that I have seen the man. I cannot take upon me to say that Hunt was the man I saw. He was a black-whiskered man. If the person shown to me be the man, he has shaved his whiskers.

Mr Noel.—In fact, Hunt has shaved his whiskers since.

The witness thought it was a black coat the man he saw was brushing. Nicholls, as well as Smith, said on Sunday that it was a gun they heard go off. Nicholls did not say he had a pistol and a knife in his possession. Witness believed he said he had been down to the spot in the lane, where he saw some blood, but he did not make the slightest allusion to the pistol, which since appeared to have been then in his possession. He said something of the hedge being broken. On Tuesday morning, witness met Mr P. Smith, in one of his fields. Witness was shooting. Mr. Smith said, " I believe there is something more serious in what we were talking about on Sunday." "Why?" said witness. "Because," said he, " I have been at the place again, and have seen some blood, and the hedge is broken, as if a body had been dragged through besides, a pistol and a knife were found." "A pistol!" said witness, in surprise; and Smith answered in the affirmative. Witness then said, "Good God! why let the matter rest so long—how could you keep it a secret?" Smith replied, that it would not rest now, and on witness asking where the pistol was, he said he supposed the Magistrates had got it by that time.

The Coroner here remarked, that Mr. Nicholls having complained, in a letter addressed to him, of the observations which he had felt it his duty to make, on his conduct in keeping the fact of finding the pistol a secret, he desired it to be understood, that the present examination was to show that those observations were fully justified. He was now more than ever convinced in his mind, that he was correct in his remarks, and that Mr Nicholls had acted improperly in keeping this matter a secret.

Witness proceeded—Nicholls said, that a knife had also been found, and that both the articles were in the hands of the Magistrates. Witness observed, he was glad it was so, and that the matter ought not to rest so

The Coroner.—Nicholls, shortly after the commission of the fact, having placed in his possession a pistol with a quantity of blood on it, and likewise a knife, both of which he carried home with him; and having also heard from his son-in-law, that a pistol had been fired near the spot, was it not his duty to have given information?

Witness.—I would have done so, ten minutes after. I always blamed him for not mentioning the circumstance. After witness left Smith on the Tuesday, he met Nicholls, who said to him, "Why, this is likely to be a serious matter that we were talking about on Sunday night;" and he added, that it seemed as if there had been a murder committed. He saw Nicholls on the Wednesday, and lunched with him, because he thought that he would perhaps say more. At the time he was with Probert on the Tuesday, not the slightest notice was taken of the business. There were no pecuniary transactions between Probert, Nicholls, and himself. It was contemplated to change the property, but nothing more. No money passed between them. It would have saved him trouble if there had.

Some conversation now took place between the Magistrates, the Coroner, and Mr Noel, the Solicitor for the prosecution, as to the course which it might be expedient to take, with respect to the confession of Hunt.

The Coroner observed, that a bag had been found in Hunt's lodgings, containing property belonging to the deceased. It appeared to him that Hunt was an accessary before the fact. It was his duty to inquire into all the circumstances of the murder, and use every exertion in his power to unravel the whole affair; he should therefore have Hunt brought before him, and whatever he thought proper voluntarily to state, it was his duty to hear; but he would hold out no promise, nor would he give him any hope from any disclosure he might choose to make.

The prisoner Hunt was then called in. His whiskers had been shaved off, and he came forward, apparently not much affected by his situation.

The Coroner then addressed him to the following effect —" I have thought proper to send for you, Hunt, to ask you whether you choose to make any statement to the Inquest which is now assembled? I think it my duty, however, in the first instance, to explain in what manner I shall receive what you may think fit to say. I shall not receive it as evidence, nor shall I examine you on oath; if you think it right to say any thing, I am ready to hear you; but from me you are to understand that you have no sort of promise either of reward or otherwise. I have nothing to do but to receive your voluntary account of the horrible transaction, to which our attention is now directed '

Hunt said he was ready to repeat what he had already

Mr. NOEL, still appearing anxious that the prisoner should not act under a misapprehension, interposed and said, he felt it necessary to observe, in addition to what had fallen from the Coroner, that the confession made by Hunt before the Magistrates could not, in any way interfere with the proceedings in which they were engaged that day. The Magistrates would, in good faith, and at the proper time, submit the confession he had made to them to the consideration of the Court, in order that it might operate in his favour. What he might now say, in no way compromised the Magistrates, and must come from himself on the terms stated by the Coroner

HUNT.—Thank you, gentlemen; I am now ready to answer any question.

CORONER.—I am now ready to hear any thing you have to say touching the death of William Weare

Mr NOEL, being yet anxious that the prisoner should not be led into any mistake, desired that he might retire.

Having left the room, a conversation took place as to the expediency of taking his statement, when the Coroner thought, that with the caution he had received, his story might be fairly heard, and he was bound to receive it

Hunt being again recalled. Mr NOEL addressed him thus —" Since you have been out of the room, a discussion has taken place on the part of the Magistrates to whom you made a confession under a pledge, and they think it proper that you should understand their pledge does not extend to any thing you may say here. They will state your confession to the Under-Secretary of State, with the circumstances under which it was taken, and it will, no doubt, receive a fit consideration. You will now use your own discretion, and either tell your story to the present Jury, or not, as you think proper."

The CORONER.—We are willing to receive any statement you may give us, but we do not ask you to commit yourself in any way before this Jury

HUNT.—I perfectly understand, and I shall tell the whole truth

He then proceeded to give the following statement in a cool, collected, and precise manner, occasionally sighing heavily, as he paused for it to be written down

HUNT'S CONFESSION.

In consequence of an indictment for conspiracy against John Thurtell and Thomas Thurtell, for defrauding the County Fire Office of 1,900 and odd pounds, Thomas and John Thurtell left the Cock Tavern, in the Haymarket, and took up their residence at a Mr Tetsall's, (the Coach and Horses), in Conduit Street, Bond Street I was invited to dine with them I called there on Friday morning, when John Thurtell invited me to take a walk.

I walked with him as far as High Street, Mary-le-bone. We stopped at a jeweller's shop, and while we were looking there, John Thurtell observed a pair of pistols, which he said he would go and look at, for he wanted such articles. They were marked 1*l*. 17*s*. 6*d* John Thurtell observed, he wanted them to kill cats, and paid for them 1*l* 5*s*

From there we returned to the Coach and Horses, and dined John Thurtell asked me, after dinner, if I knew where I could get a gig. He gave me 1*l* 10*s* for the gig, for which I paid 1*l* 5*s*. He told me not to say that the gig was going to Hertford, but to Dartford

I returned with the gig to the Coach and Horses about a quarter before five John Thurtell immediately got into the gig, and said he could not wait any longer, as he had a gentleman to meet.

After he was gone, Mr. Probert said to me, "As John Thurtell has gone down to the cottage, have you any objection to take a seat in my gig, as he is obliged to be out of the way, in consequence of the warrants being out against him for the conspiracy, and most likely we shall spend a pleasant evening together " About six o'clock on Friday evening, Mr Probert's gig was brought to the door of the Coach and Horses I took a seat in his gig, we proceeded as far as Oxford Street Mr. Probert said we must take something home for supper, we stopped at a pork shop, where I got out and purchased a loin of pork. We proceeded from there as far as Mr. Harding's, a publican, in the Edgware Road, where we had a glass of brandy and water.

From there we proceeded as far as a Mr Clarke's, another publican, and had two more glasses of brandy and water, from there we proceeded to this house We had three, but from what appears from the landlord (Mr Field) we had five more glasses. We did not get out of the gig here. Mr. Probert observed to Mr. Field that the friend that was with him could sing a very excellent song; Mr. Field said he should be very happy to hear one. Mr. Probert wished me to sing a verse, but I declined.

We proceeded from this house about a quarter of a mile. Mr. Probert stopped the gig, and said to me, "Hunt, you get out and wait my return." I did so. About half an hour or more might have elapsed when Mr. Probert returned, and desired me to get into the gig, and we would make the best of our way to the cottage.

When we arrived at the cottage, John Thurtell was in the stable. Mr. Probert said to me, "Hunt, take that loin of pork out of the gig, take it into the kitchen, and desire the cook to dress it immediately." I took the pork into the kitchen, and remained in the kitchen about ten minutes, when John Thurtell and Mr. Probert followed. We went into the parlour. I was introduced to Mrs. Probert.

John Thurtell then called me and Mr. Probert into the garden, and said, "I have killed that —— that robbed me of 300l. at *blind hookey*." "Good God!" said Mr. Probert. "John, surely you have not been guilty of so rash an act?" John Thurtell immediately took from his pocket a very handsome gold watch, and said, "Do you believe me now? and if you will go with me, I will shew you where he lies dead behind a hedge." Mr. Probert then said, "This has taken such an effect on me that I must retire and get some brandy."

We then went into the parlour. The supper was brought in, which consisted of pork chops, the loin I brought down having been cut into chops. I ate two chops, and so did Mr. Probert. John Thurtell declined eating any, as he complained of being extremely sick. Mr. Probert and I then went into the garden again, when Mr. Probert said to me, "Surely, Hunt, this man has not been guilty of murder?" I observed, it looked very suspicious, he (John Thurtell) having so valuable a watch.

John Thurtell followed, and asked Mr. Probert and myself if we would accompany and assist him in carrying the dead man. During this time Mrs. Probert was gone to bed. John Thurtell said, "If neither of you will assist, I will go myself." He accordingly went by himself, and was gone about ten minutes or a quarter of an hour.

During the time he was gone, Mr. Probert said to me, "If this is the case, Hunt, that John Thurtell has murdered the man, it will ultimately be the ruin of me and my family

After this conversation was over between me and Mr Probert, John Thurtell returned, saying, "This —— is too heavy for me, and if you won't assist me, I shall put the bridle on my horse, and throw the dead man across his back." He accordingly put the bridle on his horse for that purpose.

Mr Probert and I, while he was gone the second time, went into the parlour, and he said to me, "Hunt, this has taken such an effect on me, and I am so agitated, that I don't know what to do." He said, "What will my wife think?" I observed to him—"You may do as you please about going to bed; I shall not go to bed, as I am confident I shall not be able to sleep, after having heard this horrid account from John Thurtell."

John Thurtell then returned to us in the parlour, and said to Mr Probert and myself, "I have thrown the dead man into your fish-pond." "Then, by G—, Sir," said Mr Probert, "I insist upon your immediately going and taking him away off my premises, for such conduct will evidently be my ruin." I and Mr Probert and John Thurtell went to the pond, where we saw the toes of a man, or at least we had every reason to believe it was a man, according to his own statement. John Thurtell then got a line or rope and threw it round the feet, then dragged it to the centre of the pond. John Thurtell then said to Mr Probert, "Don't give yourself a moment's uneasiness, the man shall not remain here long; you well know, Probert, that I would not do any thing that would injure you or your family." We then went into the parlour. John Thurtell threw himself upon some chairs, and I lay on the sofa. Mr Probert went up to his wife, I believe. He was ill.

Next morning, after breakfast, Mr Probert said, "You are going to town with John Thurtell, but I shall expect you will return to-morrow (Sunday) to dinner," which I promised, and did. Mr Probert said to John Thurtell, "Mind and bring a piece of roast beef with you, or we shall have nothing for dinner."

We then left the cottage, and went to London. I left John Thurtell at Mr Tetsall's (the Coach and Horses) with his brother Thomas. On Sunday morning we left Mr Tetsall's in a horse and gig, taking with us a piece of roast beef and two bottles of rum. John Thurtell said to me, when we got as far as Tyburn, "My brother Tom is a-head, and Thomas Noyes," (Thomas Noyes is the brother-in-law of Mr. Probert.)

When we got to the bottom of Maida Hill, we took up Thomas Thurtell, who joined us for the express purpose of seeing his two children, that had been on a visit to Mr Probert's When we had travelled three or four miles from Maida Hill, we met Thomas Noyes. John Thurtell got out of the gig, leaving me and Thomas Thurtell together in it, to make the best of our way to the cottage, in order that Thomas Thurtell might put Mr. Probert's horse into his gig to fetch John Thurtell and Mr Noyes

When we arrived at the cottage, the horse that we went down with was taken out of the gig, and Mr Probert's put in

After Thomas Thurtell had gone to fetch Noyes and John Thurtell, Mr Probert said to me, "Hunt, I have not had a moment's peace since I saw you last, in consequence of that man lying in my pond." My reply was, "I am sure you have not had a more restless night than myself." Shortly after that, Thomas and John Thurtell, and Mr Noyes, arrived at the cottage We then, I mean the whole four of us, (Hunt, Thomas and John Thurtell, and Mr. Noyes), walked across a ploughed field into a lane, and returned to the cottage When we arrived at the cottage, there was a gentleman, whose name I do not know, but I believe him to be the gentleman that owns the estate, came in

T Noyes, the Thurtells, and myself, walked about the grounds till we were called in by one of Thomas Thurtell's children to dinner. After dinner we had some rum and water, and sat for the space of three hours, and then had tea After tea we had some more rum and water, and then we went to the stable to see the horses We then had supper

John Thurtell, myself, Thomas Noyes, and Mr. Probert, sat up till about half-past one Mr Probert and Thomas Thurtell then went to bed, leaving me, John Thurtell, and Noyes up About half an hour after they were gone to bed, Thomas Noyes followed, leaving John Thurtell and myself in the parlour John Thurtell desired the servant to bring in some coals I said to John Thurtell, "I shall lie down on the sofa," he said he would sit up and smoke I left him smoking by the fire, with his back towards me, and I laid down, pulling my great coat over me

About half-past six in the morning the servant came

When Mr. Probert said he would take you down in the chaise, did you consider that he was taking you down for the purpose of singing? Yes, certainly.

Did you sing? Yes.

Who was present when you sang? Mr. Probert, Mrs. Probert, her sister, Thomas and John Thurtell, and Mr. Noyes.

On what day was this? On Friday night, or more properly speaking, Saturday morning. It was after twelve I dare say.

Then, of course, it was after John Thurtell had come into the room and informed you of the murder? Yes.

Did you hear John Thurtell say he kept six pounds for himself? No, Sir.

Then after John Thurtell had called you and Probert out, and told you of the diabolical deed, you returned quietly to sing in the parlour? Yes, Sir.

How long were you absent? About ten minutes.

You did not say any thing in your statement to-day, of your being employed to sing? No, I did not.

Did you go out with a lantern? No, I am ready to take my oath I did not.

Did Mr. Probert? Not that I know. I never saw any lantern on the premises, except one in the stable.

Who had that? The boy.

Did no further conversation take place respecting the murder than what you have stated? No.

You were fully aware of the murder? I was not fully aware of it. I was told of it by John Thurtell.

You saw the watch? Yes, and I thought that was suspicious.

In the presence of Mr. J. Thurtell, Mr. Probert, &c., and after the former had told you he had murdered this unfortunate person, you amused yourself by singing? Yes, Sir.

And you made yourselves merry during the evening? Yes, Sir.

And you considered that the 6l. you received was for your exertions on this evening? I was there on the Sunday.

Did you consider that you received the 6l. for no other reason? No, certainly not.

You have stated where John Thurtell bought the pistols, and that he said they were for shooting cats? Yes.

After they were bought, did nothing pass between you and him? Nothing whatever.

Do you know where the sack was bought? Sir? [The prisoner evidently must have heard this question as well as any that preceded it, but he did not wish to answer it. His deafness recurred on one or two occasions afterwards.]

Do you know where the sack was bought? Yes. (Reluctantly.)

Who bought it? I did.

Do you know where the cord was bought? Yes.

Who bought that? I did.

Where did you buy the sack? In Broad Street.

Do you know the shop? Yes, very well.

Do you know the number? No.

Is it Broad Street, St. Giles's, or in the city? It is in St. Giles's.

Near what place in St. Giles's? Near—Oh, bless my soul, what is the name of the place?—near a kind of turn-stile—Middle Row, I think, they call it.

Is it called Hind Street? Sir?

Is it called Hind Street? Sir, I don't know.

You have lived in London all your life, you must know the name of the street. It is near Hind Street.

What did you do with the sack, after you bought it? I took it to John Thurtell, he said it was for the purpose of putting game in.

What was the cord for? I am sure I can't tell. I suppose it was to tie the game up.

Had you no conversation with John Thurtell respecting the purpose for which the rope was bought? None.

Where did you take it? I took it to Mr. John Thurtell, at the Coach and Horses.

Where did he say he was going? He said, that he had to meet a gentleman; but he did not say where he was going.

Did John Thurtell pay you before the singing, or after? After Mrs. Probert had gone to bed.

Did he take the money from his pocket? Yes.

Not from a pocket-book? No, it was a kind of note-case.

Do you know why he gave Mr. Probert 6l? No.

Nothing passed about the murder, except at the beginning of the evening? No.

You were all extremely cheerful? Yes.

Did you see a purse?—Mr. John Thurtell had a brown purse.

Did you see him have a bill-case? I saw a small note-case, which he threw into the fire.

What did he do with the purse? He threw it into the fire also.

Did you see any papers?—Nothing but a betting-book, which was thrown into the fire.

Did you not hear John Thurtell say, when he paid you and Probert 6*l*., "That is your share of the money found?" He did not say, "That is your share," but "That I consider your share," or something to that effect.

I will take your own words, but of what was the money a share? I do not know.

Did not Thurtell say it was of the "money found?" Never.

The following statement, which the prisoner had previously made to Mr. Noel, after his examination by the Magistrates, which he had himself signed, was here handed to him, and he read it. "On the return of Thurtell, after the body was removed from the lane, and sunk in Probert's pond, Thurtell produced the *reader* (flash for note-case), out of which he took three 5*l*. notes, and also a purse, from which he took four sovereigns. He gave Probert and myself 6*l*. each, as our share of the property found; he then burnt the note-case and the purse; he also burnt a betting-book, which was a red one. At the request of John Thurtell, I purchased in Hind Street, Bloomsbury, a sack and some cord, which went down in Thurtell's chaise. Further, John Thurtell told me, when describing the manner in which he had tackled with Mr Weare, that at one time he had nearly mastered him, and got above him, upon which he took out his knife and cut his throat. *The blood of Mr Weare in consequence, came on his face and into his mouth in such quantities, that he was nearly choaked.* It was in consequence of this that he was seized with sickness at supper, and could not eat any pork. After he had cut Mr. Weare's throat, the unfortunate gentleman's strength failed, and he threw him off. He then took his own shawl, and wrapped it round the neck of the corpse, to prevent the effusion of blood." (This shawl was found round the neck of the deceased, when he was taken out of the pond.)

Is that statement correct? It is.

Then he did say, "That is your share of the money found?" Yes, Sir.

What else passed that evening, after the money was divided? I do not recollect that any thing was said.

Where did you hire the horse and chaise? At Mr. Probatt's, the Golden Cross, Charing Cross.

Is he any relation to Mr Probert, of Gill's Hill Lane? No.

Do you know of your own knowledge, or from any information which you have received, where the clothes of the deceased are? I do not. I wish I did, I would freely tell. I should consider they were near the pond, as they were cut off.

You say the clothes were cut off? I should consider so, as the body was naked when Mr John Thurtell carried it.

And you do not know where the clothes now are? I have not the slightest knowledge.

Had you ever any of the deceased's clothes on your back? Never.

What became of them after they were cut off? I don't know.

How do you know that they were cut off? I was told so by Mr John Thurtell.

Had you any clothes on but your own on Sunday? I had on a suit of black, belonging to Mr John Thurtell.

Why did you change your dress? It was Sunday, and I wished to appear decent and respectable.

What dress did John Thurtell wear on Sunday? He had on a blue coat, and I think light small-clothes and gaiters.

What became of your own clothes? I left them at Mr Probert's, I have them on now.

Have you never seen the clothes of the deceased from Friday up to the present time? Yes. I am given to understand that the clothes which Mr. John Thurtell sent to my lodgings were the property of the deceased, and I gave that information to the officers.

Did you give that information after you were in custody? Yes, on Wednesday night. Prior to that time, I had every reason to believe that the property belonged to Mr John Thurtell.

Do you know what property John Thurtell took with him to town? I know that there were a carpet bag, and a great coat, in the gig.

If you did not see the clothes, how could you give a description of them to the officers? I did not say that I did not see them.

How did you come to know the contents of the carpet bag? Mr. John Thurtell opened the bag at my lodgings, took the clothes out, sorted them, and put them in my drawers.

Where did the bag originally come from? It came from Probert's in the bag, with a gun, a powder flask, and a coat.

Did you see those things put in the gig? No, when I first saw them they were in the gig.

What has become of the box-coat? I really don't know.

You said the things were deposited in your lodgings? Yes, and they ought to be there now.

Did you see a box among the things? There was a backgammon-box, so Mr John Thurtell called it.

Were you and John Thurtell in the lane near Mr. Probert's house, any time between five and ten o'clock on the Saturday morning? Mr Probert, Mr John Thurtell, and myself, as I told you before, went across a ploughed field, and broke into a lane through a sort of thicket.

What did you do when you got into the lane? We merely took a walk and went back again.

Did not Mr. John Thurtell say any thing to the individuals whom he saw in the lane? Not to my knowledge.

You understand my questions to apply to Saturday morning? Oh! Saturday? I thought you meant Sunday.

Did you not, between five and nine o'clock on Saturday morning, go into the lane with John Thurtell? Yes.

Whom did you see there? We met two men.

Did John Thurtell speak to them? Yes.

What did he say? He said he had lost a handkerchief and a knife.

How far from Mr Probert's house was the spot where you spoke to these men? About a quarter of a mile.

Had you and Mr Thurtell been looking for the knife? No, I did not know he had lost it till he told the men.

Did he say he had been capsized? Nothing of the sort.

Did John Thurtell say any thing about the lane whilst you were walking with him? No.

Then am I to understand that the only conversation which passed respecting the murder was that which took place at Probert's house? Yes.

And you thought so little of it, that you sat down to singing? Yes.

Coroner's Inquest.

JUROR.—Which way did Probert go when he set you down from his gig on the night he drove you from town? He went on the road, and came back in half an hour

What excuse did he make for leaving you in that way? Oh, he did not say any thing, but told me to wait there till he returned

What did you pay for the sack which he bought in St. Giles's, on the evening of the murder? I do not remember.

Was that sack the one the body of Mr. Weare was put into after his murder by John Thurtell? I presume it was

[At this time the prisoner took up the snuffers and trimmed the candle which stood on the table before him]

The CORONER —What did you suppose Thurtell to mean when he spoke of the "money found"? I have not the least idea I was not very *compos mentis* that night, and did not take particular notice.

Did you see a piece of sponge about Probert's house? I saw a sponge in the chaise, which was taken out of a pail in the stable

Did you ever sponge a coat at Probert's house? No, I brushed Mr John Thurtell's coat

For what purpose did you bring a spade with you from London? It was at the request of Mr John Thurtell

Did you ever use that spade, or see it used, or have any conversation about it? No

On what day did you take it down? On Sunday morning

Who took the spade, when you got to your journey's end? Mr T Thurtell threw it over a hedge, near the gate where the dead man was brought out Mr. John Thurtell bought the spade on Saturday night.

You did not see the spade used? No, when I saw it bought, I thought it was for Probert to be used in gardening

A JUROR.—On Friday you went to Probert's with thick mustachios and whiskers, what has become of them? That is very evident

For what reason did you shave them? For nothing particular, my beard is very strong, and grows fast

Did you shave in the country, or in London? In London, at my lodgings.

The prisoner's statement, as taken down by the Clerk, was then read to him, and he was asked whether he would sign it as a correct account of his voluntary statement He replied, " Yes, certainly " He then took the pen, and signed his name on every page We watched his hand whilst he was writing, but could not perceive the slightest tremor. His self-possession whilst under examination was perfectly astonishing; he never changed countenance, not a muscle of his face was ever moved, and while every one shuddered with horror at his dreadful narration, he betrayed not the least emotion. After the examination was over, the handcuffs were put on him, and having thick wrists, as they were being screwed on by the gaoler, he cried out, "Curse it, don't torture me!—don't put me in purgatory," and appeared very angry. By the direction of the Coroner, a larger pair of hand-cuffs was placed on him.

During the examination of Hunt, the room became so hot, from the number of persons present, that a window was opened on the side next to the road. A person of genteel appearance, immediately under it, was then heard talking loudly and vehemently, expressing a desire to see the Magistrate. "I want to see him!—I must see him!—I will see him!" was exclaimed with such vociferation, that the Coroner, suspending the proceedings, required to know what the man wanted, observing that he had better be brought into the room.

A JUROR.—He only wants to get admittance, I believe.

HUNT (turning round to the window, which was behind him, and then to the Coroner), Oh! it's a person of the name of ———, he is a friend of the Thurtells, and a madman, I assure you.

Mr NOEL.—That may be, but he should be spoken with.

Mr Noel then went out, and remained in conversation with the supposed madman (who, however, appeared in manner and conversation, quite rational) for upwards of half an hour.

WILLIAM PROBERT was then brought, handcuffed, into the room. He is a tall and robust man, and has black hair and eyes. His countenance betrayed an expression of fear and anxiety, and his deportment was not so composed as that of Hunt. The handcuffs were taken off him, and the Coroner addressing him said, that as he had heard Mr Hunt's statement, he thought it right to give him (Probert) an opportunity of saying what he wished. At the same time he would advise him to abstain from saying any thing which might criminate himself, and begged him to understand that he must expect to receive no favour for any disclosure which he might make.

Probert expressed a desire to speak, and immediately proceeded as follows:—On Friday afternoon I dined at Mr Tetsall's with the two Thurtells, Mr Hunt, and Mr Noyes, and one or two other gentlemen, whose names I do not recollect. John Thurtell asked me to lend him five or six pounds. I borrowed 5*l*. of Tetsall, and gave them to John Thurtell. I also gave Hunt 1*l*. for John Thurtell, which made 6*l*. I think about six o'clock I left to go home. John Thurtell asked me if I would drive Hunt to my house; if not, he said he would hire a horse for him. I said, that as I was going home, I would drive him. Thurtell said, "I am coming down to spend a day with you, and shall bring a friend with me." I said, "Very well, I shall be happy to see you." He said, "My brother and family have been down so much with you, that I do not like to trouble you."

I then left Tetsall's in the gig, with Hunt, and came to the Bald-faced Stag, a little way before you come to Edgware, where I stopped. Hunt said, "I must not go in there, I have not returned the two horse-cloths which I borrowed." He walked on to Mr Clarke's, at Edgware, where I took him up, and drove on very near to Mr Phillimore's lodge, when he said, "I must wait here for Mr John Thurtell, and you may go on."

The CORONER.—Did you not stop at this house as you went down?

PROBERT.—I beg your pardon—we did, and had three or four glasses of brandy and water. We waited here nearly an hour. About nine o'clock we left here, and went near to Mr Phillimore's lodge. Hunt said, "I must wait here for John Thurtell, and you may go on." I got within an hundred yards of my house, and then I met John Thurtell. He said, "Where is Hunt?" I said, "I have left him on the road, waiting for you." He said, "You must drive back then, and fetch him; for I have killed my friend, and do not want him." I said, "Good God! I hope you have not killed any person." He said, "I have, and now I am happy, for he has robbed me of several hundreds."

I then returned for Hunt, and brought him to my gate. Hunt said to Thurtell, "Where could you pass me, John?" Thurtell replied, "It don't matter where I passed you, I have done the trick." I said, "For God's sake, who is the man you have killed?" Thurtell answered, "It's no matter to you; you don't know his name, and never saw him." He added, "If you ever say a word about it, by G—d you shall share the same fate. Joe and I thought to have had your brother-in-law that is to be, the other day, only he ran too fast when he saw the house."

The CORONER.—Whom do you suppose he meant by Joe?

PROBERT.—Joseph Hunt. Thurtell also said, "I have got more to kill, and if you do not do what is right, you will be one of them." We then went into the parlour, and had something to eat and drink. Thurtell pulled out a purse, and shook it, and said, "I believe this is all I have got for what I have done." I do not know how much was in the purse.

The CORONER.—Did Thurtell produce any thing else?

PROBERT.—A gun and a watch. After some time had elapsed, he pulled out several papers, and began to look at them and throw them into the fire. Both Hunt and Thurtell threw papers into the fire. They handed them to each other. I then had occasion to go up stairs to Mrs. Probert, and I saw no more of the papers. When I came down stairs again, Thurtell said, "Now we must go and fetch the body, and throw it into your pond." I replied, "That you shall never do." He said, "You must do as I tell you, and I will come and fetch it away to-morrow." Thurtell and Hunt then fetched the body, and threw it into the pond. I saw them throw it in. After that, Thurtell produced three 5l. notes, which he took out of a small note-case. He said, "Here are the 6l. which I borrowed of you yesterday," and he gave me a 5l. note and a sovereign, and said, "I was answerable for it to Mr. Tetsall."

CORONER.—Is Mr. Tetsall in the room? Yes, he is.

MAGISTRATE.—He ought to withdraw.

CORONER.—It is now unnecessary.

PROBERT.—That and the sovereigns in the purse was all the money I saw. In about half an hour I went to bed, and left Hunt and Thurtell with a bottle of brandy on the table. Mrs. Probert and Miss Noyes were both in bed at this time, and had been in bed about an hour and a half. About half an hour before Mrs Probert went to bed, she pressed Hunt and Thurtell to retire to bed. One of them made answer, "You need not trouble yourself, Mrs Probert: we have a good deal of night-work to do, and wish to use ourselves to it." When I went to bed, Mrs. Probert was crying, and she said, "For God's sake what are you, Mr Hunt, and Thurtell doing up? If I knew what it was about I would inform against you.' It was then one o'clock. I replied, "My dear, I am doing nothing that will ever hurt me. I am not guilty of any thing." I then went to bed, and I believe I lay until past nine o'clock on Saturday morning. Not an hour did I sleep all that night; neither did Mrs. Probert, for she was fretting all night. When I came down stairs, both Hunt and Thurtell were standing in the parlor, and the cloth was laid for breakfast. We had some breakfast, and afterwards the boy put the horse to the chaise, and Hunt and Thurtell left my place about half-past ten o'clock. The boy put one or two bundles, a gun, and a carpet bag, into the chaise I suspected that these things belonged to the deceased. I went into the yard, and Thurtell said, "We shall come down and dine with you to-morrow, and bring my brother and Noyes, most likely." On Sunday, Thomas and John Thurtell, Hunt, and Noyes, came to my house. As we sat down to dinner, Hunt and John Thurtell observed that I scarcely ate two mouthfulls, and John Thurtell said, " You will never do for a *Turpin*." This was said before the females, Mrs Probert and Miss Noyes, who did not perceive what it meant

CORONER.—They must have known what was meant; Turpin was a notorious highwayman and murderer, and what John Thurtell meant was obvious

The CORONER and Mr NOEL observed that the prisoner ought to be cautious to say nothing that could criminate himself.

PROBERT.—After dinner we walked in the garden. Whilst we were there, John Thurtell said to me, "Do you see how my Joseph is dressed to-day, does he not cut a good figure?" Hunt had on a buff waistcoat and a plaid handkerchief Thurtell said they were the deceased's clothes I said, "If they are the deceased's clothes, good God, how can you wear them?" Hunt replied, "What is that to you? they are not your clothes."

The CORONER and Mr NOEL again cautioned witness to be careful of what he said.

PROBERT —I hope you will tell me when to stop —We retired into my house, and a Mr. Hoeward called upon me, then about six o'clock

The CORONER —If you take my advice, you will give us no more

PROBERT.—If you please, Sir I can only say that I

E

am not a murderer. I never saw the man, and I never knew his name; I declare to God

CORONER —I again advise you, though I am not bound to sit here to give advice, that you shall say no more, for what you say of occurrences after this can only injure you

PROBERT —I thank you, Sir, I will only say that I am not the murderer, and I declare solemnly before my God and Saviour, that I never knew the man, or saw him, or even knew the name of the man, or that he was coming down from London; God Almighty knows that I am not guilty of this horrid murder. I knew of John Thurtell coming down, as he said to me, with a gentleman, but I did not know who the person was; he said they should shoot on Lord Essex's estate

Mr. NOEL.—On the part of the prosecution. I advise you to say no more

CORONER —I have one question or two to ask Mr Probert

PROBERT —I will answer.

CORONER —Did you take part of the deceased's money? No, I did not

Did you see the deceased's clothes taken out of your house? No, my boy put the gun into the chaise

Did Hunt come down to sing professionally? No

Did he sing on the Friday night, after you had been informed of the murder, in your parlor? I rather think he did sing one song, but I cannot swear

Did Hunt receive any money from John Thurtell on that night? I think he did, but I am not positive

Did you order John Thurtell to bring you a new spade down from London? Never

Did you ever see a spade that he brought down? Yes, I found one on my grounds after the murder.

A JUROR.—You called at this house on the Friday night, with Hunt, about the time of the murder? Yes, I did.

You said to the landlord that Hunt was a good singer? Yes, I did

Were you both inebriated? A little

Probert then withdrew

Mr. NOEL said, that the confession of Hunt was disproved in many important parts; that he had grossly prevaricated, and though he had been admitted a witness for the Crown by the Magistrates, yet the Court of King's Bench had the power by law, upon proof of such confession being false, to reject it, and put the man upon his trial. This question was, however, quite distinct from the present inquiry

The CORONER asked if a gentleman named WOOD, from London, was in the room, and was informed that he had waited for some hours to give evidence, but supposing, from the length of time occupied in taking Hunt's evidence, that the inquiry would not terminate that night, he had returned in a chaise to London

One of the Magistrates regretted the circumstance, as his evidence would have developed a most atrocious system, which had been planned in London, for a series of murders

FOREMAN.—It would be a pity if this cold-blooded villain should escape justice, for he is in my mind the most guilty of all; he evidently assisted in planning the murder, he bought the sack in which the victim was to be deposited after his murder; and also the spade to dig his grave, and the cord to tie up the sack; and assisted in buying the pistols. I consider Mr Probert an innocent person, in comparison with Hunt. The manner in which he made his statement to the Jury, proves him to be the most unfeeling, cold-hearted wretch alive; he showed no signs of compunction for the horrid deed, no regret that he had assisted in the murder of a fellow-creature.

The CORONER then proceeded to charge the Jury in the following words:—

GENTLEMEN OF THE JURY,

Such a body of evidence, affecting the persons who are in custody, charged with the crime which you have, with extraordinary patience, been employed for the last two days in investigating, has been laid before you, that it will be quite unnecessary, in my opinion, to detain you long in commenting upon the facts which have been detailed; for a more horrid, a more cruel, more premeditated case of assassination and robbery, I think, never took place in this or any other country

Your first inquiry is this—Are you of opinion that John Thurtell is the person who committed the murder?—Of this fact, I think there can be but one opinion

The second inquiry is—Were Probert and Hunt accessaries *before* the fact?

Gentlemen, I will offer a very few words upon the law of murder, as laid down by the most eminent authorities; I shall take the opportunity of stating that a Coroner's Jury cannot take cognizance of a party accused who are accessaries *after* the fact, you must come to the conclusion, that Hunt and Probert were accessaries *before* the fact, before you can return a verdict of Murder against them; and I think that you, wishing, as you evidently must do, to put these parties on their several trials, will not be long in coming to that conclusion.

It is not necessary to make them accessaries before the fact, that they should be on the spot, or near the place where the murder was committed, at the time of its perpetration; it is enough if they have in any way aided, or countenanced, the commission of the crime. That Hunt premeditated and concerted the assassination and robbery with John Thurtell, cannot be doubted by any rational and thinking person. What could have been his object in purchasing the pistols, sack, cord, and spade, on the day of the murder; and why should Hunt have been set down by Probert, from his chaise, near Phillimore Lodge, but for the purpose of joining J. Thurtell, to aid him in murdering Mr Weare? That such was their object, Gentlemen— that such was the previous agreement between Hunt and J. Thurtell, I think, is evident, from the language used by Hunt and J. Thurtell, at Probert's Gate, directly after the murder was committed, and also from Hunt stating to Probert, " that he had to wait for J. Thurtell, by appointment."

The language used at Probert's cottage gate, is this:— Hunt said to John Thurtell, " Where could you pass me?" Thurtell replied, " It don't matter where I passed you, I have done the trick." What was meant by " the trick," is evident enough; it could mean nothing else but the murder and robbery previously planned.

Now, Gentlemen, what are the facts that inculpate Probert in this foul proceeding? These, Gentlemen, are, in my opinion, the main facts, besides many circumstances of less prominence in the plot of this singular drama. First, his dining with the party, in their lodgings in London, on the afternoon, and only a few hours before they left London with their victim. In the next place, Probert says, in his statement to you, " that he agreed with John Thurtell to bring Hunt down to his cottage;" but instead of bringing him down to the cottage, he puts him down from the chaise, at some distance from it, with the avowed purpose of waiting for John Thurtell. Why should he wait for John Thurtell? Was it possible that Probert could be ignorant of the intention of the party? Did he not know that the intention of Hunt was to assist in dispatching Weare? Is it possible he could be ignorant of it? I think not; and I think I am justified in that opinion, by an admission of Probert's, which I have a right to take advantage of, as he made it, after repeated warnings, given by me and Mr Noel, viz. —that Thurtell said to him, " This is all I got by the job." after which he receives part of the money. Hunt also stated in his confession, that on Probert receiving the six pounds, John Thurtell said, " This is your share of the money found." Found where, Gentlemen? found on the man for whom he had " just done the job," as he had previously asserted to Probert.

Gentlemen, the actual spot where the murder was committed, I think, is clearly identified. This place was in Gill's Hill Lane, by the side of the hedge which was broken, and where the blood was found in streams; and I think it very likely, that after the deceased was murdered, he was dragged by his murderers, through the hedge into the ploughed field, where the body lay, till Hunt, Probert, and John Thurtell, left the cottage while supper was being prepared (as is sworn to by Probert's cook and his boy, Haddis,) with a lantern, when they no doubt removed it to Probert's pond. In fact, Gentlemen, Probert admits that he saw it put into his pond, and this is in less than an hour after the man was murdered.

Another fact I will just advert to, affecting Probert. It is this:—The men who saw John Thurtell and Hunt in the lane, looking about the spot where the pistol and knife were found, stated, that they saw a tall man come down the lane after Hunt and John Thurtell, with a large dog; and Probert's servants stated, that Probert was in the habit of going out with his dog, and I draw this inference from that fact, that Probert's object in going down the lane at that time in the morning was the same as that of Hunt and Thurtell, viz. to recover possession of the lost pistol and knife left there by the murderers. That it was Hunt who accompanied John Thurtell early in the morning down the lane, is proved by the witnesses stating that he had large black mustachios and whiskers, which he wore at that time, and has admitted he since shaved them off. And I must remark that Hunt went too far when he stated, " that the clothes were cut off the dead body," for that proves that he participated in its removal which is further confirmed by the fact of his discovering the pond, or pit, to which he states that John Thurtell removed the body, and in which the police officers, by him directed, found it.

In addition to these strong circumstances, all tending to shew that Hunt, John Thurtell, and Probert, were participators in the murder, we have another fact of very considerable importance—I mean the fact of the bloody shirt and handkerchief, cut off the deceased's body, in Probert's yard, after the body was taken out of the pond, being found under a heap of dung in Probert's stable.

From the whole of these facts, devoloping an act of more than fiend-like barbarity, you can come but to one conclusion, in my mind, that John Thurtell is a principal in the murder, and that Hunt and Thurtell are accessaries *before* the fact. If such be your opinion, you will say so, and if you cannot at present arrive at that conclusion, it will be necessary for me to read through the whole of the body of evidence, making such comments thereon as the case may require

JUROR.—If we should be of opinion that Probert was only an accessary *after* the fact, or, in other words, that he did not know of the murderous intention of Hunt and John Thurtell, till after the deed was done, have you no power to send him for trial?

CORONER.—I cannot commit him under the Coroner's Inquest, without you find that he was an accessary *before* the fact, though, of course, the Magistrates have the power to commit him for trial.

The Jury consulted for a few minutes, and returned a verdict of WILFUL MURDER against JOHN THURTELL as a *principal*, and against HUNT and PROBERT, as *accessaries before the fact*

The verdict being recorded, and the presentment signed by the Jury, warrants were issued by the Coroner to commit the parties to take their trials at the next Assizes for the county of Hertford, and they were conveyed the same night to Hertford gaol

After the verdict was returned, the Coroner and Magistrates assembled gave orders for Thomas Thurtell to be brought before them. He was brought into the Jury-room handcuffed, but the handcuffs were then taken off.

The CORONER congratulated him that he was not inculpated in the dreadful transaction that had alarmed the whole county.—T. THURTELL, who has an impediment in his speech, endeavoured to reply, but, for some time, such was his agitation, he could not give utterance to a syllable At last he said, " It was a horrible transaction, but I thank God I had not the remotest idea of the dreadful intentions of my brother, or that the murder was committed, till it was communicated to me after my apprehension "

The County Magistrates then informed him, that they were about to commit him to the County Goal, upon a warrant brought from London, on a charge of conspiring to set fire to some premises in Watling Street.

He declared, that however guilty his brother might be, and he admitted that he had led a life the most wicked and dissolute for several years, yet he was himself innocent of the charge upon which he was about to be committed. He stated that his brother had forged his acceptance to bills to the amount of 600*l.* only eight months ago, and he was compelled to pay the money to save his life

The Magistrates lamented that a person who was related to one of the most respectable families in Norwich, should have been implicated in such a dreadful accusation

Thomas Thurtell burst into tears, and said, " Good God ! what misery must my poor father and mother endure on hearing of the situation of their children ! my brother's fate, I suppose, is sealed , pray God support my father and mother !"

Before the Magistrates separated from the Inquest-room on Saturday night, they had a private examination, and we understand that they discussed a question as to the propriety of issuing warrants against persons accused of another foul transaction, a clue to which was furnished by a gentleman named Wood, and developed by a written statement made by Thomas Thurtell to the Magistrates, the substance of which we give below, omitting only those parts which, by a premature disclosure, might have frustrated the ends of justice in the apprehension of other criminals.

THOMAS THURTELL'S STATEMENT.

It commenced by stating, that on the Friday of the murder, he met his brother and Hunt, at the Coach and Horses and then goes on to state, that in the evening Hunt came up to the door in a gig, drawn by a grey horse, into which John Thurtell got, and drove away; Hunt went away with

Probert. He saw two pistols with his brother John, and asked him what he wanted with them? Hunt made use of a dreadful expression, and asked, "What was that to him?" and then turning to Probert, said, "Bill, will you be in it?" Before they went away, Probert smiled. Hunt had previously brought a sack and some cord, which he put into John Thurtell's gig, and then said, "Jack, it's all right, drive away like ———"

Hunt said, before they left the house in the evening, addressing himeslf to John Thurtell, "Jack, our friends had better be civil, or they will get served out," following this threat up with the most horrible oaths. Both J Thurtell and Hunt were constantly talking of ripping people up, and shooting them, but he (T. Thurtell) thought it was only their idle bravado He was engaged the whole of Friday night, which has been confirmed by credible witnesses.

On Saturday morning he went to the Coach and Horses, and remained there all day; John came about three o'clock, and was in excellent spirits, he (Thomas Thurtell) remarked that his hands were much scratched, and asked him how it happened? John said, he, Probert, and Hunt, had been netting partridges, and that his knuckles were scratched by the brambles; he observed a gold watch in John's hand, and asked him where he got it? John told him to ask no questions, as it was no business of his.

Hunt came in shortly after with a bundle, containing a blue coat, a buff waistcoat, and a pair of leather breeches, which he had taken out of pawn for John Thurtell. On putting down the bundle, he pulled out of his pocket three sovereigns, some silver, and a 5*l* note, and said to Mr. Noyes, who was present, "Now, you ———, do any of you want change of a 50*l*. note? for if you do, I'm your man; we are Turpin-like lads, and have done the trick," and then he laughed heartily, and winked to John.

After Noyes went out, he (Thomas) feeling surprised at such declarations, said to his brother, "What have you been doing?" when Hunt exclaimed, "Why, committing b———y murder, to be sure." These words being of ordinary use in Hunt's mouth, he did not believe him, and took no further notice. Hunt then went on to say, "We have been shooting game, and Probert has been holding the bag" He did not for a moment believe they had committed murder.

In the evening he went again to the Coach and Horses,

and saw Hunt and his brother at supper, they were eating oysters, Hunt repeated that they had been Turpin-like lads, and addressing John, said, " We must have a bottle of wine —nothing else will do now," and then laughed He said, in continuation, " that the old woman (meaning his wife), was in a precious rage with him for stopping out all night, but when he pulled out the money, she was satisfied. He gave her a sovereign, and told her to get a pair of fowls, and a piece of pickled pork."

The statement then went on to detail the circumstances of Thomas Thurtell walking down to Probert's on Sunday morning, he was overtaken on the road by his brother and Hunt, who took him up; on their reaching Edgware they met Noyes, and John alighted and joined him. He went on with Hunt to Probert's, and he observed a new spade in the gig, Hunt threw the spade over the hedge, saying, " that Probert did not wish his wife to know he was extravagant."

They all dined together that day. Probert, Mrs. Probert, her sister Miss Noyes, Mr. Noyes, John Thurtell, and Hunt. Nothing particular occurred. He remembered somebody calling on Probert and accompanying him on business to Mr. Nicholls's. When Probert returned, he appeared extremely agitated. He (T. Thurtell) went to bed, with his children early, and neither heard or saw more.

[In the above statement, we have purposely omitted some facts, on which new discoveries hang. Thomas Thurtell was in the habit of going down to Probert's cottage every Sunday, to see his children.]

EXAMINATION OF MR. TETSALL

"WATFORD, FRIDAY, Nov. 7

Several of the Magistrates met this day at the house of Mr. Clutterbuck, in order to continue their examination and inquiries Mr. Tetsall was for a long time yesterday under examination before five Magistrates, and two Gentlemen of this county, but no one connected with the public press was allowed admission. The following is a detail of the examination, as accurate as it is possible under such circumstances to obtain it,—

MAGISTRATE.—What is your name? Charles Tetsall.

You are the landlord of the Coach and Horses Tavern, Conduit Street? Yes, I am.

When did the Thurtells come to lodge at your house? The two Thurtells came to my house with Probert on the Tuesday before the murder, but they did not sleep at my house till the following night.

What did they say to you when they came to your house? Probert said, these gentlemen have business that they wish to transact in private; which they cannot do in a public room like your parlor; I know you have a private room, can't you let us have it while we stop? I replied, "Most certainly, if you want it only for a short time." Probert said "it is only wanted for a short time."

Who slept at your house on the Wednesday night prior to the murder? One of the Thurtells, but I am not positive which of them; I told them I had only a double-bedded room to spare, and they said that would do very well.

Who visited the Thurtells at your house? Mrs. Walker and her husband, and other persons, strangers to me, whose business I had no knowledge of.

Who were at your house on the Thursday? I believe there were seven persons who dined at my house.

Do you know who they were? I do not know them all.

State those you do know. John and Thomas Thurtell, Hunt, Probert, and Thomas Noyes; the other two were perfect strangers.

What sort of men were the strangers; describe them? One was a fine portly man, at least six feet in height, dressed in black, fresh coloured, and had a very gentlemanly appearance.

What sort of a man was the other? He was a man of short stature, florid complexion, and what I call a good looking little man.

What was his dress? He wore a black coat and waistcoat, his small clothes I cannot describe, nor can I say if he wore trowsers or breeches.

Did you know Mr. Weare, the deceased? No, I did not.

You never saw Mr. Weare? I never saw Mr. Weare, till I saw him in his coffin, at Elstree.

Then you did not know Mr Weare at all? No, I did not, Sir.

Have you any reason to think that the deceased person you saw in his coffin, at Elstree, was the little man that you describe as having dined at your house with the Thurtells, &c. on the Thursday? I certainly believe not, he did not appear to me to resemble the deceased.

Then you feel confident that Mr. Weare was not the person? I never heard the name of Weare mentioned amongst the party, and from my observation of the deceased when in his coffin, I feel almost positive that it could not be him.

Who slept at your house on the Thursday night? They had the room to themselves, sometimes one and sometimes the other slept in the room, but which slept on that night there I do not know, but I think it was Thos Thurtell.

It is very strange that you should not know those two persons whom you have described as strangers? However strange it may appear, it is certainly the truth; they had been invited as I suppose, by the Thurtells, and my curiosity did not lead me to ask who they were, and their names I never heard.

Were their names never mentioned? If they were I did not observe it, and to my knowledge I never saw them before or since.

Do you know a man named Lemon? No, I do not.

You never heard his name mentioned among this party at your house? I never did.

To your knowledge did no person of that name visit at your house? Not to my knowledge.

Was no card with the name of Lemon on it left for the party at your bar, or in the house? I never heard of a card being left of any kind at my house for the Thurtells, and I am positive no such thing was left.

It is very material that we should discover who those two strangers were, cannot you call to mind who they were? And did you never hear either of them named? To my knowledge I never heard either of them named. (This question was frequently repeated, and answered nearly in the same manner.)

You say you never saw these two strangers at your house at any other time? I never saw them at my house except on the Thursday, at least I have no recollection of it.

Who had you at your house on Friday? Five persons breakfasted in Thurtell's private room, for which they were charged 7s 6d., as they had beefsteaks.

Who were the five persons? John and Thomas Thurtell Hunt, Probert, and Thomas Noyes.

Did they remain in your house during the whole of the Friday? They were in and out of the house frequently; they considered the room their own, and went out and came in just as they pleased.

Did they all dine at your house on the Friday? I believe that four of them dined at my house on the Friday.

Did they have any wine after dinner? They drank beer at dinner, and drank grog after their dinner, and the charge altogether came only to 8s.

Did you lend any money on that day to any of the party? Yes, I did.

What money did you lend? I lent 5l.

To whom? To Mr. Probert.

What did he say when he borrowed the money? He sent word by my boy that he wanted to borrow 5l. and I sent it up to him; it was a 5l. note, and he sent it down again to me, and said he must have smaller change, and I then sent him five sovereigns in lieu of it, which he gave with another sovereign out of his pocket to John Thurtell.

Did you see him give it to John Thurtell? I did not see him give it, but Probert said that it was for John Thurtell.

You have known Probert for some time? Yes, for a series of years.

Did you owe him any money at the time you lent him the 5l.? Yes, I did.

How much? Between six and seven pounds.

And that is all? Yes, it was not seven pounds.

Then you did not consider you were running any risk by lending the money? Certainly not, as I was in his debt, and if he had asked me for 10l. he would have had it, if I had got it, such was my opinion of him.

And had you then such a good opinion of Probert? I had no business to have any other opinion of him, from my knowledge of him, he always acted uprightly in our dealings

Did you know that he had been a bankrupt? Yes, I did

And that he had not obtained his certificate? Yes, I did

And that he had been in the Bench for some time? Yes, I did.

And notwithstanding all this you lent him money? I certainly did.

And I suppose if any of the others had asked for money they might have had it? I beg your pardon, gentlemen; I certainly would not have lent money to persons that I was so unacquainted with; there is but one besides Probert that I would have lent a shilling to.

And pray who is that one? Mr. Thomas Noyes.

And you would have lent him money? Yes; if he had

asked to borrow 5*l.* he might have had it, if I had got it by me, such was my opinion of him; as far as I know of him I always considered him a gentleman.

He is a wine merchant, is he not? Yes, he is, and always was considered a respectable man.

You are not aware that you owe Mr. Noyes and Probert about 60*l.* for wine and spirits? I am quite sure that I do not owe a shilling beyond the 6*l.* odd, as I before stated, and that was on a bill which I owed to Noyes and Probert for wine; it was a kind of partnership transaction, and my bill was in the name of both of them, and of course I could not object to lend them 5*l.*

What time did they quit your house on the Friday? Between five and six o'clock in the evening.

Who were the parties? I understood that there was a gig brought to my door, and some of them left in it, to go to Probert's cottage. I did not see the gig at all.

Do you know who got into the gig? I do not.

Were there two gigs? I heard of only one being at my door, but there might have been another; I was busy, and did not observe.

Who do you suppose went away in the gig? I suppose it was John Thurtell and Hunt.

Why do you suppose so? Because they were always in the habit of riding together, and as they had a gig before, and rode out together, I supposed it might have been them.

Who generally brought the gig to the door? Hunt.

Who held the horse's head? I can't say.

What sort of a horse was it? A dark horse.

Any marks on the face? I did not observe.

Did you observe the conduct of the party in your room at any particular time? From what I saw of them I considered that Hunt was a great blackguard, and I did not think John Thurtell was any better. Thomas Thurtell appeared to be quite a different man; but the conversation of the other two was quite disgusting.

Did you observe an air gun about your room when they were there, or in their absence? I never saw any such weapon in the house.

What time did the party generally go to bed? Generally early, Thomas Thurtell was always early to bed, except on the Friday night.

What time did Thomas Thurtell go to bed on the Friday night? He came home about twenty minutes before twelve, and instantly retired to bed.

Did you see any pistols in your house on the Friday the murder was committed? I understood that John Thurtell had a pair of small pistols, but I never saw them.

Had you any pistols? Yes, I had a pair of duelling pistols.

Did you lose one of them? Some of the party took one of them away, and I understand it was Hunt.

When did you miss it? On the Friday morning, and I told Thomas Thurtell of it, and I said some of your party has taken it; but I suppose it is a joke, and they will return it. Thomas Thurtell said it was a liberty they ought not to take, but he supposed it was done in a joke.

What time did Thomas Thurtell get up on Saturday morning? He got up at nine o'clock.

What time did John Thurtell arrive at your house on Saturday? I do not know, for I did not see him come in, but both John and Thomas slept at my house that night.

Did Hunt come to your house on the Saturday? He was there, but did not stop long.

Did you notice his dress at that time? A black coat and waistcoat, as usual.

Were his whiskers then shaved off? They were not.

Were any persons of the party, besides Hunt and Thomas Thurtell at your house on the Saturday? Not that I remember at present.

Was a piece of roasting beef brought to your house on the Saturday? A butcher's boy brought a fine piece of roasting beef, and said it was for Mr. Noyes.

Was Mr. Noyes at your house on the Saturday? I believe he did look in; yes, he did.

Who did you see at your house on the Sunday morning? Before the Thurtells got up, Mr Noyes called; he saw the beef lying on the table, and said I am going down to the cottage, and Mr. John Thurtell is coming down also, with Hunt, in a gig.

Did Noyes leave without seeing the Thurtells then? Yes he did.

What further did Noyes say? He said he should walk on, and they would overtake him, and told me to be sure they put the beef in the gig, for on their arrival at Probert's, they should have no dinner, if they went without it.

How long had Noyes been gone from your house, when the others started on the Sunday morning? About two hours, after Noyes left, Hunt brought a gig to my door.

Did you observe any thing particular in the dress or appearance of Hunt or John Thurtell that morning? Yes About half an hour before they left, I and Thomas Thurtell were standing in the tap-room, when John Thurtell came down stairs; and as he passed the door, he observed, " How fine my brother is to-day." He was then dressed in buckskin breeches, light waistcoat, without a coat, and he looked very wild He crossed the road to Collis's, and got shaved, and dressed himself elegantly on his return.

Did they take any breakfast before they left? John Thurtell and Hunt had a cup of tea each and a glass of brandy, but ate nothing.

Who left your house in the gig on Sunday morning? Hunt and John Thurtell.

Not Thomas Thurtell? No.

Had Hunt his whiskers on when he left your house with John Thurtell, in the chaise, on Sunday morning? Yes, he had.

Describe his dress? He was shabbily dressed in an old black coat, waistcoat and trowsers. The coat was torn under the right arm, and the trowsers by the right pocket. He did not appear to me to be either washed or shaved.

Did you observe that his clothes were torn on the Friday? No, I did not.

Did you put any thing in the chaise? Yes, I did.

What did you put in the chaise? I put in Mr. Noyes's beef, and a bundle of clean linen of John Thurtell's, and I told Hunt and John Thurtell, on giving them the beef, that Mr. Noyes, who was gone on, had sent it, and if they did not take it with them they would have no dinner. John Thurtell observed that he should take Noyes up on the road, and I understood afterwards that he did.

When you put these things in the gig, did you observe any thing? Yes, I did, I saw a shovel or spade across the foot-board.

Could you swear to it if you were to see it again? I could not, it was quite new, and such an one, as is commonly used to dig ground with, for setting potatoes.

Did you make any observation upon their carrying a shovel with them? Yes, I did; I remarked to a person standing by, " what the d—— can these men want with a shovel on a Sunday, when they are going on an excursion of pleasure?"

Did you make any other remark? Yes, I said, on observing that Hunt was so very shabby, and his clothes torn, that if I were Thurtell I would not ride with him in that condition, there was such a contrast in the appearance of the two. Thurtell then drove off.

When did any of them return? Thomas and John Thurtell returned on the Monday, also Noyes and Hunt.

Were Hunt's whiskers shaved off then? No, they were not.

Did some of them sleep at your house on the Monday night? Yes, one or both of the Thurtells, I cannot say positively.

Who were at your house on the Tuesday? All except Probert.

When did Hunt arrive at your house after this time? He arrived with the boy Jem on Tuesday; at that time Probert was not with him.

Did the Thurtells sleep at your house on the Tuesday night? John did, I know, Thomas did not.

Did any other person sleep in the same room with John Thurtell that night? Yes, a stranger to me slept there, in Thomas Thurtell's bed

What sort of a man was he? A short, rather stout, pock-fretted man, about fifty years of age.

Did you ever see this man before or after that time? Never.

Where was this man when Ruthven arrested John Thurtell? In bed in the same room, and Ruthven saw him.

What became of the man? He dressed himself as quickly as possible and left the house.

Are you sure that that person was not Hunt? I am positive it was not.

Did you ever hear the parties talk about shooting or murdering any one? No, never.

Did you ever see a sack or cord in any part of your house, or in Thurtell's bed room? No, I did not.

When were Hunt's whiskers shaved off? On the Tuesday I observed it.

Do you know any thing more? I have no recollection of any thing further.

The MAGISTRATES said, "We must hold you to bail in the sum of 50*l.* to appear at the next Assizes, to give evidence against the accused."

Mr. Tetsall expressed his readiness to do so. His examination was read over to him, and he signed it, and having entered into the required recognizance, he was discharged *

---

* Mr Tetsall has published the following address to the public.

* "TO THE EDITOR OF THE OBSERVER

"SIR,—I shall esteem it a great obligation, if you will be so kind as to give insertion to the following humble address which I think it essential to lay before

MISCELLANEOUS INTELLIGENCE.

The atrocity which has marked the horrid crime that for these last few weeks has aroused the county of Herts, and the intense interest which so cold-blooded an act has created, induces us to offer to the public this Report of all the proceedings connected with this foul proceeding.

The unprecedented coolness with which this deep, sordid, and revengeful act appears to have been arranged and consummated, will form a black and frightful page in the annals of crime, and will exhibit the ripenings of villainy in a most painful and appalling light

Gill's Hill Lane, the spot in which the deed was perpetrated, is considerably past the cottage, nearly half a mile, is about a mile long, very

---

the Public, to rescue my character from that odium which prejudiced and unthinking persons may attach to it, from having unfortunately, but innocently admitted to my house, which is open to the Public—persons who have been guilty of a deed almost unequalled in the annals of crime, for its atrocity

I am, Sir, your obedient Servant,
CHARLES TETSALL."

Coach and Horses, Conduit Street,
Bond Street, Saturday, November 7th.

"To the Public—As an humble tradesman, depending entirely upon public opinion, I have felt it my duty to relate how far I have been acquainted with the persons who have been the chief actors in the late dreadful deed Though my neighbours, who have for many years witnessed my conduct, and which I may say without egotism, have joined in declaring me free from every imputation which had been attempted to slur my hitherto fair fame—as will every person who is personally acquainted with me—yet the public at large do not know who "Mr Tetsall" is, and without explanation, many persons may form conclusions prejudicial to me and my family, I must solemnly assert, that when Mr. Probert asked for the use of a private room for the Thurtells in my house, I had not the remotest idea of their intentions, and wicked plottings, I relied upon the word of Probert, who said "that they wanted to be private for a few days, till they could put in bail to answer the charge of conspiracy, and which they expected to be able to accomplish in the course of that week." My acquaintance with Mr Probert, was from having dealt with him in the wine and spirit trade, and I considered his recommendation of the parties (with whom I was previously unacquainted) to be quite sufficient, nor from their behaviour in my house during their short stay, had I the least conception that they were conspiring to commit so foul a crime, or that their pursuits were at all illegal.

Of this, I believe I may say, that the worthy Magistrates who discharged me, were fully satisfied of my innocence, and lest my being held to bail to appear at the trial to give evidence should be misunderstood, and lead some to suppose that there is still remaining some doubt on that subject, it is only necessary to say, that every individual who has been a witness in this affair, has been bound over in a recognizance to appear at the trial, which is usual in all cases of the kind To my neighbours and friends, who have so kindly shown their sympathy for my situation, and which has made an indelible impression upon my heart, I can only offer my grateful thanks, and the manner in which they have evinced their opinion of me, has been highly gratifying

I am, the Public's humble servant,
CHA. TETSALL.

crooked, and so narrow as to admit only of the passage of a single gig at a time, it is enclosed on each side by a very high hedge, each side thickly studded with trees, brambles, &c that on standing in the middle, and extending your arms, you can with ease touch the hedge on each side of you It is fifteen miles from London, and about a mile to the left of the road from Elstree to St. Albans In the broadest daylight it has a dark and gloomy appearance —The gap formed in the hedge, by dragging the body through, is now filled up with brambles, and every appearance of bloody twigs, leaves, &c most carefully removed At this place, owing to the late rains, a rivulet begins, so that, to pass it, you must mount the bank, and enter the adjoining field, which alone separates the place from a public road, Being a road very little used, it is not kept in so good a state as those who have occasion to pass along it would wish It is a singular fact, that nothing had been done towards repairing the road during the last forty years, until the next morning after the murder had taken place, when some men were set to work upon it by the surveyor of the roads Those were the men whom Hunt and John Thurtell spoke to on the Saturday morning, telling them that they had been thrown out of the gig, and had lost some property After Hunt and Thurtell had gone away, one of these men said to his companion, "Let us look in the hedge, and perhaps we shall find some money." They then began to look in the hedge, and found marks of blood, and the pistol and penknife, which led to a knowledge of the murder

The above Plate conveys an accurate idea of the spot. The gig is a little in advance, and the murderer or murderers having completed their horrid purpose, dragged their victim through a hole in the hedge, under the trunk of an old maple tree, with a turnip field adjoining, where it was left till subsequently conveyed to the pond in the garden It is presumed, that Thurtell did not intend to have advanced so far before he accomplished his work of death, but was obliged to go forward in consequence of meeting a poor man who was going to fetch his wife, who had been charing in the neighbourhood On the ensuing morning some men, who were engaged in widening the lane by cutting the hedges and trimming the banks, saw John Thurtell and Hunt going towards the place, which is here represented, evidently with the view of searching for the pistol which had been dropped the night before, as well as for Thurtell's knife, with which he had cut the throat of the deceased, and which he had also lost. Thurtell addressed the men on the subject of their labours, and said he had been capsised in his gig the preceding night; after which, he and Hunt were seen searching for something they said they had lost They shortly afterwards returned with a small bundle on the top of a stick, which the peasants since suppose contained clotted blood, removed to avoid discovery. After they had returned, the men went to the spot themselves to search, and there found a pen-knife and a pistol, both bloody, with bits of human hair attached to them, and the latter with the barrel filled with human brains. These escaped the hurried search of the prisoners, from their being concealed in the long grass and brambles The branches of the maple tree, and the hedge around it, were found stained with the marks of bloody hands, and the ground beneath was saturated with gore There were also marks of blood in the turnip field, where the body had lain, but all these have since been eradicated by curious spectators, some of whom have cut off the bloody branches of the trees, and carried them away The workmen have now extended their labours beyond the maple tree, so that little idea can at present be formed of its original state The superstitious feelings of the poor people in the neighbourhood have been excited towards the spot, and none will now pass it alone after dusk. It was in a line parallel to Gill's Hill Lane, divided by one field, that Mr. Smith and his wife were, with their donkey chaise, on the night of the murder, and here they heard the discharge of the pistol, and the dying groans of the deceased.

The place of the murder was in a dark place in Gill's Hill Lane, within about three hundred yards of Butler's Green Lane, and less than half a mile from that village, where Mr. Nicholls, who owns or farms the land where the murder was committed, resides, and whose servants found the knife and pistol

The Editor of the Sunday Times thus speaks on this dismal ravine of Gill's Lane. "The very approach to it looks as if one were treading the mazes of those subterraneous labyrinths, in which banditti were used to dwell Beneath hedges which meet over head, and through which there is hardly one point of escape, it twines along for about three quarters of a mile; at the end of which it assumes a character, even more dark and gloomy. One or two bushy trees form a canopy almost impenetrable, the hedges are of unusual closeness, the lane is not above six feet in width, the banks are so high, that escape would be difficult, even though the hedges were removed. It was here, according to the statement of Hunt, that the murderer, after having promised entertainment, after having passed the preconcerted place of assassination, after having passed the cottage to which he was pledged to conduct his companion, and where he had promised to entertain him with festivities and songs—It was here—here, that this most atrocious deed was perpetrated, it was here that he, who up to that period had worn the smile of a friend, turned round upon the man who had trusted him, upon the man who, good or bad, had reposed in him, and drawing from his bosom the fatal pistol, discharged it in the face of the unsuspecting victim, dashed him out of that vehicle which had been offered for his safe conveyance, pounced upon him— dashed the discharged pistol through his brains; struggled and struggled, was almost mastered; drew forth his knife, and with the coolness of an anatomist at a dissecting table, felt for the vein, divided it, and, tiger-like, drank the blood of his victim!"

PROBERT'S COTTAGE.

The next point to direct attention is the cottage Placed upon an eminence, it commands the adjoining fields, while it can be overlooked from no other place, and is approachable only by two close frightful lanes Even from these it is appparently shut up, a high and close railing, in which the door is not distinguishable, runs along the whole front of the house, and hides it, save the antique roof, from the view This cottage is an old farm house, in a very decayed state; and till within the last six or seven years, it was the residence for half a century, of a man as decayed as itself, who lived in seclusion, and conducted himself as a miser About six years ago, Probert obtained a lease of the cottage, without the farm When Probert's conduct brought him to the King's Bench and to Horsemonger Lane gaol, he let the cottage, and again obtained possession of it a few months ago

PROBERT'S COTTAGE FROM THE LANE.

To the left is the stable, in which the coats of the murderers were sponged. The cottage is a very rude, though rather picturesque fabric; this is heightened by its peculiar form, its turret-looking chimney-stack, and the dark ivyed roof of the kitchen. The place is wild—and romantic.

The house is a gloomy, it might be said a miserable looking place. It resembles a decayed farm-house more than any thing else. The premises are situated upon very high ground, and command a very beautiful prospect. They are so retired, however, as seldom or never to be approached unless by those going immediately to them, or those engaged in agricultural labours in the neighbourhood. Indeed, so much are they out of the ordinary beat of travellers, that Field, the landlord of the Artichoke, at Elstree, although living close to the spot for upwards of thirty years, never saw them but once. The lanes approaching them in all directions are extremely narrow, and will only admit one vehicle to pass at a time. The most direct road is through Elstree to Radlett, and then turning up to the left by the High Cross Road, you pass a farm house. Then again turn to the left, and so to the cottage. The distance from Radlett is about half a mile, and the distance from Elstree to Radlett is two miles. The same lane which leads to the cottage, and which is called Gill's Hill Lane, conducts you by a steep and circuitous course, to a place called Backler's Green, and so into the road to Lechmere Heath and Watford. It was within two hundred yards of the end of this lane, in the deepest part of it, and half a mile from the cottage, that the murder was committed. It is impossible to have imagined a place better suited for such a purpose, or one in which there was less likelihood of interruption.

In the stable, the bloody and torn shirt was found under a quantity of dung, beneath the manger. The whole premises are in a very dilapidated and neglected state, choked up with the over-growth and wildness of shrubs.

On the whole, this cottage is a cheerless abode, as to its internal appearance. The kitchen is three times the size of any other room, and like all the rest, in a ruinous and neglected state. From this censure, however, we exempt the parlour, which (putting recent atrocious actions out of view) is just such a room as a retired, contemplative man would select, who could be content with passing his days in his library, and his summer evenings in his garden, though now its once tranquil and secluded pond, its willow, shrubberies, ivy, its silent and inviting solitude seem for ever fled.

'The above view represents the garden and pond, the window on the roof, is that out of which Mrs Probert saw the murderers dragging something. They were then dragging the body in order to bury it in the pond, after an unsuccessful attempt to dig a grave for it, with the spade Hunt purchased, in the hard clayey soil close by Some suppose that within an hour after the perpetration of the deed in the lane, the body was removed (while supper was getting ready at Probert's) and thrown into the fish-pond. Not succeeding in burying him in the grave they had begun to prepare, from its hard chalky or clayey substance, it was carried to the pond where it was afterwards found, about three miles from this cottage.

Among the trees and shrubs, which are extremely numerous and luxuriant in every part of the pleasure ground, is seen the top of the cottage, which is the only part perceptible from the garden. On the ground-floor is the parlor in which the murderers passed the Friday night. There are two doors to this room, one leading directly from the kitchen, and the other, a glass door, from the garden. The latter door opens to the pleasure ground, and in the direction of the stable Persons might go in and out by that door, without observation from the kitchen There is also a window in the parlour which looks towards the shrubbery—but from the thickness of the foliage it is impossible from thence to see the pond, or indeed any part of the garden, beyond the trees close to the cottage The pond, next the house, is narrower and shallower than at the other end, and is thickly surrounded with shrubs, and a weeping willow In length it is about thirty yards, the banks being covered with green turf Two serpentine walks approach it from among the trees, the one on the left, the other on the right, that on the right suddenly bursts from behind a laurel hedge, and it is opposite this, and in the shallow part of the pond, that the body of the deceased is supposed to have been first thrown, the toes remaining above water, according to Hunt's account, a line was subsequently procured, and being thrown over the legs, it was drawn down to the deeper part, where perhaps there were six feet of water. Here it remained till removed on the Monday night, on that to the right is the second gate, to which Hunt states that he and Probert were desired by Thurtell to bring the gig, into which the body was put and driven to the Elstree road. Behind the shrubbery, on the left hand, towards the gate, is a small piece of ground, in which potatoes have been grown, and it was in this spot that the attempt was made to dig a grave, but from the stiff brick earth it was found impossible to penetrate to a sufficient depth. The lane into which the second gate opens is extremely narrow, and pursuing it to the right it leads into the road to High Cross; and turning again to the right, this leads into the high road at Radlett. By this course it is supposed the body was taken, until it arrived at the pond where it was ultimately discovered.

The head of the fish pond, in which the body lay concealed more than two days, comes nearly up to the house, separated only by a small shrubbery and gravel walk. This cottage belonged a few years since, to George Heath, Esq. the barrister, who first laid out the ground and fish-pond, which before was a common ditch, nearly covered with brambles, thistles, and wild shrubs. On following the path round the fish pond, near the large tree, on the right hand, hid from the eye by shrubs and ivy, you enter a summer house, having a rustic table in the centre. It was in this arbour, close to the brink of the fish pond, that some of the dinner party at Probert's on the Sunday after the murder, took a ramble round the banks of the water. Hunt is described as being particularly elated upon this occasion, and more than once made allusions to the pond, which were not then intelligible at least to the observer, but have since been too mournfully explained.

Probert's bed-room is a diminutive, dark place. An unlighted staircase leads to a small landing, from which, by three irregular steps, you enter the chamber. Adjoining is a sort of dressing closet with a window, in which Hunt confesses to have arrayed himself in the clothes of the murdered Weare. From this room, descending again to the landing place, and turning short about to the right, by ascending three steps, and stooping almost to the very ground, you enter another sleeping room, in which Thurtell or Hunt commonly slept. This room is rendered remarkable, from one circumstance that transpired after the apprehension of the murderers. It will be recollected that Probert, in describing what took place in the night of the murder, asserts that his wife retired to bed an hour and an half before himself; and that on his going up stairs, she was still dressed, and in tears. She has since confessed, that having her suspicions excited by the conduct of Thurtell and Hunt, she was induced to leave her room, and go into that usually occupied by the murderers, from the window of which she soon after saw two persons, bearing a heavy burden, enter on the path leading to the parlour, which, as has been before observed, by closing its entrance from the kitchen, is then cut off from all communications with the house, saving by a folding glass door, at the end, opening directly upon the garden, into which a person must first enter, and take a considerable circuit, before he can gain admittance into any other part of the house. Who these persons were, and what they carried, there can be little doubt. Thurtell and Hunt sat up the whole night, and were very particular in ordering in a good supply of fuel, and keeping up a good fire. It is not to be supposed they remained idle during the night—imagination sickens, and the heart shudders at the nature of their employment. As no trace of the clothes belonging to the deceased can be discovered, it is supposed that they were destroyed that night in the cottage. It is known to many that Mr. Weare wore metal buttons on his coat. There were a quantity of cinders in the yard that deserve to be examined.

Behind Probert's bed-room is that occupied by Thomas Thurtell, in his occasional visits to his two children under Probert's care, with whom he invariably slept. These three bed-rooms, above described, are the whole which the cottage contains, excepting the two attics, each empty, where Probert's servant boy and girl slept.

Probert's cottage is now in the possession of the Sheriff, but it is visited by many persons daily. It has a most wretched and deserted appearance. There is a large kitchen on the ground floor, with a parlor and wash-house. The parlor is a small room, of a very low pitch, and is not well furnished. It still contains the couch on which Hunt lay on the morning after the murder, and the chintz covering of the squab is stained with blood in several places. Mr. Mason, the Magistrate, and the Coroner, have noticed this circumstance. The bed-rooms are of the most homely description, extremely inconvenient, and very small. The grounds are beautifully romantic, and are capable of being made extremely picturesque. The walks and trees, however, of late, have evidently been let to run wild. The pond is of considerable length, stretching from the house to the end of the grounds. The upper part, towards the house, is shallow; but the lower is wide and deep. It was drained, but no new discovery was made. From the house no view of the pond can be obtained, and the parlour-door looks in a contrary direction. Indeed, so thick are the trees and shrubs, that until you get to the pond-side, you cannot perceive it. The place where the grave was attempted to be dug has been partly filled up, it is not more than two feet deep, and then comes a strata of strong brick earth, through which it would have been impossible to have penetrated without great labour.

The anxiety of the public on this horribly interesting subject, may be guessed at by the following occasional information given in our newspapers:

"The spot at which the murder was perpetrated, and the house and grounds which Probert inhabited, have been visited by a great number of persons from the neighbouring country, and also from London It is supposed that upwards of 500 persons went to Gill's Hill Lane on Sunday The broken hedge in the lane, the pond in which the body was thrown in Probert's garden, and the intended grave in the same place, successively engage the earnest attention of the curious. The house in which Probert lived is a gloomy, it might be said a miserable looking place It resembles a decayed farm-house, more than any thing else Major Wood, a gentleman who lives in the neighbourhood of Aldenham, near Watford, was the proprietor of the house, and sold it only six days before the murder took place. The house is at present in the possession of the Sheriff's officer, who, we understand, has seized the goods in consequence of some proceeding under Probert's bankruptcy"

"Gill's Hill Lane has been the scene of unusual bustle. The lane for many days was blocked up with carriages, gigs, and horses, which had been put in requisition to convey the crowd of persons who flocked from London and other places to visit the neighbourhood which has obtained such an odious celebrity The present proprietor of the premises in which Probert resided was determined that the curiosity of the public should be a source of profit to himself, and he accordingly exacted a shilling from every person who viewed the cottage and the grounds attached to it When it is considered that the landlord is not likely to find a new tenant for his cottage for some time, owing to the horror which has been excited by the dreadful transactions of which it has been the scene, few persons, perhaps, will be disposed to blame him for endeavouring to remunerate himself in this manner The speculation did not prove to be a bad one, for about 500 persons paid for admission to the grounds Several hundreds more, however, who either could not or would not pay the sum demanded, contented themselves with a view of the outside of the cottage from the road, examining the place where the murder was committed.

The sale of the furniture in the cottage was advertised to take place lately, but it was postponed for a few days This caused a great disappointment to numbers of persons who had repaired to the cottage, in order to be present at the sale. Many had come from London The furniture may perhaps acquire a fictitious value, for reasons which are obvious, but its intrinsic worth we should judge to be trifling There is a fowling-piece of Thurtell's in the house The furniture does not belong to Probert, it was let to him with the cottage All that belongs to him on the premises are some ducks and fowls, and a little hay It is not true, as has been stated, that Probert resided in the cottage for three years. He had lived there only six months before the murder"

"The cottage which Probert occupied is still so much an object of interest, that hundreds daily visit the spot The remoteness of the situation, and the wild forlorn aspect of the house itself, mark it out as the seclusion of persons from society. The grounds were originally laid out with taste. Beds of flowers were spread about. Some fine willows shaded the spot, and the fir and beech trees formed a fence on either side where the garden might be viewed by the passenger. A portion of the front of the house is covered with ivy. The windows commanded an extensive view of plain and rising grounds crowned with woods. Several beautiful seats formed part of the prospect. The flowers and young shrubs are now trodden down—the advance of the season has scattered the leaves from the trees—and some of the branches have been rudely torn away. Indeed the hand of desolation has passed over the place, which, in its neglected and ruined state, presents only an emblem of the fortunes of its late owner."

Elstree, Tuesday, Nov. 11.

"The numbers that are drawn by curiosity to visit Gill's Hill Lane, and the adjoining cottage, are almost incredible. On Sunday and yesterday, on account of the weather, the avenues to the scite of this barbarous outrage was completely thronged by vehicles of all kinds. It is a fact, that at one period in the course of Sunday there was no less than twenty-seven post chaises drawn up before the Red Lion Inn at this place. The landlord had the curiosity to calculate the amount of money received by him for refreshments in that day, and it turned out to be no less than sixty pounds. Several parties were compelled to leave the neighbourhood without accommodation, in consequence of the landlord not having procured provisions adequate to the unexpected demand. However, as the influx of visitors seems to be rather on the increase, care will be taken that there shall be no reason in future for urging a similar complaint. A sale of the effects at Probert's cottage had been announced for Monday, but the landlord, Mr. Heward, having good reason to assume that by permitting the furniture to remain as it was, he might be able to tax the curiosity of strangers to greater advantage, postponed the sale until Friday next.

Notwithstanding the minuteness with which every fact connected with this atrocious affair has been described, and the industry which has been exhibited in tracing the histories of the parties supposed to be implicated, in all their various situations in life, public curiosity seems to be still as ardent as ever, and every anecdote, however trifling, as to the habits and practices of the parties, is received by all classes with the utmost avidity. The cottage of Probert, the lane where the murder was committed, and the pond in which the body was deposited for the second time, are now inspected every day, by crowds of persons of all ranks, from the peer to the peasant.—Carriages constantly crowd the narrow avenues leading to Gill's Hill.—Even the fair sex are seen braving all the difficulties of approach, and submitting to the greatest inconvenience, for the full gratification of their curiosity.

The neighbourhood of Elstree was yesterday crowded with persons of all ranks, viewing the cottage of Probert, and the surrounding premises—the pond in the garden—the spot in the lane in which the murder was committed—the hole in the hedge through which the corpse was pushed—the half-finished grave—the pond in which the body was ultimately found—all in their turn became objects of intense observation, and, on reflection, produced a sensation of the deepest horror in the minds of those by whom they were viewed.

The fineness of the weather on Sunday (Nov. 8), induced great numbers of persons to visit the scene of the atrocious act. At Elstree the curious made their first halt. Here the grave of Mr. Weare, in Elstree Church-yard, was visited, and the pond, about a quarter of a mile out of the village, where the body of the unfortunate man was found. The Artichoke Inn, to which the corpse was carried, and where the Coroner's Inquest was held, was, for more reasons than one, an object of great attraction. Mr. Field, the landlord, being one of the Jury, was therefore fully competent to the task of answering the numerous questions put to him by his customers. Here the sack, in which the remains of the victim had been carried from Probert's cottage, was shown. The marks of blood which it bears gave it peculiar interest in the eyes of those who coveted to see every thing in any way connected with the murder. A few persons were accommodated with small pieces of the sack, which they seemed to regard as relics of extraordinary value.

The two small inns at the end of Gill's Hill Lane were crowded. Not a few, however, of the horsemen, and the masters of the various vehicles which arrived, declined making a halt there, and proceeded up the lane. Gill's Hill Lane is a long crooked turning. It is narrow from the beginning, but up to the cottage where Probert lived, or nearly up to it, a gig can be passed by horsemen or pedestrians. After passing the cottage it gets so extremely contracted, that the smallest vehicle completely fills it, and for any thing to pass in an opposite direction is absolutely impossible. Its windings were explored for a considerable distance beyond the house, to get a sight of the spot where the crime was perpetrated. Those on foot could reach this spot by crossing a field. To approach it by the lane was no easy task, as the road had been so cut up, that the clayey mud is, in some places, almost knee-deep. Notwithstanding this, many ladies ventured through it, regardless of the injury which it inflicted on their finery, and the danger to which it exposed themselves.

The break in the hedge was originally but small; it is now about six feet wide, having been thus enlarged by the operations of those curious people, who consider a twig from the hedge, through which the remains of a murdered man had been dragged, must furnish a treat to their equally curious friends.

The cottage was very closely invested on all sides. Here the kitchen where the supper was prepared on the night of Mr Weare's death, and the small parlor in which the parties now in prison passed the night, claimed attention. The latter is a pretty little room, with a pleasant look-out. The walls which had resounded with the murderers' mirth, after the horrid business had been performed, furnished matter for serious contemplation—and the sofa, on which one of the party reclined, and which was stained with the victim's blood, was not passed over unnoticed. The cover of the sofa, which had thus been soiled, has been taken away, to secure its being forthcoming at the trial.

The persons now in possesion of the house had books to sell, containing a narrative of the murder, with a plan of the premises. They did not complain for want of custom. The fish-pond, into which the dead body was thrown before it was conveyed to Elstree—the imperfectly formed grave, between two small hedges, were severally visited, as was every part of the cottage.

THE POND NEAR ELSTREE

The body might have remained a long time undiscovered in this pond, had it not been for Hunt's confession.—It is situate close to the road from Elstree to Radlett, within a quarter of a mile of the Artichoke public house, in the former village. A small bridge crosses a sort of brook, formed from the drainage of the surrounding fields, and a pond being formed to the right of the road. Here the body was deposited, and here it might have remained for some months, but for the confession to which we have alluded. From Probert's cottage to this spot, the distance is at least three miles; and little doubt can exist that some person must have assisted in throwing the body into the water, as it was situated at a considerable distance from the edge where it was found.

Hunt seems to have guided the police officers with more certainty than that of instinct. His direction was too specific to have been obtained by hearsay: "A little this way," said he to them, after the first unsuccessful trial, "and you may depend upon finding the body." He pointed out the exact spot in which the body lay; from whence it is clear that his statement before the Coroner's Inquest "that he walked on, and that Thurtell followed him, and told him he had thrown the body into that piece of marshy pond he had just passed," is not true, and this is an additional reason for not saving him from the fate which awaits his guilty associates. We have already stated that the body was quite naked, and was enclosed in a sack, which reached about half way down the thighs. The stones in the sack, the pains which had been taken to tie it, and to add other stones to the cord which passed round the body, all tend to show that the preparations were of that nature, that more than one was engaged in the horrid work.

> "——————— safe in the ditch he lies,
> With twenty trenched gashes on his head,
> The least a death to nature."

One of our Papers of Saturday, the 1st of Nov. thus speaks of Hunt —On the road between Radlett and Elstree, near the pond of which the body of Mr. Weare was found, there are two other ponds or pits filled with water, a short distance from each other. Joseph Hunt, when he left Watford with the officers, directed the chaise immediately to the spot where the body was found. He assisted in drawing it out, and when it was brought out upon the bank he looked at it without betraying the least emotion. He joked with some bye-standers upon indifferent subjects.

This reminds one of the impressive censure of Mr. Field, the landlord of the Artichoke; and the worthy Foreman on the Jury :— "It would be a pity if this cold-blooded villain should escape justice, for in my mind he is the most guilty of all; he evidently assisted in planning the murder, he bought the sack in which the victim was to be deposited after his murder—and also the spade to dig his grave, and the cord to tie up the sack, and assisted in buying the pistols. I consider Mr. Probert an innocent person, in comparison with Hunt. The manner in which he made his statement to the Jury, proves him to be the most unfeeling, cold-hearted wretch alive. He showed no signs of compunction for the horrid deed—no regret that he assisted in the murder of a fellow creature."

The pond in which the body was ultimately found is upwards of three miles from Probert's house. What appears singular is, that the murderers should have chosen this depository, when they actually passed over a bridge which crossed a pond of water of infinitely greater magnitude. It is clear that the body never could have been carried from place to place, and finally thrown into deep water by one person.

BURIAL OF MR. WEARE.

It had been arranged that the body of the deceased should be interred in Elstree church-yard. Shortly before eleven o'clock the church-bell announced that every thing was prepared for the melancholy ceremony. The coffin was borne on the shoulders of six men; the brother of the deceased and most of the Jurors attended as mourners, several persons carried lanterns before, and on either side of the coffin, and in this manner the funeral train, followed by a considerable crowd, proceeded up Elstree Hill towards the church, which is about a quarter of a mile distant from the house at which the inquest was holden. The coffin was, as in ordinary cases, first carried into the church, which was lighted up for the occasion, and then to the grave; the funeral service was read in both places by the Rev. Mr. Addow, the clergyman of the parish. As the coffin was being lowered into the grave, the rope which was placed round the foot broke, and that part of the coffin fell suddenly to the bottom of the grave, whilst the head, being sustained by the other rope, rested against the side of the grave, so that the coffin stood nearly upright. This unfortunate accident, as might be supposed, created some confusion. but the sexton immediately descended into the grave, and by great personal exertion, in a short time succeeded in getting the coffin level at the bottom of the grave, which was about 12 feet in depth. The clergyman then proceeded to read the remainder of the funeral service, and the crowd stood uncovered. The scene which now presented itself was one which can never pass from the recollection of those who witnessed it. The unusual hour of interment—the horrible and extraordinary manner in which the man whose corpse had just been consigned to the grave had lost his life —the solemn stillness of the night, for the wind which had been loud and boisterous during the day, had now fallen, and did not even shake the branches of the high trees with which the church-yard is surrounded—the impressive nature and affecting composition which was read by the clergyman who stood conspicuous, in his white gown, at the head of the grave, whilst all around him was darkness, except where the faint light of a lantern happened to fall on the countenances of some of the mourners—all these circumstances produced an effect on the beholders which we think can hardly be surpassed. The service being finished at about half-past eleven o'clock, the mourners retired from the church-yard, and the grave-diggers proceeded to fill up the grave.

Another account is thus worded.—About ten o'clock on Saturday night, just before the Inquest terminated, arrangements having been previously made, the coffin was screwed up, and carried down stairs for interment at that hour, in Elstree church-yard. By the inscription on the coffin plate it appears the unfortunate man was 43 years of age.

The corpse was brought out in front of the inn, and four men carried it on their shoulders, over which a pall was thrown. The brother of the deceased followed next to the coffin, as chief mourner, and, after him came the Jurymen in succession.

The police officers headed the funeral, and on its arrival at the church-yard the scene was most affecting and impressive. The Clergyman, at this dead hour of the night, performed the solemn obsequies over the corpse, while the bell tolled, announcing the interment of the murdered man.

The town was in a state of peculiar excitement, and most of the inhabitants were assembled to witness the funeral. The grave is about 25 feet from the front of the chancel window. Part of the church is a venerable fabric, one wall having stood the storms of thirteen centuries.

It appears that Mr Weare was not the first victim of jealousy or revenge, who was buried in Elstree church-yard. In April 1779, the remains of the unfortunate Miss Ray, the daughter of a labourer in that parish, and the *chere amie* of the late Lord Sandwich, were buried there, she was shot by the Rev. Mr. Hackman, under the Piazza of Covent Garden, coming out of the theatre. Her enthusiastic lover and murderer was tried a few days after, and executed on the 19th of the same month.

There is something in the scenery of this church-yard and the recollections here which give a deep interest. Mr. Hackman was enamoured of Miss Ray almost to distraction—his crime arose from feelings most deeply lacerated. His heart was wrung and tortured on her account. His murder therefore was spotless compared with the cool and hardened monsters whose victim has taken up its last and long abode by the side of Miss Ray.

ANECDOTES OF THE PRISONERS.

Previous to giving the history of those persons, we cannot prevent ourselves from presenting our readers with an extract from some of those admirable reflections which the Editor of the Sunday Times has given in his paper of the 9th of November.—" That there are in this country, and especially about this metropolis, thousands of young men, who, like the Thurtells, are born of respectable parents—who like them, have been educated in the hope of respectability in the world—who, like them, have been launched upon the ocean, trimmed, and with the wind fair for the port of honour; and who, like them, at the beginning of their aberrations, esteem the brawls of the ring, before the sober offices of the counting-house, and join in the roar of gamesters and revellers, rather than in the calm and salutary sweets of honest and respectable society, is a truth which admits of no doubt. Yes, we say, here is an awful lesson to those thoughtless young men, who, in the slang of the day, are called " fine fellows;" and who, because they are such, are seduced from every thing having the least honourable pretence to the name.—When the Thurtells first left their father's house at Norwich, in all the activity and ardour, and, we doubt not, in much of the innocence of youth—when they last shook their mother by the hand, turning away with swelling hearts, from the tear of maternal solicitude which glistened in her eye—when they looked to the towers and turrets of their native city, and to the fair fields, which still retained the prints of their infant feet—when they haply said to themselves, " We will go forth into the world, we will be diligent as our father has been diligent, will be honest as he has been honest, and will be respected as he is respected;" then the Thurtells may have been, " fine fellows;" and there may have been a time when Hunt was a " fine fellow." Where is their fine fellowship now? It is now fellowship in the jail—the gloomy glimmering of light—an iron bedstead,—the pillow which knows not sleep,—the clanking fetter,—the deserting world,—the terror of retribution,—the horror of looking back. Strong is the charge against these unhappy men,—their sands are run,—and we would not bar their repentance by a single gloom. but the lesson is to the living; and where can it be preached with such effect as at the grave of the murdered, and by the gibbet of the murderer? From yonder little spot of earth,—yonder lowly grave, near the chancel window at Elstree,—from the shattered skull, the scattered brains, and the mangled throat, beneath that cold, and oblivious sod, there speaks a monitor more touching, more true in its admonition, than any which can come from the house of health. It is in our hells and haunts of dissipation that young men are seduced from every thing good. It is here that bucks, brawlers, and bloods have made the language of villains the language of fashion,"

The following are some other communications which the newspapers have occasionally given us respecting John Thurtell:—

The two Thurtells are sons to Alderman Thurtell, of Norwich, a man of the highest respectability. They have recently become notorious from the action brought by them against the County Fire Office, for the destruction of their premises in Watling Street. John Thurtell mixed with the lowest sporting characters, and was known in the prize ring. He is a tall man, not very bulky, but a very powerful man; he is all sinew and bone, and was so determined, that he was the terror of his less guilty associates.

Early in life John Thurtell went to sea. On returning to this country, he obtained a lieutenant's commission in the German Legion, then serving in Portugal, and, as we believe, still enjoys the half-pay of that rank. He served in Spain, and was at the storming of St. Sebastian. About two years and a half ago he was residing at Norwich, and was a bombasin-manufacturer at that place, but such was his general conduct that he was held in disrepute throughout the city. He came to London about that time, and received four hundred pounds for goods, which he had sold to a respectable house in London Wall; and on his return, was to pay the money amongst his creditors. Instead of doing so, on his arrival at Norwich, he propagated a story, that on his return from London, as he was walking across some rather lonely spot near Norwich, with the 400l. in his pocket, he was stopped by footpads and robbed of it. This story not gaining the belief he expected, his creditors did not hesitate to tell him that he had invented this plausible tale for the purpose of defrauding them, and to avoid their importunities, he left the place and set off for London, in the company of a very pretty girl (with whom he has lived till lately) of the name of Miss D——. His failure in business in Watling Street, and the charge against him of having set fire to the premises and defrauding the Fire Office, by making a return of his loss to the amount of 2,000l. when it was not more than 100l. (as is supposed), are facts very generally known. We lament to state that whether the fire was accidental or otherwise, the consequence to other persons was very calamitous. Three houses were burnt down by the conflagration; and the property of a Mr. Penny, a wine-merchant, who was not insured, was destroyed, as well as the property of another person whose premises adjoined those of the Thurtells. The discovery is said to be owing to Miss D——, in consequence of John Thurtell's ill-treatment and desertion of her.

Anecdotes relative to J Thurtell.

The following is an outline of the "London Life" of John Thurtell, commencing with a remarkable fact in his early history. Our readers will recollect the loss of the *Hero*, *St George*, and *Defence* line of battle ships, coming home from the Baltic some years ago. Of the whole crew of the Defence, eleven only were saved, and of those, John Thurtell was one. His first introduction to what is called "the London ring," was at the Brown Bear public-house, in Bow Street, about three years ago, at which time that house was much frequented by the boxing fraternity and their patrons, several fights were *made* there and the money deposited. Dinners to celebrate victories, and to pay and receive bets, were also held here, and it was therefore considered in a great measure as the focus of pugilistic intelligence. At the time spoken of, John Thurtell one day accosted the landlord at his door in Bow Street, and said he knew that he (the landlord) was better acquainted than most people with fighting men, and he had therefore waited upon him to ask him, if he could recommend two men who could be depended upon to *fight a cross*. The landlord told him it was an odd question from a stranger, and he could give him no information upon such a subject, even if he knew him intimately. From this time, Thurtell became a constant visitor at the house, and in a few days, was introduced to Lemon, alias Lemming, a Mr. B. and several other "sporting men," who were in the habit of meeting there. There was a room at the back of the premises, detached from the house, where the meetings alluded to always took place, and where rather high play was sometimes allowed. It was in this room that Thurtell lost the 300l., as stated on a former occasion, but Weare was not present, nor did he know anything about that particular transaction until afterwards. The persons who won the money were Lemming and B. The game was *blind hookey*, or hazard—a game, perhaps, which affords a better opportunity for the dexterous to play upon the unwary than almost any other. The whole 300l. were won in a very short space of time. It is but fair to state, that Thurtell was strongly cautioned by the landlord not to play, as he was a novice at the game, but he persisted, and soon found that the advice of the landlord was valuable, and ought to have been acted upon. He was extremely angry at his loss, but his new *friends* contrived to conciliate him. It happened that about that time matches were on the tapis between Hickman (the *Gas Man*), and Oliver,—and Randall and Martin, Hickman and Martin were under training at Wade's-mill, in Hertfordshire; and John Thurtell was found to be so good a *flat*, that it was determined to get him down to that place, gratify his vanity, by allowing him to assist in the training, and fleece him of whatever cash he might have left. Weare was appointed as the *plant* upon this occasion—that is, he was to come down as a stranger to all parties, and so to conduct himself as to appear to be a good subject for fleecing. The plan answered completely. Weare was pitted at play against Thurtell, who was suffered to win at first, but who finally lost another 300l. He was afterwards played upon again in

G

London; and these repeated losses irritated him so much, that he made use of threats, which alarmed the fraternity, and it was thought best to adopt some mode of conciliation. After some consultation, it was agreed upon, that a *cross* should be fought between two of the pugilists then matched—namely, Randall and Martin, and that Thurtell should share in the profits. An attempt was at first made to buy over Randall, but that pugilist was proof against all their offers, and their attention was next turned to Martin, with whom, it is well known, they succeeded. One bet was made of 1,100l. to 600 guineas, by Lemming and B. with a celebrated sporting character, and Thurtell had his share of the 600 guineas. This bet was made at a masquerade, at the Opera house. It was about this time that Thurtell was examined before the Commissioners of Bankrupts, and he stated that he was robbed of a large sum in notes, on the highway, coming from Norwich. Payment of these notes was consequently stopped at the Bank of England; and when one of them (for 100l.) was presented by B. who had that and other notes as his share of the winnings from Thurtell, the Bank refused to pay it. The opinion of counsel was taken by B. upon the subject, and after some lapse of time, we understand, the Bank paid the note. Thurtell having in the interim admitted that he lost his money at gaming.

Since the above transactions, Thurtell has been the constant companion of the principal actors in them, and has been concerned in many plans of the same description as those of which he was first the dupe.

On the night that he and Hunt were taken to Watford, their conduct was marked with extreme levity. The writer of this statement was in the room with them, at the Essex Arms, before the investigation commenced, and they had scarcely been there half an hour, when Hunt commenced singing. He sung one entire song, and detached verses of several others, until checked by the officers.

Thurtell smoked his pipe, and conversed with seeming ease upon pugilistic subjects. After he had been before the Magistrates at Watford, he conversed with the officers in whose custody he was, with great freedom. One of them said to him that Hunt had confessed all. He replied, "I thought the —— —— would be the first to split." The officer said to him that Hunt was not present at the murder; he replied, "Before I die, the whole truth shall come out." The officer said, "you could not have done the deed alone, as the horse would have set off when you fired the pistol, had no one held him at the time." Thurtell replied, "I was not the person that shot Bill; the truth will come out in time."

Since his commitment, he maintains, in general, unshaken firmness; his health and appetite continue good; his manners are decorous, and he eats, drinks, smokes his pipe, and sleeps, with the apparent enjoyment of comfort. There is nothing in him of the bravo. He talks of his situation like a man who is perfectly sensible of the peril in which he stands; he has only once asserted his innocence, and that was in a conversation with the chaplain of the prison, who very properly checked him for the assertion, and entreated him to weigh well the importance of every declaration which he made in his present awful situation, and its possible effect upon his future condition.

The chaplain has been unwearied in his attendance upon the prisoners: he furnished them with books suited to their unhappy situation, as the Bible, a Prayer-book, and Sherlock on Death. He expressed a wish for some law books, and Phillips's Speeches, which he says he has in London, to prepare himself for his defence, as he is aware of his privilege to address the court. He reads the books which have been presented to him to compose his mind to a sense of his awful situation, with attention; but the great difference between his manner and that of the two other prisoners, is, that he evinces the utmost repugnance to converse upon the horrible nature of the crime laid to his charge.

He declares that in proper time he will establish his innocence; but when the conversation is introduced, he becomes dejected, his features assume an agitated expression; his eyes become half closed and sunk, he vainly endeavours to suppress a heaving sigh, and seizes the first instant, still without coarse abruptness, of changing the subject; and then, as if a weight was removed from his heart, his constitutional spirits and firmness of nerve return, and he will converse fluently, and with seeming satisfaction, upon any other subject to which he can recur he, however, talks of his trial with calmness, and when asked, whether he had not better hasten to avail himself of the assistance of counsel, his reply was—"I shall certainly do so in due time, but if I write now, they are all too busy to give speedy attention, for to-morrow will be the first day of term."

He has, however, written to a Mr. Jay, a respectable attorney at Norwich, desiring his early attendance. He expresses a great anxiety to refresh his memory upon the facts deposed in evidence against him, and more particularly regarding the testimony of Hunt, giving as the motive for his anxiety the very natural reason, that upon these he must ground his defence. So intent is he upon making these preliminary arrangements, that he wrote a letter to the Coroner, requesting either a copy of Hunt's deposition, or that the Coroner would do him the kindness of repairing to the prison, and reading over the notes of Hunt's examination.

Although upon the subject of his imputed guilt in the late horrid murder, he continues incommunicative, he is yet loquacious upon all the other events of his life, and eager to disclose the source of his misfortunes, and the pernicious character of his associates. The dreadful spirit of gaming, he avows, and names the associates with whom he practised it, as well as the schemes and frauds with which they conducted their machinations—always with the too common delusion of trying to disconnect himself personally from the atrocious acts of their fellowship, willing, naturally enough, though contrary to the apparent stamp of his character, to be considered more as the dupe of their practices, than the participator of their designs and profits.

He says that he lent Hunt a good suit of black on the evening of the murder, that he might appear respectable at the cottage; these on the Saturday, he says, Hunt pulled off at his (Thurtell's lodgings), putting on an inferior suit, which he lent him; the better clothes Thurtell put on the day he was taken and accounts for the pistol being found in the coat pocket, by stating that Hunt left it there, having murdered Weare with the fellow to it, which was found underneath the hedge

When J Thurtell was apprehended, Ruthven found upon him three small bullets, or what are called buck-shot, which suited the calibre of the pistol found in his pocket, but when asked about them, he denied that they belonged to or were intended for the pistol, and said they were cast for an air-gun, which he had had for some time. He subsequently wrote a letter to a friend in whose house he had lodged, requesting that care might be taken of it, and this letter being intercepted, led to the finding of the deadly instrument

The letter was addressed to Mrs. Walker, a young woman who had lived at the Cock, in the Haymarket, as bar-maid to Thomas Thurtell. Upson, the officer, upon having this letter put into his hand, went to the Cock, where, in a room occupied occasionally by John Thurtell, he found the air-gun and its apparatus.

John Thurtell stands five feet ten inches in height, his age 32, his make and frame denote a man of superior strength and muscle, complexion sallow, and his hair and eyes dark, the latter with a dull and heavy appearance, his cheek bones prominent, his brow knitted, and his whole countenance lowering The impression which a stranger would form from his mien and appearance, is that of a resolute, intrepid, and determined man, whom no dangers could daunt, and no difficulties turn aside from the pursuit and final accomplishment of any object on which he has bent his mind His walk is swinging, like a sailor, and generally with his hands in his trowsers pockets. He admits " that play has been his ruin," and is disposed to be very communicative upon such topics, perhaps his information may not be unworthy the serious consideration of the Secretary of State for the Home Department, from the singular statements which he makes, always saving as it were his own distance, by imputing them to others : one of them is, that a person whose hieroglyphic is described as being X, assured him he paid 1000l. a year to certain parts of the police, for a species of general connivance, or early communication of intended attacks ! He was known among his flash friends by the nickname of " Old Flare." He was always remarkably reserved and thoughtful in company. He would sit for hours and scarcely speak. When he did speak, his conversation was of the most hardened and disgusting kind, and his general conduct was such, that two of his *worthy* companions made a bet of a dozen of wine that he would be hanged within three years. He appears under great mental depression, indicating a strong internal struggle, yet he sleeps soundly, and maintains an invincible silence with the men placed over him.

Early in life he went to sea, on his return he commenced business at Norwich, there he became a bankrupt in 1820. He then came up to London, joined with all the gamblers in town, and took the Black Boy public-house, in Long Acre, in the name of a younger brother, Henry Thurtell. He then took premises in Watling-street, which were burnt down, and he recovered 1,900l. of the County Fire Office.

Warrants against the Thurtells on the bill of indictment which was found, are out against them. From the time when the house in Watling-street was burnt, John continued to reside at the house of his brother, the Cock, in the Haymarket, which is now in the possession of the assignees, under the commission of bankruptcy against Thomas Thurtell.

He sent for the Managing Director of the County Fire Office, who immediately left London for the gaol; an interview took place, when Thurtell begged that bail might be taken for his brother, on the warrant for conspiring to defraud the Insurance Office, as he had a large family. The gentleman observed, that he expected the prisoner had some important communication to make; he replied, that he could confess nothing, for his brother was innocent of the charge. This observation elicited a reply, that Thomas Thurtell was as certain of being convicted of the fraud, as he (John Thurtell) was sure to be found guilty of the murder of Mr. Weare.

When Ruthven apprehended Probert, he learned from him that John Thurtell generally slept at the Coach and Horses, in Conduit-street. He induced Probert to give him a letter of introduction to Thurtell, and instantly proceeded to town. The following is a copy of Probert's letter —

"Dear Sir,—The bearer of this note, a *friend* of mine, wishes to make a communication of importance.

"Your's most truly,   "WM. PROBERT."

"Oct. 28, 1823 —Mr. John Thurtell"

With this letter Ruthven, on his arrival in London, hastened to the Coach and Horses, and gained an introduction to Thurtell's bed-room, and secured him. It is regretted that this active officer did not apprehend the man who was at the time in a bed in the same room with Thurtell. When apprehended, he was in bed, and supposing Ruthven's visit to be only about putting in the bail, he received him cheerfully; but, on being handcuffed, observed with surprise, he did not suppose it was necessary to treat him so; he had never been treated so before. "Perhaps not," replied Ruthven; "you have never been in custody before for such a crime as that of which you are now accused." Proceeding to search him, Ruthven found blood on various parts, both of his coat and waistcoat.

"Feathers, Wade's Mill, Hertfordshire, Nov. 9.

"Rather more than two years since, John Thurtell came to Wade's Mill, for the ostensible purpose of witnessing the training of Martin, the boxer. This little village, consisting of less than one hundred houses, is situate in a valley on the London and Cambridge road. Thurtell arrived in a post-chaise and four; he was dressed elegantly, and appeared what is generally understood by the term, a dashing blade. The house was then kept by a young man of the name of Denham, who left Wade's Mill about a year and a half ago, and was succeeded by its present landlord, Mr Evenett, who has brought back the trade of the house, and is much respected on the road. Thurtell and Martin were well known to each other, and almost always together. A few days after the former arrived at the Feathers, a young woman came down in a post-chaise at a late hour; she was accompanied by an elderly female, the former was received by Thurtell as his wife, the latter left Wade's Mill a day or two afterwards for the metropolis. The young woman was about 22 years of age, a fine full figure; her face rather plain than otherwise, and slightly freckled; her complexion pale; she spoke much of Yarmouth, of which place it is supposed she was a native, seldom in her own room, she freely associated with the sisters of the landlord, and often, when in the bar, assisted in the business of the house. She conducted herself, at times, with great propriety, but occasionally indulged in the narration of vulgar anecdotes, or the telling loose tales, nor would the presence of the other sex occasion any hesitation in her manner, or call the slightest tinge of modesty to her cheek. Her favourite amusement was swinging, and, for her gratification in this respect, a rope was fixed up in a shed in the yard, on which a pillow was placed as often as necessary. Jack Thurtell frequently officiated in propelling the lady, but more generally an old blind man performed that duty, and often for hours together. Thurtell remained at this house for about six weeks, and brought down Teasdale, the boxer, who went into training to fight Lenny. During his stay here he had plenty of money, lived well, and drank his wine every day after dinner, but never to excess. He had generally some of the sporting fraternity with him, and the days and nights were devoted to gambling. The deceased (Weare), Captain Elliot (who shot himself), Baird (proprietor of a hazard-table in Oxendon-street), Lemmon (who has of late figured conspicuously as Mr. L——), Donnelly, and M'Carny, were almost constantly of the party. Blind hookey and hazard were the only games played. Sundays were usually devoted to gambling. One night Weare was a winner of from 200l. to 300l, and although it is supposed that Thurtell generally rose a loser, on one occasion two of the neighbouring sporting gentlemen felt each forty pounds worth of regret that they had preferred the company of Thurtell to that of the reverend pastor, at the parish church, who is also the chaplain of Hertford gaol. Thurtell once went to the church at Wade's Mill, and recognized the clergyman at his first interview with the prison chaplain. Thurtell was accustomed to express himself in the strongest and grossest language. After Martin had beat Gipsey Cooper, the following sporting men came down to this house, in a barouche and four, dressed in uniform—white hats, green handkerchiefs, and sporting coats of the same colour—Thurtell, Martin, Elliott, Lemmon, Baird, and Hickman They kept it up at the Feathers all night, and never was the true spirit of the sporting world depicted in more glowing colours. What a change have two short years produced in the fortunes of these men!—*British Traveller.*

Wade's Mill, Nov. 13.

In our paper of the 10th we mentioned the circumstance of two sporting gentlemen of the neighbourhood having lost 40l. each in play with Thurtell on a Sunday, one was Mr. C., of Ware, the other, Mr. B. of Hertford. Jack Thurtell and Weare made the *plant* on these gentlemen; Weare played with the unwary provincialists, while Thurtell assumed the appearance of dozing by the fire-side, making only an occasional by-bet with the deceased, to inspire his antagonists with an additional degree of confidence. Martin and Hickman were also present. The latter called Mr. B. out of the room, when he had lost a considerable sum, and cautioned him of the *plant*, told him he was a fool if he paid a farthing of his loss, or allowed his friend to do so; and advised him to borrow as much money of the sharpers as he could. Mr. B. took an early opportunity of acquainting Mr. C. with the characters of their customers, and both eventually refused to pay. Weare (with that coolness which was his peculiar characteristic, and which gave him much of the appearance of a gentleman to strangers), observed, that he had played merely for amusement, and that he was perfectly willing to accommodate the gentlemen by taking their acceptances at their own dates. The young birds were, however, too knowing to be caught, and the old ones were entrapped in their own net, for Mr. B., taking advantage of Hickman's advice, had borrowed " sufficient" of Weare to enable him, by occasionally pocketting a *canary* or two, to accumulate the sum of twenty-eight pounds, having originally but thirteen pounds about his person. The upshot of the affair was, that Mr C., on being called upon for his note of hand, "*payable in seven years, if more convenient,*" gave as a reason for his refusal, that Mr. B. had given him the *office (Anglice, put him up to trap)*. Mr. B. gave Hickman up as his authority, on which Martin threatened to beat the head of Gas to a mummy. M'Carthy (another of the firm) swore by St. Patrick that he would break every bone in Mr. B.'s skin at the ensuing fight on Crawley Downs; and Jack Thurtell exhibited his usual ferocity of character, by swearing to be avenged on the lives of the —— —— who had *done* the *macers.* Mr. B. is the son of a widow, hostess at Hertford; and, when Thurtell was lodged in the gaol of that town, he said he would have his dinners and wine from that —— inn, as the landlord (meaning Mr. B.) was indebted to him in the sum of forty pounds —*British Traveller.*

Thurtell indulges greatly in smoking, and in the absence of visitors his pipe is his constant companion He expressed much satisfaction at the expectation of Mr. Noel having the conduct of the prosecution. He has written to a friend for " Phillips's Speeches," to amuse him during his imprisonment; and when the

Rev. Chaplain observed, that he could put a book in his hand that would be more serviceable to him, he remarked that he wanted "Phillips's Speeches" to enable him to draw up his defence, which he meant to deliver himself

The following extract of his Examination, in March, 1820, will be read with interest, in consequence of the disclosures it contains. He accounts for the absence of £1500, which it was proved he had recently received, by pretending to have been knocked down and robbed of it in the City of Norwich. Nobody believed the tale, and the identical notes were afterwards traced to his gambling connexions, to whom he had subsequently staked them. Weare, it is said, was one of those persons; he won £300 of Thurtell at "Blind Hookey," as has been already stated.

It will be instructive to view the rapid transition from gaming to robbery, from professions of friendship among villains to their betraying and murdering one another—from the hazard table to the gaol—from the scene of drunken revelry to the place of execution.

"Where did you change the note for 500*l.* which you received at Barclay and Co's., and for what species of notes did you change the same? At the gambling-house, No. 10, King Street, St James's Square, about half-past one at noon, on Thursday, the 18th of January last, to the best of my belief I changed it for four 100*l.* Bank of England notes, and ten 10*l.* notes of the same bank. Where did you change the note for 300*l.* which you received at Barclay and Co's, and for what species of notes did you change the same? Either at the gambling-house, No. 28, Bury Street, or at the gambling-house, 32, Pall Mall, but for what species of notes I cannot recollect. Where did you change the three 200*l.* notes which you received at Barclay and Co's, and for what species of notes did you so change the notes? At some of the said gambling-houses, or at some other gambling-house, but I cannot say at what particular house, nor for what species of notes I so changed the same. Did you endorse your name, John Thurtell, on all the notes you received in change for the notes you received at Barclay and Co's, and if not on the whole, on how many, and what was the value of each of those notes so endorsed by you? On Sunday evening, 21st of January last, I endorsed my name, John Thurtell, on thirteen one hundred pound notes of the Bank of England, and on no others, and those notes I brought to Norwich on the following day; I endorsed them at the Golden Cross, Charing Cross, but whether a waiter at that inn saw me endorse them or not, I cannot say."

The assignees refusing to grant their certificate to John Thurtell, he was under the necessity of carrying on his subsequent dealings in the names of other persons. He took the Black Boy, in Long Acre, in the name of a younger brother, Henry Thurtell, who subsequently went for a soldier, he then employed a Mr. Cowdry, as his *locum tenens* in that house. This person, in the trial with the Fire Office, deposed to Thurtell's having proposed to him to take a certain house, which he named, offering to furnish it, insure it, remove the goods, set fire to the premises, and get a thousand pounds from the Insurance Office. The young man refused to have any thing to do in such a transaction, and immediately broke off all connexion with him. In the Spring of last year, he took the Cock, in the Haymarket, in the name of his brother Thomas; but Thomas was at that time, and for a long time afterwards, a prisoner in the King's Bench, at the suit of John Thurtell, for a trifling debt, having previously, in an application for relief, under the Insolvent Debtor's Act, stated that he had no property whatever, and was supported by the assistance of his friends.

It appears that Probert, after he was in custody, told Mr. Field, the landlord of the Artichoke, that on the night of the murder, he put Hunt down at the end of a lane near the Lime-kilns, on the road from Elstree to Radlett, at which place he had agreed to meet John Thurtell, and that he afterwards drove on through Radlett to his own house. On his arrival there he saw John Thurtell, to whom he mentioned that he had left Hunt waiting for him, on which Thurtell said, "Oh, I've done the trick without him." Probert then said he must go back for Hunt, and he did accordingly turn round, and went back for him in the gig.

It would seem from inquiry on the spot that John Thurtell drove Weare past Probert's cottage, down Gill's Hill Lane, as he was seen at a turning in the lane at eight o'clock, by a man who noticed the distressed state of his horse. Thurtell had then got out of the gig, and seemed to be feeling in the breast of his great coat for something (now supposed to be the pistol), and it is believed, but for the interruption he received, he would have effected his purpose on the spot. Finding himself disturbed here, however, he drove on down the lane till he arrived at the place where the dreadful tragedy was performed. This was about eight o'clock, as Freeman and his wife, who heard the report of the pistol, followed by the groans, and the man who met the parties, both agree. The scene of action was nearly half a mile from Probert's house, and after the murder was accomplished, the victim was drawn through the hedge into a turnip field, where the body remained till it was subsequently removed to the pond in the garden.

It would appear, from what has been stated by one of the prisoners (Hunt), that a desperate struggle took place between John Thurtell and Weare before the latter was completely overpowered. Hunt says that John Thurtell shot Weare whilst he was sitting by his side in the chaise. Thurtell had intended to blow out the brains of his victim, but the ball struck upon Weare's cheek bone, and stunned him; upon which the assassin threw him out of the chaise. When Weare fell upon the ground, he recovered in some degree from the effects of the shot, and got up and ran a few yards. Thurtell then jumped out of the gig, ran up to Weare, and drove the barrel of the pistol into his head. Weare closed upon the assailant and, to use Hunt's words, "a sharp scuffle took place, and Weare was near getting the better of him once or twice," until being at length exhausted, Thurtell succeeded in cutting his throat with his penknife. Hunt was asked how he knew all this. He answered, "Why Jack told me himself."

In all gambling speculations, Thurtell and Hunt (where they were not known) generally dropped in as accidental spectators, and took odds on the game, when decided against the favourite, who having a show of bets himself, led others to suppose that he would not bridge or sell them. However, in games of science, such as billiards or cards, this is easily accomplished by stratagem. If the stakes were considerable, and that the favourite could not break down without a palpable disclosure of fraudulent play, a row was commenced, by which the game was put an end to, and the stakes drawn. In all cases of this nature, Thurtell and Hunt were generally the champions or bullies, and though they occasionally met their deserts, they were neither dismayed nor deterred from pursuing a profession having less of honour than profit, and Hunt's expression in such cases invariably was, "that he never regarded a few ———— kicks or cuffs, so that he made the blunt." On such occasions, Mr. Weare and the fourth person, already alluded to, were passive spectators, or interfered only to bring about an adjustment, which made their conduct appear even more disinterested, as they had generally money at stake.

Nov. 14.—The gentleman who came from Norwich (Mr. Jay) was allowed the proper confidential communication with Thurtell, the three attendants were removed from the apartment, and he remained nearly two hours with the prisoner. Thurtell's demeanor, we are informed, was cool and collected; he persists in an unqualified denial of his guilt, and, as has been already stated, attempts to prove that he was not, and could not be, on the spot at that time. He does not complain of harsh treatment in the gaol, he has a good bed, and the irons are not the very heavy ones reserved for felons— they are not more than 15 pounds weight; there are flannels round the ankle-ring, and that space enables the prisoner to undress at night, and he sleeps well. He expressed great solicitude about his family to the gentleman who visited him yesterday, declared his perfect readiness to meet his trial, and positively and repeatedly denied, not only this particular murder, but that of the Polish officer at St. Sebastian. He also peremptorily denies the statement respecting a coral dealer named Sparks, who was said to have been invited, with his goods, to the house in Manchester Buildings, as well as any present knowledge of a woman named Dodson, who cohabited with him. He states that he never was taken before a police magistrate, antecedent to the present time, except for an assault, when in the vicinity of Covent Garden he accosted and sat down in the box of an eating house with two females of loose character, whom he accidentally met, and knocked down a person who put his head into the box, and made some offensive remark to the females. For this assault he was brought, as he asserts, for the first time, before the police magistrates, and gave bail, but the charge was not further prosecuted.

ANECDOTES OF JOSEPH HUNT.

The examination of Thomas Thurtell, which we have already inserted at length, at p. 59, truly pourtrays the hardened character of this monster. Hunt, in his solicitude to clear himself, has not only been successful in catching Thurtell, but also in catching himself. Still it may turn out that more than Thurtell had a red hand in this murder.

Hunt is a professional singer, one of his sisters was married to Captain O'Rielly, of the Austrian service, who died about eight months since, and he himself married to a woman of respectable family. His mother formerly resided in Bride's-lane, and now in Mary-le-bone. His sister-in-law kept the Naval Coffee-house, in St. Martin's-lane, and he subsequently kept it himself, frequently presiding at a club, where his vocal powers made him an agreeable member. His love of dissipation, however, soon ruined him; he gradually subsided into his present hardened and profligate course of life, and his manner of subsisting himself has, for some time, to say the least of it, been not a little suspicious.

On the evening of the day following the murder of Mr. Weare, Hunt went into the public room of the Northumberland Head, in St. Martin's-lane, and being well known by the compny, he was asked to entertain them with a song, which he refused, and amused himself by flourishing a pistol, which he took out of his pocket. His conduct, on that occasion, appeared remarkably strange

The following anecdote is a proof that Hunt was one of a set of atrocious characters. A short time since, he and a young man drove up to an inn in St Albans, in a one horse chaise. They had breakfast, lunch, wine, &c. and the bill came to 24s. After lunch, Hunt told the landlord he was going to serve a writ upon some individual, and begged that he would lend him a smock-frock, to serve him for a disguise. It was accordingly brought, and Hunt and his companion were about to leave the house in the gig. At this moment the landlord intimated that it would be agreeable to settle his bill; Hunt said that he was coming back to dinner, which he proceeded to order. The landlord assured him that the dinner should be served up to his perfect satisfaction; but at the same time informed him that the bill must be paid before the gig left the door. Hunt, finding his host inflexible, ordered the chaise to be put back, and left the house, putting the smock-frock over his coat.

The landlord being determined to watch their motions, left the house, accompanied by the ostler, and each took a different route, both, however, keeping Hunt and his companion in view. They had not proceeded far before Hunt and the young man began to run, and entered a field of standing corn. The landlord followed them, and found them lying concealed at some distance from each other. He asked them what they wanted there? Hunt replied, that they had been playing at cards on the preceding night, and had lost all their money; and seeing somebody coming to whom he was indebted, he ran into the field to hide himself.

The landlord now seized both of the men, and told them they should go back to his house and pay their bill. They resisted, some blows were exchanged, and the landlord would have been overpowered, had not the ostler come up and assisted in conducting Hunt and his friend back to the tavern. Both now declared they had no money, but, after some time, each of them pawned his coat, and then they drove away in the gig.

The landlord saw Hunt at one of the recent examinations. Hunt recognised him, and said, making use of an oath, "If it had not been for the ostler, you would not have been here now."

On his apprehension, Hunt gave Ruthven the following letter to his wife, to be delivered on his going to search the apartments occupied by him in town.—

"My dear Wife,—Please to give the bearer, Mr. Noel, the whole of John Thurtell's property, consisting of the gun, the shirt, waistcoat, breeches, boots, shoes, powder-flask, and every thing belonging to him. Keep up your spirits, I hope all will end right.

J. HUNT."

Across the letter were written these words—"You shall hear from me soon." The letter was addressed to "Mrs. Hunt, No 19, King-street, Golden-square, or at Mrs Mountain's, 4, St. Martin's-lane."

On the authority of this letter, Mr. Noël and Ruthven went to Hunt's lodgings. Mrs. Hunt was out, but they broke open the door, and found the whole of the clothes of the deceased. There was a complete change, which he was in the habit of taking with him, when he went out for a few days. Part of these clothes Hunt wore at Probert's on the Sunday. Hunt always studiously described these as John Thurtell's things, so as to save himself from suspicion of being a party concerned. Part of the cord bought by Hunt to tie round Mr. Weare's legs, was also found at his lodgings.

During his examination, he was attired in a suit of black, which he said belonged to John Thurtell. A person who knew him when he was in London, would scarcely have recognized him. He was then a frequenter of all the public places, dressed fashionably, and was what is termed "a regular swell." He usually wore a blue surtout, suffered his whiskers to grow to an extreme length, and wore mustachios.

His appearance on Saturday was very mean; he had shaved himself nearly close to the temples,* and his features bore a death-like paleness. He stands about five feet seven inches high, and is stout made.

* At the suggestion of Mr Wilson, the Governor of Hertford gaol, Hunt is now allowing his whiskers to grow. This may be important, as it relates to personal identity.

Much has been said of a promise of mercy to Hunt, but it has never been distinctly stated how this conditional promise was made. We shall here give a correct account of the transaction.

When suspicions of the murder were first excited, the Magistrates were indefatigable in their search for the body of the supposed murdered man. The country for two miles round was searched most minutely, without success. It was then concluded, that there were several concerned, and therefore it was afterwards felt desirable to withhold Hunt's confession from the public. The apprehensions which were now entertained that the body would be removed out of reach, and thus the principal link in the chain of evidence be broken, inclined the Magistrates to take advantage of any assistance which Hunt might be disposed voluntarily to give, and the more especially, as they believed that his was not the hand that perpetrated the foul deed.

Hunt was then called in, and was addressed by Mr. Noel to the following effect:—

"Now, Hunt, as I understand you have expressed some desire to make a confession, I have inform you, that the law has frequently permitted accomplices in a murder—I mean those who have not been the individuals by which the murder has been effected—to become witnesses for the Crown; therefore, if you are disposed to make a *full* and *candid* confession of all you know, touching this horrible affair, the Magistrates are prepared to hear you, with a pledge that they will submit your confession, and the circumstances under which it has been made, to His Majesty's Under Secretary of State, for him to judge how far it may be desirable to extend mercy to you. After this information, and without any further pledge, it is for you to say how far it will be prudent to carry your intention into effect."

Hunt was about to reply, but Mr. Noel desired him to retire, and consider for a few minutes before he formed his determination. He did retire, and in ten minutes came back, and said he would tell *all* he knew of the transaction. His confession was then taken, but subsequent discoveries prove that it was *neither full nor candid*, and that he was disguising his own concern in the affair, while he did all he could to fix the entire guilt on John Thurtell.

How far this breach of condition may affect the implied pledge given by the Magistrates, circumstances will show; but from inferiority of guilt he can have no claim; he seems to be quite as horrible a miscreant as John Thurtell. His confessions, however, led to the finding of the body, which, from the place where it lay, might have remained undiscovered for months. The pond is situated close to the side of the road, and, from its publicity, is the last place to which suspicion would have attached. It was certainly from accident, deep, but its appearance is otherwise insignificant. Under all the circumstances, the Magistrates were perfectly justified in the course they pursued. Hunt appears to entertain no fears for his own acquittal, and exults in the idea of being admitted as a witness.

Mr. Clutterbuck having waited on the Secretary of State for the Home Department, with the depositions, we can state with certainty that Hunt's confession will be of no avail, as far as regards his own personal safety, and that he will be put on his trial with the other prisoners. We are satisfied, from his prevarication and want of candour, that this circumstance will afford general satisfaction. He appears to be an ignorant and illiterate man, and continues to manifest the same indifference which he has hitherto manifested under the dreadful circumstances in which he is placed. A day or two ago he observed, that if he should get off, this affair (the murder) might hurt him in his singing business.

Hunt writes to his mother for money, and in his letters calls God to bear witness to his innocence. He complains much of his *quondam* friends, who, on being applied to for assistance, have expressed their anger at his taking so great a liberty.

We understand that a letter from Mrs. Hunt to her husband, in Hertford goal, has been intercepted, which may lead to some important results. One of the local Magistrates came to town yesterday, and had an interview at the Home Office on the subject.

Hunt is known to many persons in this town and Lewes. At the latter place he sang a few months since, at a dinner at the White Hart, with great applause; and he was considered one of the best room singers at Free and Easy Societies, and other convivial meetings, in the metropolis.—*Brighton Herald.*

The Government (which has taken a very active part in the business), and the Magistrates, are fully determined to put Hunt on his trial, conjointly with Probert and Thurtell. The part which this man has had in the perpetration of the deed, together with the inhuman and dastardly spirit which he has since betrayed, would render an act of mercy to him extremely ungrateful to the world; so that unless a material link in the chain of evidence can no otherwise be supplied, we may calculate on seeing him arraigned with his colleagues in crime, before the tribunal of justice. Hence the Magistrates have directed all their recent efforts towards the collection of such evidence as will establish the guilt of these parties. Two fresh witnesses have been examined; the first was Rutlingham, the man in whose house, in Hyde-street, Bloomsbury-square, Hunt represented that he had purchased the sack and a piece of cord. He again declared, he had no doubt as to the identity of the person who bought these articles from him. The other witness was Thomas Herm, an ostler belonging to the stables adjoining those of Mr. Probatt, of Charing Cross. Hunt, it will be remembered, hired a gig at this place on the Sunday, and returning on Monday, had a fresh horse put to it. He returned on Tuesday, when this witness saw him. Hunt seemed to be greatly agitated, and appeared to be averse to holding any communication with any person. His demeanour on Sunday and

Monday was very suspicious. His language was very disorderly. On Tuesday he was still more wild; and after he had brought in the gig and horse, walked away in a very hurried manner. The gig and horse were quite dirty, and the cushions were wet, and daubed with mire. This witness was certain as to the person of Hunt. He described his whiskers and appearance, in such a manner, as leaves no doubt of the identity of the man Such is the purport of these examinations, and it will be seen that the efforts of the Magistrates, under the immediate controul of the Secretary of State, have been directed to the establishment of a case against Hunt, whose services as an approver, it is now hoped, can with safety be dispensed with. The Magistrates who principally conducted the examination, are Messrs. Clutterbuck and Haworth.

BIOGRAPHICAL SKETCH OF PROBERT.

Mr. William Probert is the son of a respectable farmer who formerly rented a considerable extent of ground at Ross, in Herefordshire, where the unhappy subject of our memoir was born, about the year 1782. His mother, who has re-married since the death of his father, still resides at Lydbrook, in the same county; and he has a brother, a farmer, in the adjoining county of Gloucester. Of the pursuits of his early life we are unable to speak, and we believe they are generally unknown, but they are supposed to have been passed in a more humble sphere than he has since moved in. The character in which he figured when he first came within the observation of the writer of this brief notice, was as clerk to Mr Bramwell, a wine merchant of extensive business at Pimlico. This was about 1815, in the December of which year he was married at the church of St George, Hanover Square, to Elizabeth, the daughter of Mr. William Crook Noyes, formerly an extensive brewer at Foxfield, near Hungerford, and afterwards farmer of his own freehold estate at Langley, near Andover, from whence he retired with a handsome fortune to Hampstead, where he lived for some years highly esteemed and respected. Mr. Probert received a handsome property with his wife, and soon after his marriage he commenced business on his own account as a wine merchant, taking apartments at the house of Mr. Lambert, silversmith, in Coventry Street, Piccadilly, and opening extensive wine cellars in the Haymarket, where he continued till the middle of 1818, carrying on his business with apparent credit. He removed from thence to No. 112, High Holborn, into the premises now occupied by Mr. Kleft, the oil merchant, and where he remained rather more than twelve months, when his circumstances becoming insolvent, he appeared in the Gazette as a bankrupt towards the end of the year 1819. He failed for a large sum, not one shilling of which have the creditors, we believe, ever recovered.

From the quantity of wine which was repeatedly brought into prison to him, and which he was known to sell to the keeper of the coffee-house, and also to several private individuals, it was suspected that he had also a stock of wine in some quarter of the town which he had withdrawn, by some means or other, from the grasp of the law.

The following anecdote has been transmitted to us. Probert before his bankruptcy kept a very large establishment, and was perpetually driving about town in a tilbury, attended by a servant lad in livery. One of his creditors was so much taken by his manners, his equipage, and his apparent extensive dealings, as to declare after his bankruptcy, that he would have given him credit, had it been asked, for as many hundreds of pounds as he had obtained of tens. On this declaration being communicated to Probert, his expression was, "what a cursed fool I was not to know my own value, and to stick it in the fellow for a few thousands Alas! alas! a man never knows what he is worth, until he is ruined"

Mr Probert is a man of collossal stature, being upwards of six feet one inch in height; he is a bony, muscular, and powerful man, with a short neck and round shoulders, like most very tall persons, his hair is a jet black, his complexion extremely swarthy; his features are not large for so large a man, and his countenance is rather heavy and inanimate except about the eyes, which are very dark, and sometimes lighted up with remarkable expression. His gait is slovenly, and his general appearance, though assuming in his manner, such as comes within the description of being neither prepossessing nor repulsive.

Some years ago he kept an extensive range of wine vaults in the neighbourhood of Holborn, and contrived, by the respectability of his appearance, the plausibility of his manners, and the apparent great business which he carried on, to obtain very large quantities of wine, spirits, &c. upon the credit of his bills, from various wholesale dealers in Mark Lane. When the bills became due, the greater part of them were dishonoured Legal measures were taken to recover their amount, and, after much litigation, a commission of bankruptcy was issued against Probert On his appearing before the Commissioners to surrender to his commission, he refused to answer certain questions which they put to him relative to his assignment, to one of his relations, of the lease of several tenements which had been in his possession. He remained in the King's Bench Prison for three or four years. He was removed from the King's Bench to the gaol in Horsemonger Lane about two years ago, on a charge of making too free with the till of the coffee-house-keeper in the King's Bench On his trial for that offence at the Sessions, he pleaded not guilty, stated that the charge originated out of the jealousy of the prosecutor, and contended that he had taken the money by the consent of the prosecutor's wife, with whom, as well as with the prosecutor, he declared himself to be most intimate. This defence, however, was of no avail, for the jury returned a verdict of guilty against him, and he was sentenced to imprisonment for six months. On the expiration of his imprisonment, he returned to the King's Bench, from which he contrived to get himself liberated by means of the Insolvent Act.

The interest which this transaction excites in the public mind is such, that fresh points of information relative to the prisoners turn up every day.

In the year 1821 (January 20th, at Guildhall), there was an action tried before the Lord Chief Justice, "The Assignees of Bague, v. Holding." Bague (the bankrupt) swore upon the trial, that in 1818, keeping a liquor-shop in Piccadilly, he became acquainted unfortunately with Probert and Holding. At that time his affairs were on the decline, and his new friends persuaded him that it would be easy to get goods to a large amount; make away with them; and then fail, without paying his creditors a farthing. On this occasion a trip was made to Holding's country house, near St. Albans, where the matter was pressed, as immediate, because Probert himself was going to fail shortly : Holding had failed, and "made a good thing of it," a little while before. Eventually Bague obtained wines and spirits from different persons to the cost of about 3500l ; of which 2000l worth was put into the hands of Holding (who took a house as a wine-merchant to receive them), and 1200l. worth to Probert. In addition to this, the man was so deluded as to give Holding an acknowledgment for 2000l. money lent—all this being, as he expected, to be proved under his commission, and the dividend, as well as the produce of the wines taken by Holding and Probert, returned to him when he got his certificate. In the end, as might have been expected, Bague was thrown into prison; and neither Mr. Probert nor Mr Holding gave him any assistance. He was then persuaded by his wife to confess the whole transaction to his creditors; and the result of that measure was the action in question.

The Jury, without hesitation found a verdict against Holding.

No proceeding appeared to be taken against Probert—probably he was not considered worth pursuing.

In consequence of the newspapers publishing the above statement, Mr Holding has, in vindication of his character, addressed the following letter to the Editor of the Times.—"Sir,—An attempt has been made to mix up my name with the parties concerned in the late horrid murder, in consequence of my having, four or five years ago, been on terms of intimacy with Probert, at a time when he was carrying on a respectable business, and was on terms of intimacy with some of the first merchants in London. That such intimacy between us ceased as long ago as April, 1821, is well known, and that I have subsequently been put to an immense expense and inconvenience in consequence of his hostility towards me, and particularly by his causing a fraudulent commission of bankruptcy to be issued against me, which the Lord Chancellor, upon my petition, superseded. It is true that a verdict was obtained against me, as stated, by Bague's assignees, in January, 1821; but it is equally true and well known, that upon my final examination in November, 1821, under the commission issued against me, the chief commissioner, after a long and most patient investigation, declared himself convinced that I was a most injured man by such verdict, which appeared to him to have been obtained by perjury; and he was satisfied that could I myself have been heard as a witness (which I could not, being the defendant), a verdict must have been given in my favour, and my ruin have been prevented. After this being publicly declared in Guildhall, it is base and unmanly thus to attack me. It is true, as stated, that Probert is my debtor in upwards of 3000l as appears upon my balance sheet. Though I am far from shrinking from a cool and impartial investigation of my conduct through life, still I do protest against being thus dragged before the public in the details of a horrid transaction to which I am no party.

"It is mis-stated in all the public prints, that I took the cottage for Mr. Heward, and let it to Mr. Probert; but the real fact is, that I entered upon it immediately after George Heath, Esq the barrister, and I kept it until the latter end of 1819, when I sold the lease and furniture to Mr. Heward; and Mr. Heward lived in it from that period until within the last six months, when he let it to Mr. Probert.

"Under these circumstances, I rely on the justice of the press not again to connect my name with those horrid details.

"I am, Sir,
"Your obedient servant,

Nov. 10, 1823. "WM. HOLDING."

It may be thought extraordinary, that having been so recently released from prison, Probert should have been in possession of the villa at Gill's Hill, but the history of the cottage is briefly this — About five years ago George Heath, Esq who had for some years occupied the cottage, disposed of it to Mr. Heward—a gentleman of respectability, unknown to and wholly unconnected with any of the subsequent occupants. After a short residence there, Mr. Heward disposed of it to Holding, in whose possession it remained until occupied by Probert.

Since his imprisonment Probert appears in the deepest and most unaffected distress at the ruin of his family, which he ascribes to his unfortunate connexion with Thurtell, but he emphatically persists in declaring his innocence of any previous knowledge or concurrence in the murder, or even the slightest acquaintance with Mr Weare He admits that he had invited Thurtell to his cottage, but did not expect he would have been accompanied by any other person He repeats over and over again the statement he has already made, with the strongest asseverations of his innocence He admits the receipt of 6l. on the night of the murder, but declares it to be in payment of a loan to John Thurtell, 5l of which he borrowed at the time, and for the purpose, from the landlord of the Coach and Horses His spirits are entirely broken, and his bodily health is evidently affected by his anxiety

We have already given Probert's statement before the Coroner

He has made a subsequent declaration, of which the following is the substance

"John Thurtell pretended to be paying his addresses to my sister-in-law, Miss Noyes, and therefore frequently came to my cottage on the Friday on which the murder was committed, he came to me, and said he wished I would give Hunt a seat in my gig, as he was a good singer, and would much amuse Miss Noyes, and greatly contribute to the conviviality at the cottage he observed that he could not take him down with him, as he had promised to give a gentleman, a friend of his, who was going into the country, a lift on the road as far as he was going

"I consented to his request, and Hunt left London with me in the gig We stopped at several houses on the road, which I had at different times served with liquor, and drank several glasses of brandy and water, when we arrived within a mile and a half of the cottage, Hunt desired me to stop, which I did, he got out, and then said, he had promised to meet John Thurtell there, I drove on, and when I arrived at the cottage I was surprised to find Thurtell there, I told him Hunt was waiting for him in the road, when he uttered an exclamation to the effect that he was too late, for the job was done, he then left the cottage in the gig, and returned shortly afterwards with Hunt, it was on their arrival that I was first informed of the horrid murder, and both of them said they would blow my brains out if I dared *split*" [Here Probert appeared completely overwhelmed, covered his face with his hands, and said he could not go on.]

"Hertford, Tuesday, Nov 4

"Probert is most sorrowful and dejected, each successive day his mind appears to lose a portion of its ease and vigour, last night he was very ill He this morning received a letter from his afflicted wife, she states that she has not slept since his apprehension, and who can doubt it?"

Probert appears perfectly wretched, and extremely depressed. He wishes his wife to see him, but has been dissuaded from an interview He observed, "I am sure Thurtell's life will be taken, and I am afraid my own will too" "Not if your statement (which we have already given) be true," replied his spiritual adviser. Here a pause ensued, but it did not elicit any observation in reply Probert, however, rather courts than shuns the subject of the murder, and, unlike Thurtell, abstains from entering upon any other topic when started by another

He is without a shilling to buy himself a dinner; and Thurtell learning this expressed his willingness to pay his expenses as long as he had money, adding that he would not advance a farthing for the —— ——, Hunt, if he were starving

Probert has heard of the arrest of his wife and Mr. and Miss Noyes he deplores very much the situation of his family, but denies altogether that any of them knew any thing of Thurtell's act.

ARREST OF PROBERT AND THOMAS THURTELL.

The precise circumstances attending the arrest of Probert and Thomas Thurtell have not been accurately stated. Upon the information given to the Magistrates of Hertfordshire, of the supposed commission of a murder, a warrant was issued for the apprehension of Probert Forster, a constable, was chosen to execute this warrant, and he went to the cottage at Gill's Hill on the Tuesday morning He there found Probert, whom he seized in the garden Probert at first expressed surprise, but upon being told that the charge against him was of a serious nature, he declared his readiness to go wherever the constable might think it necessary to conduct him At this time there was a waggon at the door, which was loaded with goods. Mr Mason and other Magistrates then came up and asked Probert whether the goods in the waggon were his? He answered in the affirmative, and they were examined, and such things as were considered important to the charge were taken away, and the rest were permitted to be removed Probert was then taken to the house of Mr Nicholls, the farmer, in whose possession the pistol found in the lane remained, where he underwent an examination. He then described the persons who had been at the cottage on the night of the murder, and the subsequent days, and from his information it was ascertained that Thomas Thurtell was coming down the same night. Forster, with proper assistance, in consequence went to the cottage on that night, and ascertained that a person had just arrived in a gig, he entered and saw Mrs Probert, he asked her if any person was in the house? She said, "No," but her manner being confused, Forster took a candle and ran up stairs, where he found Thomas Thurtell with his coat and waistcoat off, he immediately took him into custody, and carried him before the Magistrates.

ANECDOTES OF Mr WILLIAM WEARE.

Mr Weare was living upon the town without any particular occupation. He was passionately fond of sporting, and had some good dogs, which he occasionally kept in Lyon's Inn, where he was often seen airing them He had been about three years in Lyon's Inn, and was much respected. Billiards was a favourite game with him, and he played well He had a great distrust of banks, and kept his money about his person—a circumstance which perhaps led to the attempt on his life. Some time ago Mr Noel, his solicitor, induced him to open an account at Morland's, and he lodged 500*l.* He could not be satisfied, however, and drew the whole out to keep it in his own possession. He was paying his addresses to a young lady living at Bayswater, who had 300*l.* a year in her own right, and there was every probability of a union. It was in consequence of his having agreed to make a call on this lady, on Friday evening, that he appointed to meet John Thurtell at Tyburn turnpike. He was always remarkably neat in his dress, of diminutive stature, but active, and inured to fatigue. He had much of the cunning look of a Jew, and there was a peculiar hardness in his physiognomy His cheek bones stood out so much, and his chin was so small and pointed, that his face below the eyes, was quite a triangle. It does not appear that there was any fraud in his dealings, except the systematic fraud of the gaming-house. He was extremely suspicious of every body, and would not trust even a banker with his money, but usually carried it about his person. He was in the habit of attending races, and other sporting amusements, with an E O table. The only thing which could entice Weare from his retirement and his gaming was shooting, for the indulgence of which he would, at any time, travel to any distance; and in all probability, it was the hope of gratification in this way that betrayed him into the hands of his murderers. His elder brother is a highly respectable seedsman at Coventry, and he has another brother, a tailor, in the Borough. It was the latter brother that attended the funeral, and was so deeply affected, as to be unable for some time to rise from the grave. It is believed, from the offer of Hunt to change a 50*l* note at the Coach and Horses, that the booty was more than has been admitted. Indeed, it will be recollected that Hunt actually produced upwards of 8*l*, having previously given money to his wife. Mr Weare was reputed to be worth about 2000*l*. He was a prudent man, and rather more covetous than extravagant. We have heard that he was formerly a marker at a billiard-table, and that his livelihood depended upon his gambling speculations. He was well known in all the gambling circles.

Mr Weare resisted the attack of Thurtell with great energy, and had he been apprised of the treacherous attack, would, no doubt, have mastered his antagonist; but Thurtell is celebrated at gymnastic games, and overcame him by superior presence of mind and determined villainy.

The unfortunate deceased was slow and cautious in his play at the gaming-tables, and from his systematic course of action was deemed to have been very successful. It is supposed that it was this uniform success, and some late winnings from John Thurtell, (who had made what is called "a set" at him, and been foiled by the prudential calculations of the deceased), which excited the mixed spirit of cupidity and revenge to which he fell a victim. Some clue is afforded to the motive of the murderers (if more than one should eventually prove concerned) for cutting the clothes off the deceased's back, from the fact, that Mr Weare was in the habit of carrying, in a pocket inside, and attached to his flannel shirt, a considerable sum of money, to meet the possible exigencies of play (if circumstances should prompt him to pursue his speculations), in the event of his losing the ordinary sum with which he sat down at the table. Upon finding, therefore (as it is presumed) that his outside pockets were only supplied with his usual travelling sum, the murderer or murderers must have cut away the clothes in the hope of getting at the supposed concealed capital he was sometimes known to carry within his flannel shirt, but which, it is thought, he did not carry into the country on the night of the murder. Mr. Weare, if we are not misinformed, was one of the persons who were some time ago taken into custody, and examined at one of the police-offices, on a charge of being a co-proprietor in a gaming-house in Pall Mall.

There is no foundation for the story that he had won 1700*l.* from one of the Thurtells, nor does a subsequent report of a more disgraceful nature, as to his having been concerned in a swindling transaction, by which a gentleman was lately plundered of 7000*l.* appear to be better founded. It seems, however, but too evident, that the deceased was very closely connected with some of those disgraceful establishments at the west end of the town, appropriately called *Hells*.

In the months of March and April last, a co-partnership was formed betwixt Weare (the deceased), John Thurtell, Joseph Hunt, and another person, whose name has not yet been introduced, but who, there is every reason to suppose, was not entirely ignorant of the intentions of the murderers. The object of this association is easily defined. Mr Weare's attachment to play is already known, and in most English games he attained very extraordinary proficiency. Of those recently imported from the Continent he knew but little, and therefore rarely played for money, except now and then *rouge et noir*, in which he was generally successful. In regard to birth and education, they were both decidedly superior to their associates, one whom (Thurtell) was called "the bully," and the other, who had less prowess, was pretty justly dubbed "the blackguard." In spite of circumstances, Weare and the unknown still wore the air of gentlemen, and both have more than once exchanged cards with persons of honourable character in the more respectable gambling-houses at the west end. Thurtell, at one time, assumed the character of a gentleman, which he contrived to sustain, when sober, for some time, and, through his acquaintance with the groom-porter of a fashionable hazard-table, got admitted to the house, though an entire stranger to those gentlemen by whom it was generally frequented. Inflated to an extraordinary degree one night by wine and good fortune in the game, he forgot the masquerade in which he was moving, and the company by whom he was surrounded. He accordingly broke forth into a vulgar and disgusting boast of his success, and taunted his antagonist, an Irish gentleman well known in those circles, with his continued ill-luck; the other, perhaps really piqued by the circumstance, or else aggravated by his consummate assurance, rose from the table and pulled his nose, which the other resenting more like a ruffian than a gentleman, was, with the simultaneous consent of the entire party, kicked down stairs by his exasperated opponent, who then resumed his place.

It appears that the unfortunate murdered man was at Doncaster, during the races, with an extensive firm of gamblers. He was also half proprietor of *Rouge et Noir* and *Roulette* tables, in the neighbourhood of Pall Mall.—*Doncaster Gazette.*

Mr Weare kept a gambling-house at Bath last year, and netted handsomely, from the sporting propensities of the fashionable visitors of that city. His death has created a powerful sensation among those who were acquainted with him.

Although humanity shudders at the fate of Weare, still it appears that his character was not of the purest nature, and that, in fact, he has only fallen by the hands of some of the infamous association of which he was a member.

FURTHER PARTICULARS,

Which has occasionally appeared in the Newspapers, as to the Prisoners generally, and as to the Murder.

THE following letter appeared in the Morning Chronicle:—"SIR, —It is utterly impossible to describe the sensations I felt on perusing the account of the horrid murder near Watford. You must allow that the mere perusal is enough to make any feeling mind sicken; but when a reader ssupposes that he knows the cause of the crime, the sensations emanating therefrom are truly distressing.

As there can be no reasonable doubt but Mr Weare was the unfortunate murdered person, I beg to inform you that he was well known for what is called a sporting man. Thurtell resided at Norwich, and was known to what is called "the Fancy" in London, as a bit of a fighting man, and about three years ago he abandoned Norwich, and came to London with a large sum of money, which being well known, as a matter of course, his company was courted by "*Sporting Men*" Thurtell knew something of gaming, and thought he knew every thing, and it is not likely that the "*Sporting Men*" would undeceive him. After a *Sporting* dinner in the neighbourhood of Covent Garden, Thurtell lost a large sum of money, some say 1,700*l* or less, but certainly 1,000*l* by the unfortunate Mr Weare. Shortly after Thurtell became perfectly acquainted with the means by which he lost his money. These are the facts not to be disputed, and in this short statement cannot the origin of the crime be clearly traced, supposing Thurtell guilty.

Oct 31, 1823   A CONSTANT READER."

This most atrocious deed still occupies the public attention, to the exclusion of almost every other subject, and the most trivial circumstance connected with it is caught at with avidity, and listened to with intense interest. The parties implicated were generally known, especially in what are called "the sporting circles," and they were also equally well known at singing and other convivial societies, from the "tip-top" taverns at the west end of the town, down to the lowest pot-houses in the east.

After the examination had concluded on Thursday morning, Thurtell was placed in a small room, and attended by two constables. He was strongly ironed, and very narrowly watched throughout the day. His bearing on Wednesday night was exceedingly bold, and there was a great degree of levity in his manner, but after the examination he became exceedingly dejected, and sent for Ruthven, with whom he continued in conversation for a long time, in the course of which he accused Hunt of having committed the murder, but admitted that he himself was concerned in it. In the afternoon the Magistrates issued an order for the conveyance of Thurtell to the county gaol at Hertford, and he was taken there in a chaise by two constables of Watford well armed. On his arrival, he was placed in a cell by himself, and was watched during the night. Hunt remained in custody at Watford.

Hunt and Probert arrived at Hertford gaol, between four and five o'clock on Sunday morning, in two post chaises, and well guarded.

The visiting Magistrates have ordered the three prisoners to be kept separate, and to be double ironed, and that no person whatever be permitted to see either of them, unless by the special order, or in the presence of a Magistrate—excepting the Chaplain of the gaol.

On the Magistrates' order being alluded to, Hunt betrayed considerable alarm, and entreated that he might not be kept in solitary confinement. "Why should you fear being alone?" was asked, the reply was evasive, Hunt only observing, "that he should greatly prefer the company of three or four persons." Although it is determined to keep the prisoners apart from each other, it is nevertheless ordered, that two men should always be with each, and Hunt's desire is therefore, at present complied with.

On Sunday the three prisoners attended divine service; they were in three distinct pews, the text was appropriate—"Do justice, love mercy, and walk humbly with thy God." A pin might have been heard drop during the sermon. Beyond mute attention, nothing peculiar was observable in the conduct of the prisoners.

The boy and girl who were in the service of Probert, are at present in the workhouse at Aldenham, and are not allowed to have any communication with strangers.

No unnecessary severity is practised upon the prisoners, they are safely, but not closely, confined, they are properly allowed that self-possession, free from intrusion or severity, which their case at the present moment requires. The Magistrates occasionally visit them, the chaplain daily—not intruding into the judicial topics, which are the peculiar province of the former, but assiduous and ready to offer the consolations of his office, whenever the parties shall voluntarily call for their application.

Nov. 4.—Both Probert and Thurtell express much anxiety to see the newspapers, but this is denied them. The latter and Hunt have something less than 5*l.* each. Probert is without a shilling to buy himself a dinner, and Thurtell hearing this expressed his willingness to pay his expences as long as he had money.

Thurtell evinces no desire to be communicative with any body. When spoken to respecting the murder, he continues irritable, and, within the last day or two, rather coarse in his abruptness, wishing not to be talked to "*about such ——— stuff.*" He cannot bear to hear Hunt's name mentioned without imprecations. He hopes that that "villain will starve upon the gaol allowance"—a diet that, in allusion to his profligate habits, he thinks Hunt must find intolerable.

Nov. 6.—Other persons were examined by the Magistrates, among these were Mr. Probatt, the landlord of the Golden Cross, Charing Cross, and his servant, Stephen March. It will be recollected that Hunt, when he was examined before the Coroner, stated that he hired the gig in which John Thurtell and Mr. Weare proceeded to Gill's Hill Lane, on the night of the murder, at the Golden Cross, which is kept by Mr. Probatt. Hunt's statement about hiring the gig is correct. Mr. Probatt was not at home when Hunt came to the yard, but one of his men, who knew that Hunt had been in the habit of hiring horses there, said it was "all right," and Hunt was allowed to take the gig. On Saturday evening, when Hunt brought back the gig to the Golden Cross yard, his manner was extremely wild. He asked for a glass of brandy and water at the bar, and proceeded to talk on a variety of subjects without observing any kind of order. Whilst he was standing at the bar he produced a pistol, and said, "This is the fellow to do business." Mrs. Probatt was much alarmed, and told him, "for God's sake to put the pistol in his pocket," which Hunt did, after brandishing it about for some time. On the next morning (Sunday) Hunt hired another horse and gig, within which he and Thurtell drove to Gill's Hill Lane to dinner. He brought back the horse and gig on Monday morning, had a fresh horse put to the gig, and drove away again, saying he would return on Tuesday evening. He, however, came back in the gig about two o'clock, and then said that he should want a horse and gig next day, to take his wife to Dartford. March, Mr. Probatt's servant, observed that the horse was very much distressed, and on looking at the chaise, he saw some blood at the bottom. He supposed that some accident had happened in the chaise, and took no notice of the circumstance. The blood, however, must have proceeded from the body of Mr. Weare, when it was removed from the pond in Probert's garden to the pond at Elstree.

About a week ago a man brought a part of a box coat to the office in Bow Street, which he said he found in Brook Street, Bond Street, on the morning after the murder. It had marks of blood and dirt upon it, and the sleeves and skirts had been cut off. The body of the coat has since been identified as the property of Weare. It remains in the care of Bishop, at Bow Street.

In consequence of information received by Ballard, one of the officers of Marlborough-street Police Office, that two persons, an swering the description of Hunt and J Thurtell, had a short time back hired lodgings for some persons in Cumberland-street New-road, Ballard communicated his information and suspicions to Mr Conant, the Magistrate, who lost no time in dispatching Plank, in company with Ballard, to make the fullest investigation. Those two officers proceeded at an early hour to the house, respecting which they had obtained the information, No. 4, Cumberland-street, New-road, and having gained admission, questioned the landlady as to the persons that occupied her apartments. The woman, in the most unreserved manner, related the following particulars :—She said, that on Monday, the 24th of October, two men, one of whom was a tall man, with a white hat, and the other a short one, dressed in shabby black clothes, came to her and agreed to hire the first floor by the week. The agreement was made by the man in the white hat, who gave his name as Brown, referred her for character to Mrs Hunt, who gave a good character of him. The next day they brought a cart with a quantity of furniture, including feather beds, which were put into their apartments, and she was told to take care of them, particularly of the beds, which Brown (whom she now believes to be John Thurtell) requested she would put under her own beds to air them, which she accordingly did. From that day, until the Tuesday after the murder of Mr Weare, she neither saw nor heard any thing of the two men; but on that morning the shorter man, who, she thinks, is Hunt, called at about ten o'clock, and asked for Brown, she told him he was not at home, he then inquired in a very smart manner if a black hat was left there for Brown, to which she replied there was not. Hunt went away, and was not gone over a few minutes when he returned with Brown (Thurtell), still wearing the white hat, and asked if a black one was sent there for him. The two stopped for a short time, went away, and locked the door of their apartments after them, Brown saying to her that they would be back in a day or two, but she never saw them since. Plank, on receiving this information, had no doubt that Hunt and J Thurtell were the two men who took the lodgings, and though unprovided with any warrant, he did not hesitate to take the responsibility on himself, and forced open the doors. The first thing he discovered was a dressing-case, containing a set of razors, with the name "J T Cock, Haymarket," marked on them. Plank then broke open a chest, and found a variety of property, among which were some towels marked "T. S T" (Thomas and Sarah Thurtell). The officers having accomplished their object in identifying the suspected parties, locked up and sealed the rooms until they particulars should be communicated to the Magistrates at Watford. At a late hour on Saturday night last, Craig informed Mr Conant, that he had reason to believe that a man in the neighbourhood had been down with his caravan and horse to Gill's Hill cottage, a day or two after the murder, to remove some goods form thence to town. Mr Conant ordered this man to be immediately brought before him. He gave his name Thomas

Duffern, carrier, 35, Old Compton-street, Soho, and declared that he knew nothing whatever of the business, as it was his man, William Franklin, that always went out with the caravan and horses, on being closely pressed, and obliged to answer the questions put to him, he said that on Monday after the murder of Weare, Mr Thomas Noyes, of Castle-street, waited on him, and told him he must send down a caravan at a very early hour next morning (Tuesday) to Probert's cottage, to remove some goods to town. He sent his man with the caravan, and they arrived at the cottage about nine o'clock in the morning, they immediately loaded the caravan with every thing valuable in the house, but just as they were about to depart, Mr Norris, a Magistrate, arrived, and ordered all to be unloaded. He closely examined the property, to see if any thing was there that might lead to a discovery of the murder, but being satisfied that there was not, he suffered the caravan to depart, they arrived in town about seven, and the goods were taken, according to the directions, to a house in Titchfield-street, where they were refused to be taken in. The carman then conveyed them to Duffern's, in Compton-street, where they had scarcely arrived, when they were seized by a Sheriff's Officer, who had followed them up to town, and in whose possession they now are. This statement was corroborated by Franklin, and nothing appearing to throw suspicion on either of them, they were discharged.

Of Hunt, Mr Wardell says he knows nothing, never having seen him in all his visits to the cottage. On the night of the murder, he says, his attention was particularly attracted by the rapid passing and repassing of gigs near his house, and remarked to his family that something extraordinary was taking place.

The rent of Probert's cottage, including all taxes, and about four acres of land, was but 35*l* per annum. The property, as before stated, had recently been purchased before the murder, and the new proprietor had signified his intention of pulling down the old cottage, and erecting a new one near it.

The chambers of the late Mr Weare in Lyon's Inn, have not been as yet examined. They are padlocked, and the examination is not to take place till the arrival of his elder brother in town. It is suspected, however, that they were visited by Hunt on the Saturday after the murder. It will be recollected that he left the servant boy of Probert waiting for him behind St Clement's Church while he went on some errand. The key of the chambers, and the key of the escrutoire within them, were always kept by Mr Weare, attached to the purse which fell into the hands of the murderers, so that means were afforded of rifling the rooms of their valuable contents.

The Magistrates have been extremely anxious to discover the clothes which the deceased wore when he was murdered. It is remarkable that Hunt should yet maintain silence with respect to the manner in which the clothes were disposed of. On Sunday last, the pond in Probert's grounds, in which Mr Weare's body was thrown, and a well also in Probert's garden were drained by order of the Magistrates, in order to ascertain whether the clothes had been concealed in either of those places. The search, however, was fruitless, for nothing was found. It has not yet been ascertained what has become of Mr Weare's watch. John Thurtell, who, as well as the other prisoners, is very communicative to those who come in contact with him, being asked what he had done with the watch, said, ' I was offered 26 guineas for it by a Jew, but I'd see him d—d before I'd give it him for that, for it was worth 60*l*. " But what have you done with it?" he was again asked. The reply was, I threw it over a hedge near Bushey, as I was coming down in the chaise. Thurtell here alluded to the period when he was being conveyed to gaol. There is, however, every reason to believe that this story of throwing the watch away is quite fictitious, for Thurtell was closely searched by the officers when he was apprehended, and, besides, the watch has been looked for in vain at the spot pointed out by Thurtell.

On Saturday (Nov 8), there was a meeting of the Magistrates of the county at the Town Hall, their deliberations were private, but it was resolved that an order should be issued to the Governor of the gaol prohibiting the admission of any person to even a sight of either of the three prisoners confined there, and recommending it to all gentlemen in the commission of the peace, not being visiting Magistrates to the gaol, to forego the exercise of their usual privilege: this order was signed by upwards of twenty Magistrates of the neighbourhood. A warrant was some days since issued for the apprehension of Leman, who is supposed to be now in Paris, which being backed by the French Ambassador to the Court of St. James's, was addressed and transmitted to Sir C. Stuart, to be laid before the French Minister of Police. It has been reported that it is the intention of Leman to surrender himself; this, however, we rather doubt. The prisoners continue to conduct themselves very well.

Hertford, Nov 10

The interdiction of access to the prisoners continues, nor can any information be procured respecting them beyond the gossip of the townsfolk.

Thurtell, if questioned, or if he suspects himself to be examined on the late murder, has uniformly replied in a hurried tone, ' For God's sake be patient, I shall clearly prove an *alibi* sufficient for any reasonable man." Hunt is still confident and unembarrassed. Probert continues greatly dejected.

Bow-Street, Saturday, Nov 15.—Sir Richard Birnie has been actively engaged in arranging and sifting the mass of evidence got together by the Watford Magistrates. It is natural to suppose that, in the alarm first occasioned by this deed of blood, many statements were listened to, and many voluminous depositions were taken, which do not bear upon the case; and it has been, and still is, the labour of the chief Magistrate, to select and arrange from this mass of irrelevent matter, a clear, concise, and well-connected chain of evidence. In the course of his labours, he has found that many connecting links were wanting, and these he has spared no pains to supply.

It will be recollected, that Thurtell was stated to have met Mr Weare, by appointment at the end of the Edgware-road, on the evening of the murder, previous to his taking him down in his gig to Gill's-hill cottage, but there was no direct evidence of their having met at the place so said to have been appointed. This deficiency Sir Richard has supplied, by finding out the hackney-coachman who drove Mr Weare on that evening from his chambers in Lyon s-inn to the place in question. This man underwent a long examination in private before Sir Richard, at Bow-street, early yesterday morning, and his evidence is said to be of importance.

Mr Weare's brother has also been examined, and also the female servant of the deceased. Of course the examination of these persons has been strictly *en secret*, but we have been given to understand that they complete a chain of evidence which will be sufficiently clear for the purposes of justice, without the assistance of the would-be approver—Hunt.

We understand that the great coat worn by John Thurtell on the night of the murder, has been found, with the lining of the sleeves cut out as if for the purpose of removing the marks of blood, there are such marks however on other parts of the coat. It is also rumoured, that the bloody clothes of Weare have been found in the lodgings of some of the parties.

The shirt which Mr Weare had on when he was murdered, and which was found in the stable at Probert's cottage, was yesterday taken to the house of Mr Clutterbuck. It is ripped up in front.

In the course of Monday, many applications were made for a sight of the prisoners. Some of the applicants were of high rank, but they were refused.

Nov. 23.—A gentleman thus describes an interview with Thurtell —He was standing in the little yard before his cell, dressed in black, and heavily ironed but not handcuffed; he seems still unbroken in spirit, and of a collected and resolute demeanour, but is far from expressing any thing of improper confidence; his manners are rather humble, though his look and voice are firm; he is a man whose expression is marked with a great deal of peculiar character; his countenance is quite a contrast to that of Hunt, the latter implying feebleness of mind with an expression very like that of a smart coffee-house waiter. But the conformation of Thurtell's features indicates decided energy and inflexible stubborness of purpose. His eye is sharp and intelligent, and to those who are under the impressions connected with his name, would appear revengeful. His address at present, however, is very mild and rather conciliating. He was asked if he had any complaint to make. He said the gaoler had treated him with great kindness, and he had no complaint to make of him. He was asked if he was satisfied now with the arrangements for his defence. He observed that he was in all but one respect, that of not having been allowed to see Mr C. Pearson, he said that gentleman's advice he had very much desired. He felt it would have been of great importance to him if he could have had a communication with him for but ten minutes, and the want of it had put him to great expense and trouble. It appears that even before and since the above interview, he has frequently lamented his not having been able to see Mr C Pearson.

Hertford, Nov 27.—The most important circumstance which has transpired during the day, is the fact of Mr Nicholson having, as Solicitor for the prosecution, called upon Hunt this morning, and officially announced to him, on the part of the Crown, that he is *not to be admitted as a King's evidence*, but is to be put upon his trial for his life. The effect produced by this communication on the wretched prisoner was painfully apparent. He seemed to be at once struck with the horror of his situation, and to sink beneath the weight of his apprehensions. In a moment he lost all that flippant confidence which he had before displayed, and prayed that the hopes with which he had been buoyed up might not be withdrawn. Mr Nicholson could not soften the notice which he felt it his duty to give, and retired, leaving Hunt in a state of dreadful alarm.

MRS. PROBERT, MISS NOYES, AND MR NOYES

Bishop having been directed by the Magistrates to apprehend some persons in London, he succeeded in taking into custody *Thomas Noyes*, the brother of Mrs Probert, who was at the cottage, on the Sunday after the murder; and *Mr. Tetsall*, the landlord of the Coach and Horses, in Conduit Street.

Noyes was taken into custody between twelve and one o'clock yesterday morning. At six o'clock yesterday morning, Bishop carried his prisoners in his post-chaise to Watford, where it was understood they were to undergo an examination. Noyes was handcuffed, Tetsall, we believe, was not. Noyes was extremely agitated during the journey, and frequently wrung his hands, but said little. Tetsall betrayed no emotion. At eleven o'clock Noyes and Tetsall were conveyed from the Essex Arms' Tavern, where they had been taking some refreshment, to the house of Mr Clutterbuck the Magistrate, and their examination immediately commenced. As was the case on Tuesday, no stranger was permitted to enter the room where the investigation was carried on; the nature of the evidence given, we are therefore unable to state.

Noyes was called before the Magistrates several times, after leaving the room on the last occasion, he was fearfully agitated; the perspiration flowed from him profusely, he struck his hands violently on his forehead, and appeared to be nearly choked in endeavouring to suppress his feelings. At 7 o'clock the examination being concluded, Noyes was committed to St Albans gaol, for further examination, until Saturday. Tetsall, Mr. Probatt, and his servant, and the landlord of the Bald faced Stag, on the Edgware road, at which place Probert and Hunt stopped on the night of the murder, entered into recognizances to give evidence against the persons accused of Mr Weare's murder at the next Hertfordshire assizes. It is but justice to Mr Tetsall to state, that it is generally said that nothing resulted from the examination which could be supposed to implicate him in the horrible transaction in which it appears that his lodgers were so deeply concerned. Some respectable persons were prepared to become his bail, if required, to the amount of 2,000*l*.

Noyes was apprehended at 35, Castle-street, where he and his sister occupied lodgings on the second floor. There was an appearance of extreme poverty in the house, and Noyes was entirely destitute of money, Mrs Probert was also apprehended in these lodgings.

On Monday evening, Nov 3, Mrs Probert and Miss Noyes were apprehended and taken to Bow-street Office, but the examination was so strictly private, that not a word transpired. They were afterwards taken to Watford, in the custody of Bishop, the Officer. Yesterday they underwent a long examination, at the house of Mr Clutterbuck. The result of this examination is likewise kept private. Every precaution was taken to prevent the proceedings from obtaining publicity, but it is whispered that the Magistrates have obtained some highly important information from Mrs Probert and her sister.

Mrs. Probert and her sister were taken down to Watford on Monday night, in separate post-chaises. Miss Noyes seemed to be much more sensibly affected than Mrs Probert. She cried almost incessantly. After having had tea in the same apartment with the officers, they retired to rest in separate chambers, in which they were locked up for the night; Miss Noyes entreated that she might be allowed to have a light during the night; but this was refused, as well as a subsequent request that the chamber-maid might be allowed to sleep with her; she in consequence spent the night in darkness, and we understand in the greatest agony, not venturing to go to bed at all. In the morning they breakfasted again with the officers, and soon after ten, were conducted on foot to Mr Clutterbuck's house.

Their examination was protracted to eight o'clock on Tuesday evening, when they were taken back to the Essex Arms, and were immediately conveyed from thence to St Albans, in separate post-chaises. The female servant and boy lately in the employment of Mr Probert were also examined. The former described the circumstance of her seeing Hunt lying on the sofa, on the evening of the murder, and also spoke of the circumstance to which we yesterday alluded, namely, the sofa squab being stained with blood.

During the time that they were in custody, and under examination, they were both much affected, and were with difficulty prevailed upon to take any refreshment. The Magistrates, acting upon the intelligence which they derived from the inquiry, issued warrants for the apprehension of some persons in London. The warrants were placed in the hands of Bishop.

On Wednesday evening, Mrs. Probert informed the gaoler at St. Albans, that she had something to communicate to the Magistrates Mr Clutterbuck being informed of this, immediately sent for her to his house, where she remained until four o'clock yesterday morning, when she was taken back to gaol. We understand that she imparted some important information to the Magistrates, and no small surprise, by producing from her bosom, the chain which was attached to the watch of Mr Weare, and which Thurtell asserted he had thrown, with the watch, over the hedge on the Watford road.

RE-EXAMINATION OF MRS PROBERT, MISS NOYES, AND MR NOYES

At half past eleven o'clock this morning (Nov 8), the above-named prisoners were brought from St Albans to this town, the two former in separate post-chaises, and the latter in a gig, between two officers. They were conducted to Mr. Clutterbuck's house, and placed in separate apartments, no communication having been permitted between them since their first apprehension Mrs Probert appeared to be more collected than when she left the Magistrates on the Thursday morning, but still she evinced a good deal of uneasiness, and when the name of her husband was mentioned, she expressed the strongest anxiety for his fate She wrote to him, she said, before she was herself apprehended, but since that she has not heard from him either directly or indirectly She is equally anxious as to her children, who, it seems have been consigned to the care of a friend

It has already appeared from the statements both of Hunt and Probert, that Mrs P had manifested considerable uneasiness at the mysterious whisperings on the Sunday as well as on the Monday night, and that Probert, when called upon to assist in removing the body from the pond in his garden into the gig, actually expressed his fears that his wife would suspect something Indeed it is impossible to suppose that Mrs Probert should not have feared something wrong was going on, and the more especially when we reflect on the unguarded, if not hardened and profligate exclamations of Hunt, and the jeers and indirect insinuations of Thurtell as to the clothes which he (Hunt) wore on the Sunday, and which Mrs Probert must have perfectly well known were not his, but had remained in her house from the night of the murder In every view of the case her testimony, if given with candour, must be of the utmost importance, and the danger in which she has conceived herself to have been placed, has induced her to be extremely explicit in her disclosures

Miss Noyes is not presumed to have known so much, although from her residence in the house, she must have made observations on what was going forward On her way from St Albans this morning, she was considerably affected, and shed tears Her situation is certainly of a very painful nature, whether as it regards herself, her sister, or her brother-in-law

As to Mr Noyes, it does not appear from any thing that has yet transpired, that there exists any ground of suspicion against him, beyond the facts of his intimate acquaintance with all the parties—his presence at the cottage on the Sunday, and his repeated interviews with all the parties both before and after the murder. The Magistrates deem it impossible, with all the opportunities he had of hearing and observing the prisoners, that he should have been altogether ignorant of what had happened, and therefore felt the less reluctance in subjecting him to temporary imprisonment. An acquaintance of his, thus speaks of him, "that respectable, quiet, and inoffensive being, Mr Thomas Noyes."

Mr Clutterbuck, Mr Haworth, and Mr Mason, resumed their labours this morning (Nov 11), Mr Noyes and his sister having been brought frought from St Albans, underwent a long examination.*

---

* MRS. PROBERT'S STATEMENT.

When first taken before the Magistrates, she betrayed great agitation, and expressed the strongest reluctance to make any statement at all. She declared she knew nothing about the matter, and could not, therefore, give any information, but upon being pressed, and warned of the consequences that might accrue to herself and those connected with her, she became more communicative. She stated, that on the night in question, her husband and Hunt (the latter of whom had been there before) arrived in Mr. Probert's gig, and Hunt brought a loin of pork into the kitchen, desiring that it might be cooked, and then returned to the stable. John Thurtell arrived almost immediately after her husband and Hunt, and remained in the stable with them for nearly three quarters of an hour, when they all three came into the house. They had been seated but a few minutes, when Hunt and Thurtell went into the yard, and got the stable lanthorn, with which they proceeded through the garden, and out of sight. Her husband remained behind. She thought all this was very singular, but took no notice at the time, because she knew that Hunt and Thurtell were men of irregular habits, and therefore supposed that they were only after some "lark," as they termed it. When they returned, they appeared in high spirits, and sat down and ate a hearty supper, John Thurtell somewhat less so than Hunt, or her husband, but he did eat a considerable quantity. Hunt was by far the most merry of the party, and was once or twice betrayed into expressions of an indelicate kind, and was reproved by John Thurtell. He sung several songs in a firm unembarrassed manner. Soon after supper, Thurtell took out a very elegant looking watch and seals, and they examined it, he observing that it was a nice "thimble" (flash for watch). The chain was not offered to her that night. Her sister, Miss Noyes, retired to bed some time before she did. She (Mrs Probert) heard many remarks between Hunt and Thurtell which induced her to believe that something wrong had been done and when she went up stairs, she partly undressed herself and returned to the stairs, placing herself as near to the bottom as she could, so that she might if possible, hear what passed. The conversation was in so low a tone, that she could only catch here and there a word. She heard a rustling of paper, like that of bank notes, and heard something heavy thrown into the fire. She then heard it proposed that the three should "go and finish the job." Her husband said something which she could not hear, and Hunt and Thurtell went out together. She was sure her husband did not go with them. She did not like to venture down stairs, and returned to her room and opened the window, in order to watch the return of Hunt and Thurtell. She had been standing there for some time, when she observed a light approach from Gill's Hill-lane, and presently saw John Thurtell and Hunt enter the garden. Hunt had a light in one hand, and with the other was assisting Thurtell in dragging along some heavy substance. She could not see what it was, but it was something very heavy, and was enveloped in a sack. They went towards the fish-pond, which is concealed from the view of a person in her situation at the window, by a small shrubbery. They were out of her sight for about ten

It is clear that the only object the Magistrates can have in examining these witnesses, is to connect the chain of evidence against all the parties implicated, without the assistance of Hunt, whose wilful misrepresentations have certainly disqualified him from becoming a witness for the crown. Mrs Probert's testimony cannot legally be received against her husband, she will therefore, be relieved from the pain of saying any thing directly to his prejudice.

The proceedings of the Magistrates were not brought to a conclusion till nearly six o'clock, when Mr Noyes and his sister were again sent back to St Albans.

Two other witnesses were examined during the day, namely, Rushingham, the man from whom Hunt bought the sack and cord, and Thomas Heron, the ostler, to whom he delivered the horse and gig, the morning after the removal of the body of Mr Weare from Probert's garden. The latter man describes the cushions of the gig to have been extremely wet and dirty when brought home, and also says that the horse was much distressed. The manners of Hunt, he adds, were extremely agitated.

The Magistrates have been all day, (November 12th,) engaged in the examination of witnesses, and have just concluded their labours. At eleven o'clock this morning Mr Noyes and Miss Noyes were conducted from St Albans Castle, as on Saturday, to the house of Mr Clutterbuck, at this place. Mrs Probert remains at St. Albans, her examination having been concluded on Saturday night. They were brought in separate chaises. The examination of Miss Noyes elicited nothing which allows the least ground for presuming that she was acquainted with the horrible transaction in any of its stages. She has become more reconciled to her situation, and seems now to entertain no fear for her personal safety. She has been reconducted to St Albans gaol. The examinations of the different parties are regularly laid before the Secretary of State for the Home Department

---

minutes, and then she saw them return to the house, but the candle had been put out. It was more than an hour after this that her husband came to bed. She told him she was sure those men (meaning Hunt and Thurtell) had been doing something wrong; her husband, in an under tone, desired her to make herself easy, for there was nothing the matter. He seemed much depressed in spirits. The next morning she renewed her inquiries as to the proceedings of the previous night, and he said that Hunt and Thurtell had been snaring partridges, "and that you know, my dear," he added, "is against the law, and must be done secretly." Hunt and Thurtell breakfasted with them in the morning, and then went away. On the Sunday they came down with Noyes, her brother, and in the course of the evening John Thurtell said he had a little thing in his pocket, which he intended to make a present of to her (Mrs Probert). He then took a gold chain from his pocket, and putting it over her neck, accompanying the action with this remark —" This chain was given to me by a favourite little Quakeress of mine, at Norwich, as I have done with her long ago, I cannot do better than give it to Mrs. Probert, as a token of my respect for her."—[This chain she produced to the Magistrates.]—Mrs Probert stated nothing else material. She was questioned very closely, as to whether her husband had not a greater share in the transactions than she had admitted, but she declared she had told the whole truth.

Miss Noyes was next called in, and interrogated, but she professed an entire ignorance of the whole business, and said she went to bed early, and therefore could give no evidence of the conduct of the parties after supper.

It was the intention of the Magistrates, according to report, to liberate Mr Noyes and his sister, upon merely binding them over to attend the trial as witnesses, but they have been perplexed so much by the examinations, that they have deferred this measure until they know the opinion of the Secretary of State as to its effect

The father of Mr Noyes was an extensive and respectable brewer at Flozfield, in Wilts, who, after having realized a considerable sum in business, lived respectably for several years in retirement at Hampstead,

Some mistake has arisen with respect to the Miss Noyes, to whom it has been represented that John Thurtell, and a Mr Woods paid their addresses The female at present in custody, is not the Miss Noyes alluded to The lady who had excited this rivalship is a younger sister, named Caroline, a pretty girl, about 22 years of age. Woods had been attached to this girl for three years, and whilst he was in France about six months back, she resided with her sister, Mrs. Probert, at the cottage. Whilst here, John Thurtell used to persecute her with his attentions, which she always rejected When Woods returned from France, about three months ago, Caroline Noyes informed him of Thurtell's conduct, in consequence of which Woods removed her from the cottage, to which she has never since returned

Mr Clutterbuck has lately called at Bow-street, and had some consultation with Sir Richard Birnie and Mr Minshull on the subject of the examinations taken, and particularly with reference to Mrs Probert He was desirous of knowing, in the event of his binding this lady to appear as a witness on the trial, what sureties he should require for her appearance

Sir Richard Birnie asked, whether her evidence was essential to the ends of justice?

Mr Clutterbuck said, that he certainly considered her a witness of great importance, against Hunt and John Thurtell, although he very well knew that she could not be permitted to give testimony against her husband

Sir Richard Birnie said, that if this were the case, she should either be called upon to find sureties for her appearance to a very considerable amount, or should be detained in custody, in order to be produced as a witness on the trial. If the latter were the case, she should of course be treated with every possible indulgence In a case of murder, and especially in this, where the connexions of the parties implicated were considered, he thought that a Magistrate could not be too cautious It was expedient that this woman should be kept from communication with others, and it was equally expedient that her personal safety should be secured. He should have no hesitation, as a Magistrate, on his own responsibility, to detain her till the hour of trial arrived

Mr Clutterbuck went away, we believe, with the intention of adopting the course suggested With respect to Mr. Noyes and his sister, they are, we believe, to be discharged upon producing sufficient securities for their appearance on the trial

It is due to the Magistrates to state, that they have been indefatigable in their exertions, and from the commencement of their painful inquiry, have evinced a degree of shrewdness and promptness, highly creditable to their official situation

We cannot conclude or dismiss this department of our present publication, without a few articles from the Press, on our Gaming Houses

The loose Gamblers of the metropolis have been thrown into consternation, by the warrants issued against some of their fellows, by the Magistrates who are conducting the enquiry into the circumstances of Weare's murder. Like all marauding confederacies, the moment a link in the chain of fellowship is broken, suspicion awakes, and renders the whole a prey to their several guilty recollections. It is this "compunctious visiting" which has no doubt induced some of those against whom warrants were lately issued to abscond, although it was notorious that their arrest was only intended to elicit collateral evidence against the parties implicated in the murder, without involving themselves in any of the guilt connected with it

We are not without hope that gambling-houses may receive a severe shock by the late dreadful occurrence. These are the seminaries of self-murder and assassination. It was in these that Thurtell and Hunt spent their nights. It was the gambling-house that murdered Weare; and when his murderers shall approach to their frightful end, it will be to the gambling-house that they will look back as the birth-place of their crime, and the office from whence issues the warrant for their execution

Those hells—haunts of dissipation among characters of all ranks—have been brought more immediately into public notice by the murder of Mr. Weare, than they ever were by a common gaming-house accident; and, therefore, we think, a page or two cannot be better applied, than to such an exposure of them as will warn the unthinking against the certain ruin, of principles and of character, to which the habitual attending of them naturally leads. It is said, that the entrance to those hells is difficult; be it so, but the object is only to exclude the officers of justice, and all who might put the thoughtless on their guard against the ruin which awaits them there. The hell is usually a very splendid apartment, in which the frequenters are treated with the choicest viands, and the most costly wines, at the expense of the house, at least this is the case in those of the *most respectable*—or, as one should call it, of the deepest and most destructive class. Before a stranger can be admitted, he must pass three, four, or even five sets of doors, strongly barricadoed on the inside, and watched by cunning cerberi and club-armed bullies. At each of those doors, a small slip only is at first withdrawn, and passwords and signs, like those of a freemason, have to be exchanged ere the stranger can get within side. This caution is repeated at every door, and one would naturally suppose, that a person possessing even the slightest degree of penetration would hesitate, ere he entered where so many guards against the knowledge of the public had to be set. It turns out, however, that the difficulty of access does not lessen the number of visitors, and the throng to these hells is full as great as if the admission were easy and the visit profitable. In proportion, too, as the getting in is long and laborious, the getting out is summary and involuntary; for no sooner is the visitant *stripped* of all his cash, than he is insulted, jostled, kicked down stairs, and tossed into the street, without ceremony and without pity. The causes of so much crime cannot be too frequently or too forcibly held up to public reprobation; and while it is the duty of the administrators of the law to follow the detected knot of pests of society into all its ramifications, and visit upon every part of it the full measure of punishment which the offended statutes of the country demand, it is equally the duty of those who legislate for the public, so as to strike at the roots of the evil, as to preclude the possibility of its future growth,—to prevent the practices which have ruined these men from being again the ruin of others,—and by thus saving from crime, to save the country the pain and the odium of another such occurrence as the murder at Gill's Hill.

An offer of a general disclosure of the gambling system was made to a person high in office, by means of an anonymous letter, in the early part of last week, but, as the gentleman to whom it was addressed never attends to communications of this sort, no further notice was taken of the affair until either Wednesday or Thursday, when the proposal was verbally made through a third person, and after some consideration, was finally accepted. The principal was subsequently introduced, and pointed out the tendency of his information, demanding as a preliminary measure, that his name should in no wise be coupled with any ulterior proceedings that the Magistrates, under the circumstances, might think proper to adopt. This condition being considered perfectly reasonable, was immediately granted, with a further promise of special protection, should circumstances at any future period dictate such interposition. On the following morning (Friday), a scroll was exhibited, on which upwards of *two hundred* (¹) gambling-houses of various ranks and notoriety were described, with a minuteness and accuracy that none but the most intimate of their visitors could have accomplished. In addition to the names and characters of the keepers and servants of those houses, were superadded those of the persons who chiefly frequent them, together with their respective callings, whether real or fictitious. From this document, copies are being taken for the private possession of the different Police Magistrates, who will, no doubt, apply their information to the public good. It was at first suggested to publish the whole in the newspapers, with a view of guarding inexperienced young men from these haunts of vice and misery; but on reconsidering the subject, the former measure was adopted, as apparently more conducive to the ends of Justice, and affording more ample protection to the public at large.

Mr Cobbett too, in his admirable sermon on Gaming, published in 1821, forcibly paints in every page, the horrors of this passion

"Of all the fraudulent practices of which we have any knowledge, those of the Gamester are the most odious in themselves, and most baneful in their consequences The object of every gamester, is, to get, doing injury to his neighbour It is to get his money or goods from him without yielding him any thing in return, and thus, disguise it under what name we may, is *extortion* and *fraud*

It is invariably found, that gamesters are amongst the most *unfeeling* as well as the most fraudulent of mankind In Virginia and the Slave-States of America, nothing is more common than to see the gamester, whose purse has been emptied, call in a domestic slave, man, woman or child, as a *stake* to be *played* for against a sum of money Thus the drawing of a card, or the turning of a die, may, and frequently does, separate instantly and for ever, wife from husband, and child from parents! Look at the poor creature that stands trembling by awaiting the result of the game, and then find if you can, words to express your abhorrence of those who can give to a deed like this, the appellation of *play!*

In this country, indeed, the gamester, thanks to the laws which we inherit from our brave and just forefathers, cannot make the stake consist of human flesh and blood But, amongst its *consequences*, gaming never fails to bring *want of feeling* towards others The mind, constantly agitated by selfish hopes and selfish fears, has no time to bestow on country, friends, parents or children. The pride of ancestry, the inheritance of successors, the past, the future, and even the present, even ordinary pleasures of the day have no attractions for the gamester, nay, as thousands of instances have proved, *Love* itself, the great conqueror of the human heart is compelled to yield to the cards and dice, for, all-powerful as that passion is in every other case, here it tries its powers in vain

Hence it is, and many are unfortunate enough to know the fact by experience, gamesters are the most unsocial, cheerless and gloomy of mortals They appear constantly lost in care ' They are plotting against others, or, are absorbed in reflections on their own losses A want of affection for others, brings in time its natural return, and, at the end of a few years, men, or women, of this description become objects of contempt, or, at least, of indifference with all around them

Accustomed to practise deceit, insincerity becoming habitual to him; the gamester suspects every one, confides in no one and is completely excluded from that inexpressible pleasure and advantage which good and generous minds derive from the placing of unlimited confidence in friends. Confidence to be real, must be mutual, and, as the gamester never confides, so no one confides in him. Indeed, his very habits render him unworthy of trust or belief. What he calls his *play* is a regular practising of hand His success depends wholly on ability in deceiving, Even the language of the gaming-table, the very terms of his art, are such as to render the commission of fraud familiar to his mind *Shuffle—cut—trick*, words which express the divers acts that he performs, and all indicating something in the way of lying or cheating, or both.

How numerous are the instances, wherein crimes the most heinous have been committed, for the purpose of obtaining the means of pursuing gaming, or, for that of making up for losses sustained at the gaming-table! Masters defrauded by apprentices and clerks, defaulters defrauding the public; forgeries innumerable on friends as well as others, children stealing from their parents theft and robbery, in all their various forms, murder aggravated by every cruelty, and acts of suicide without end! These, O cards and dice, are your works! And yet, not *yours*, but the works of those Lawgivers, Magistrates, and Parents, who, deaf alike to the commands of God, and the cries of nature, neglect the most sacred of all their duties. The annals of the jail and the gibbet blazon forth the triumphs of gaming

Disconsolate father! Distracted mother! You, who are sinking into the earth over the corpse of a self-murdered gaming son! There you behold the result of your own misconduct! It was you who created the fatal taste, it was you who taught his little hands to shuffle and to trick, it was you who taught his infant looks to lie, it was you who implanted in his heart the love of enchanting fraud! Take then, your just reward—sorrow, remorse, and shame, and constant fear for the remainder of your days, to hear even an allusion to him, who, but for your fault, might have been the comfort and pride of your lives, and have borne your name with honour to posterity!"

We are now bringing to a conclusion, our pages which have thus illustrated the transition from gaming to murder, and the fatal consequences of ungovernable passions, by observing, that the trial for this most guilty act, was fixed for the 5th December, at Hertford, on which day, the Court after hearing the arguments of counsel as to the prejudice which so generally prevailed against the prisoners, thought the ends of public justice better attained, by putting off the Trial until the 6th of January, when the reporter whom we have specially retained for that purpose, will send us by express, a faithful account of every occurrence that takes place in Court, which shall be when printed, immediately added to this our present work

TRIAL

OF

THURTELL, HUNT, AND PROBERT.

HERTFORD, TUESDAY MORNING,
January 6, 1824

THE delay which has taken place in the prosecution against the prisoners does not appear to have at all diminished the feeling of the public interest, which the circumstances of their case have excited.

During the night the town has been one continued scene of bustle. As early as four o'clock, numbers were waiting outside the Court-house, hoping to gain admission, and at five o'clock it was surrounded by a crowd. However, although thus early, it was of no avail---seven o'clock being the hour fixed by the Sheriff for admission, excepting Magistrates, and for some few of their friends.

As usual, a flourish of trumpets announced the approach of the awful hour of trial, which was repeated at various parts of the town. At twenty minutes past seven o'clock, a post chariot drove towards the gaol, which being noticed, was instantly followed by a multitude of people. Precisely at half-past seven, the chaise having drawn up close to what is called the Mill-gate of the gaol; the clanking of chains gave notice of the approach of the prisoners, and an assistant of the gaoler entered the chaise, and was followed by Thurtell, heavily ironed. An officer mounted the box of the chariot, and was followed by Hunt, with heavy chains to both legs. The two prisoners being conducted to the place appropriated for them, the chariot returned to the gaol for the purpose of bringing down Probert, and very shortly returned with him. But few minutes elapsed before a post-chaise brought Mrs. Probert, we believe from St. Alban's.

The Prisoners on alighting, were conducted to the *Nisi Prius* Court, where breakfast was brought to them, and served on the Barristers' table. Instead of eating a hearty breakfast, as when last up, Thurtell took but a quarter of a round of toast, and then he seemed to eat with difficulty.

K

Hunt's appetite was equally bad. Neither of them spoke to the other. The prisoners' irons were knocked off in the Court.

The hour of eight, the time appointed for the sitting of the Court, having arrived, precisely as the clock struck, the Learned Judge entered the Sheriff's carriage, and proceeded, attended by the proper officers, at a slow and solemn pace to the Court, where having arrived, another flourish of trumpets announced the moment so pregnant with importance to the individuals charged,

The Court was crowded to excess in every part, and particularly the gallery, from which we learn that several persons have been taken out in a fainting state. Even the stairs leading to the gallery were thronged in the extreme, and a vast number of anxious persons, many of whom came from a distance, were unable to obtain so much as a glimpse of the prisoners, or to hear a word of the trial.

The Witnesses who had arrived the preceding night, were now brought to the Court-house, and placed in a room by themselves. Thomas Thurtell came down in the care of the Turnkey of Newgate. Mrs Probert was accompanied by a friend, and on being brought into the passage of the Court, she was greatly affected, and cried with much bitterness, when she subsequently heard that her husband had been removed from the bar, she became more calm.

Every Evening Paper had its reporters down, and in order to facilitate the publication of the proceedings on the same day, each had engaged from four to six horses, which were employed in carrying up the reports at a later hour in the evening; and it was calculated that there were not less than one hundred horses placed on the road for this purpose. While alluding to this subject, it is due to the High Sheriff, the Rev. Mr. Lloyd, and Mr. Nicholson, the Under-Sheriff, to state, that every thing in their power was done to assist the views of the different reporters; and although, in some instances, the rudeness of persons holding high rank was to be regretted, still, upon the whole, and considering the difficulties which were to be encountered, the Gentlemen who were engaged in these duties, had every reason to feel grateful for the politeness with which they were treated.*

---

* The Times thus judiciously remarks on the confusion, on the outside the Court-house —On the last occasion, Upson, one of the officers on the Bow-Street establishment, gave every facility of ingress and egress; and from his

Proclamation having been made, the Judge ordered the prisoners to be brought to the bar

Mr. Justice PARK. All who have seats, and don't sit, must go out: the heat will be intolerable, if this order is not attended to.

The bustle and noise which had prevailed from the first opening of the Court had not yet subsided In this interval, Mr Jay and Mr Fenton, the attorneys for the prisoner Thurtell, were struggling to find their way through the crowd for the purpose of obtaining places near the prisoner's Counsel, and having reached the point intended, and there being great noise and confusion in the effort;

Mr Justise PARK inquired who were the persons thus increasing the disturbance?

Mr. Fenton and Mr. Jay respectfully intimated that they were the Attornies in the case.

Mr. Justice PARK, with considerable warmth, said, "Nonsense; it is only just to make a fuss; you ought to be here at seven o'clock in the morning."

---

being accustomed to act in a crowd, was enabled to meet the difficulties to which a crowd generally gives rise, but on the present occasion, a party of rustic constables, unaccustomed to any other mode of assuaging the slightest disturbance than the application of a cudgel, impeded, instead of facilitating, the approach to the Court house The Rev Mr Lloyd and the High Sheriff were particularly obliging in their efforts to obtain admission not only for the reporters, but for all persons who had orders for admission at the private door But even they were unable upon several occasions to make the constables listen to reason Mr. Nicholson, the under sheriff, who was understood to be standing at the inside of the door, was requested again and again to state whether he intended that admission should be given to the orders which he had himself signed The only answer which could be obtained to this question, which in all probability never reached the ear of him for whom it was intended, was a push in the body from a constable's staff, and an order to remove from the steps of the door The Constables, however, were not the only persons who were guilty of much brutality upon this occasion, indeed, their rank in life, and the novelty of their situation, may be some excuse for the savageness of their behaviour But what excuse can be given for similar conduct on the part of those to whom, if they were really the parties they pretended to be, education and good breeding ought to have taught better manners? A fellow who was called by his companions Lord Errol, but whom it would be an insult to the peerage to suppose to have been that respectable nobleman, was particularly remarkable for the outrageous brutality of his behaviour Under the pretence of making way for the High Sheriff, but in reality to make way for himself, he pushed a gentleman who was standing on the steps against the wheel of the high Sheriff's Carriage, and whilst he was thus unable to make any resistance, placed his elbow on his throat and nearly strangled him. On being told of this circumstance, this dandified gentleman, who usurped Lord Errol's title, damned the party, complaining of his violence, for a fool, and swore that he would keep him in that situation as long as he thought proper We really hope that the proper authorities will take care that scenes of such danger and confusion do not occur again during this trial There was no occasion for them, had the police been properly acquainted with their duties, but, unfortunately, they were deficient in two of the main qualifications of peace-officers—urbanity and good temper, and so created difficulties, which, under a better management, would not, and ought not, to have existed.

Mr. Jay respectfully suggested, that himself and Mr. Fenton had occasion to communicate with their client.

Mr. Justice PARK: You ought to be here early in the morning. It is nonsense—only just to make a fuss.

Messrs. Jay and Fenton not being able to find accommodation, and upon the Learned Judge waving his hand, they withdrew to the space between the dock and the seats allotted to Counsel.

The noise, bustle and confusion still prevailing,

Mr. Justice PARK said, If those who have nothing to do with the proceedings, will feel for the responsibility of those who have, they will make way.

Several persons occupying the seats appropriated to Counsel, were ordered to make way, and some Gentlemen at the Bar, who do not usually attend at the Home Circuit, having been attracted by curiosity to hear the trial, were accommodated with seats. Messrs Jay and Fenton still remained standing in the body of the Court. The bustle then in some degree subsided.

A buzz of expectation immediately prevailed, and Mr Wilson announced that the prisoners were ready.

Hunt was then brought to the bar, and then Thurtell.

The appearance of the prisoners was considerably changed from this day month, but Hunt much less so than Thurtell. The latter was considerably paler and thinner, probably from the effect of a long confinement, he betrayed, as before, no trepidation.

The Prisoner PROBERT was then introduced, and he also bowed respectfully. He was not brought close to the Bar, but kept in the centre, about half a yard from each of the other prisoners. Mr. Wilson and an assistant respectfully interposing between him and the others.

APPLICATION FOR THE ADMISSION OF HUNT AS A KING's EVIDENCE.

Immediately after the prisoners had been brought to the bar,

Mr. THESSIGER rose and said—I wish to address to your Lordship an application in behalf of the prisoner, Joseph Hunt, and to show cause why his trial should not be proceeded in.

The JUDGE—Is it founded on any thing that has arisen since the last time I sat here?

Mr. THESSIGER. Not exactly so, my Lord,

The JUDGE. Then I made a rule at the time of the former adjournment, that I would hear nothing respecting further application for putting off the trial, and that the issue should be peremptorily tried this day.

Mr. THESSIGER. My Lord, it is founded on affidavits, which I wish to put in and have sworn.

The JUDGE That might have been done at my lodgings This is all a waste of time

Mr. THESSIGER —Not by the prisoner, my Lord?

Mr Justice PARK—Is it from one of the prisoners? I beg pardon. Oh, let him be sworn.

The affidavit that had been prepared was handed to Hunt, who signed it steadily, and was sworn to the truth of its contents

The usual time was then consumed by the Judge and the Clerk of Arraigns looking over and signing the sheets of the affidavit.

The JUDGE What is the substance of this affidavit?

Mr. THESSIGER The object of it is, to show facts to prove that Joseph Hunt should be admitted as an approver

The JUDGE Can this application be entertained, after the pleadings of the prisoners to their indictment?

Mr THESSIGER On the last day of meeting here, your Lordship ordered that the prisoners should plead before any application was made, and as the application made immediately after on the part of John Thurtell, for a postponement of trial was successful, and the Court was immediately adjourned, there was no opportunity for making this application.

The JUDGE Then I'll hear the facts.

Mr. KNAPP then read the affidavit, but as he turned his face towards the Judge, and read it not in a loud tone, he was not distinctly audible throughout. The substance, however, which we were enabled to collect, was a statement that the deponent (Joseph Hunt) having been apprehended on a suspicion of murder, he was applied to by Mr Noel, who had been employed by the Magistrates of Hertfordshire (Mr. Mason and Mr. Clutterbuck) to discover certain facts connected with the supposed murder That Noel had said to him, " We have clear evidence in every other respect· we only want to know where the body is deposited; and if you will discover that, you shall be admitted as an approver, provided you were not the actual perpetrator of the murder." That Mr. Noel, after some hesitation on the part of deponent, repeated the application to him, and said, " For God' sake, Mr. Hunt, tell us where the body is, and you shall be safe." That after repeated asseverations on the part of Mr. Noel, in the presence of the Magistrates, the deponent consented, and Mr Noel then said to him, " Mr. Hunt, I hope you are now perfectly satisfied Take a seat, and let us know all about it " That deponent then stated various facts in relation to the murder, as far as from the agitation and hurry of his mind he was able to recollect them, and that he (the deponent) did himself particularly shew them where the body was deposited. That subsequently, other facts having occurred to him, which he had omitted in his first statement, he sent for the Magistrates, and communicated the said facts to them and to Mr Noel. That he was subsequently taken before the Coroner's Inquest, and that the Magistrates pressed the Coroner to allow him (Hunt) to be examined upon oath; that the Coroner, however, objected to this, but took from him a statement of facts, and that he answered such questions as were put to him.

Another affidavit was then put in, and sworn to by Mr Noel,

The affidavit stated that the deponent, Thomas Noel, was personally acquainted, and professionally employed by the late Mr. Weare, and that having had reason to suspect that Mr Weare was murdered, he went to Hertfordshire to make investigations respecting his fate; that having applied to Mr. Mason and Mr Clutterbuck, two Magistrates for Hertford, and represented to them the relation in which he had stood to the deceased, they requested him to give his professional assistance in the investigation of the supposed murder ; that in consequence of the information he gave, certain persons were apprehended, but that many facts remaining in doubt, and particularly where the body of Mr. Weare was deposited, it was thought advisable by Mr Clutterbuck and Mr Mason, to make overtures to Hunt, that he might be admitted as an approver, on condition of his making a full and true confession; that the deponent did make the offer to Hunt to become an approver, with the full approbation of the Magistrates, and he, with their knowledge and consent, promised that he (Hunt) should be admitted an approver, if he had no hand in the actual commission of the murder. That Hunt consented, and in pursuance made a confession, and pointed out the place where the body was deposited: that the Magistrates then expressed their opinion that from the nature of the concealment, but for the confession of Hunt, it never could have been discovered where the body was laid; and that this deponent verily believes it could not.

Mr. Justice PARK then called on Mr Thessiger to proceed with his application.

Mr. THESSIGER wished to know whether the Counsel for the prosecution would resist an application founded on such affidavits?

Mr. GURNEY having said a few words in a low tone, we believe asking whether it was necessary to offer counter-affidavits

Mr Justice PARK said, "I can give no direction; if you think fit, after the affidavits that have been made, to proceed, I shall not interfere You must use your own discretion.

Mr. GURNEY. Then I will put in answers to the affidavits.

Mr. Mason and Mr. Clutterbuck then came forward from the Magistrates' box.

[An interruption was then made from the officers bringing in a person making a disturbance in one of the passages, who was ordered to be committed for the present.]

The affidavit of Messrs. Mason and Clutterbuck was then sworn.

The affidavit was read, and stated that it having been represented to them, that a murder had been committed in the county of Herts, they had issued warrants to apprehend J. Thurtell, J. Hunt, and Probert, who were brought before them, and that witnesses were examined as to the fact of a murder having been committed That it was suggested by Mr. Noel, that Hunt would make a confession, but that they gave no authority whatever to offer to Hunt to be admitted as an evidence; that they fully understood that if he made a full and true disclosure, an application would be made to the Court to admit him as an approver, but that no assurance was given him to that effect, and that from circumstances that have come to their knowledge, they believed that the said Joseph Hunt did not make a full and fair disclosure.

An affidavit of the Coroner, Mr. Rooke, was then put in. It stated that he made no promise whatever to Joseph Hunt that he would endeavour to get him admitted as an approver.

Mr. GURNEY said he would bring forward another affidavit to show very material facts not stated in the confession of Hunt.

The JUDGE. I hope you will not state what those facts are in the affidavit. That is the difficulty. On the former occasion an affidavit was read, which at the time of reading had been actually printed and published. Will it not answer your purpose Mr. Gurney, to state merely that important facts were admitted by Hunt, or will it be sufficient if Mr. Thessiger read the affidavit himself?

Mr. GURNEY Our wish is to show that there were facts omitted by Hunt in his pretended confession; and that it is evident, from his conversation in private, that he was aware of the importance of those facts. We wish to show, in short by clear testimony, that Hunt did purposely omit in his confession facts which alone could give it the character of being full and true.

After the affidavit had been sworn, Mr GURNEY, by consent said, he would state the substance of the affidavit. It was, that Hunt did not state in his confession, that he had had previous knowledge that a murder was to be committed, and that he consequently endeavoured to show, that he was not an accessary before the fact; that other testimony showed that he omitted facts which would have given the crime a character very different from that which he actually gave it, and that consequently his confession was not full or true

Mr. THESSIGER then rose in support of the application, and begged to premise, that he had not been empowered on a former occasion to bring forward this application They had been taken by surprise, by being called on by an order of his Lordship to plead before any application could be made. The situation they were now placed in was the result of his Lordship's own act, and he sincerely hoped, therefore, that if the prisoner, Joseph Hunt, was conceived to have had any original claim on the mercy of the Crown, he would not be prejudiced by the delay of the application. In the King *v* Banfield, and the King *v.* ——, it has been laid down, that Magistrates had no direct power to say a prisoner should be pardoned, but on account of the evident advantage to the cause of justice, it had been [the uniform practice of the Courts to pay attention to the recommendation of Magistrates, so that practically, the Magistrates possessed the power of pardon to accomplices. This practice had superseded the old doctrine of approver, and for 170 years there was but a solitary instance in which this recommendation had not been attended to, and that case was so peculiar in its nature and circumstances, that it had no affinity to the present case. The affidavits had informed them, that in the absence of the confession of Hunt there had been, wanting the evidence of the necessary preliminary to the investigation of the crime committed, viz. the body—and that the Magistrates had displayed the utmost earnestness to supply this defect in the proof. He admitted that in ordinary cases it was the practice for Magistrates to make an offer of pardon, on no other condition than that of a full and true confession. But the *power* of the Magistrates was limited by no such condition, and provided some one fact was necessary to be disclosed for the purposes of justice, which could only be disclosed by an accomplice, the Magistrates had right, and might, with the utmost propriety, offer pardon for the disclosure of that one fact. No person would question the importance of the fact disclosed by the prisoner Hunt

Mr. Justice PARK. I question it. I don't know that it bears at all on the case.

Mr. THESSIGER. It has been laid down by the highest authorities, that no man should be convicted of murder or manslaughter, without the absolute certainty that a homicide had been committed, which the finding of the body, in such a case as that which was to be brought before the Court, could alone give. There was a confused idea that a murder had been committed on some one, before the disclosure of that important fact; but he took it on himself to say, that but for that fact, so disclosed by the prisoner Hunt, they would not have been at this time assembled there. The whole foundation of the charge rested on that. And after he had been so important an instrument in the investigation of the truth, was the prisoner Hunt to be thrown away as useless, in defiance of the solemn promises made to him, in consideration of his disclosing that fact,—for to the disclosure of the fact in question, and to that alone, the repeated promises to him could be supposed to apply. The affidavits put in on the other side did not contradict his with regard to that important fact, that it was not known before Hunt made his confession, where the body was to be found. If that fact was discovered by Hunt's voluntary agency, on the faith of a solemn promise made to him, did it not lay the ground of the strongest claim to a merciful consideration of his application? Some thought, probably, that the Magistrates had acted incautiously, because, now that all difficulties had vanished before the confession, persons could not conceive the obstacles which the absence of the confession would have thrown in the way of the proof. But even if the Magistrates had acted incautiously, which he did not admit, it was better, for the purposes of justice, to hold their promises inviolate than to give an example of their violation He was sorry that Probert had been admitted as an approver, that the facts stated in the affidavits had not been laid before his Lordship, who professed himself entirely unacquainted with the proceedings in the case, and who had not read even the statements in the Nawspapers. His Lordship could not have been aware of the promise held out, and that the application in behalf of Probert was founded in a violation of a promise to Hunt. As to the nature of the confession of Hunt, the affidavit on the other side did not contradict that of the prisoner, and Hunt himself stated that he had not at first, from the hurry, confusion, agitation, and exhaustation of his own mind, stated all the facts he knew. He had sent subsequently to the Magistrates additional facts as they occurred to him And was this, and the fact of a conversation of his (Hunt's) over brandy and water (for that was the allegation), in a moment of foolish exultation, to satisfy a wonder-seeking hearer in a moment, perhaps, of intoxication itself? Were expressions under such circumstances to override the merits of his confession, and of the important fact he had communicated? The learned Counsel then alluded to popular feelings.

Mr. Justice PARK said, He felt no impression from public applause or public censure.

The Learned Gentleman proceeded.—It was important for public example, and for strengthening the hands of Magistrates in discovering crimes, that the promises of Magistrates should be held valid to the utmost extent.

Mr. Justice PARK was decidedly of opinion that none of the arguments applied to him, whatever weight they might afterwards have with his Majesty's Government. There was no reason for delay. The Magistrates had no authority, and did not consider that they had authority to admit a man a witness for the Crown. No objection had been made to the admission of Probert; and if there had, there could be no reason for refusing the proposition of the Counsel, who thought his evidence necessary. He dared not put off the trial, or to listen to the arguments used for not trying Hunt. The Magistrates had not done wrong in receiving the disclosures which Mr. Noel thought proper to make, through Hunt.

Mr. Thurtell requested to be permitted to be near his Counsel.

His LORDSHIP said most certainly, but he might stand as he was till the challenges should be over.

The following Jury were then called into the box, those challenged were not desired to go into the box, though their names were called.

THOMAS BROWN
THOMAS BRIGS, Hertford
REGINALD JENNETT
RICHARD PRIOR, Bishop Stortford
GEORGE STARBRIE, ditto
CHARLES FOX, Hitchen
JOHN RUSSELL, ditto
THO^s. CHALKELEY, Stevenage
WM. FONLDING, ditto
JOHN HOPEWELL
SAMUEL PRITCHARD
WM. KIMPTON.

The Jury having been sworn, Mr. KNAPP, the Clerk of Arraigns, stated the indictment against Thurtell and Hunt, and the Coroner's inquest against Probert.

Mr. GURNEY rose and said, That he had no evidence to offer against William Probert, and the Jury would therefore give him their verdict before he should state the evidence which he was prepared to give, against the other two prisoners.

Mr. Justice PARK said, That as the Counsel for the prosecution gave no evidence against William Probert, he was entitled to their verdict.

The Jury accordingly found him *Not Guilty.*

Mr. Justice PARK. Let him be removed.

All the witnesses were then ordered out of Court, excepting such medical gentlemen as might be called.

Mr. BRODERICK then stated the counts of the indictment.

Mr. GURNEY opened the case. They were now, he said, assembled for the trial of the two prisoners at the bar, after a month's delay, which the Court had ordered. It had been obtained on the ground of the great excitement of the public which had shortly before taken place, and had not then subsided. It was on the former occasion thought by his Lordship that it would conduce to the more satisfactory dispensation of justice, to allow the operation of a short delay to suffer passing events to subside, some of which were of a melancholy character, and capable of producing a prejudicial effect. The jury had now assembled after the delay which had taken place, and prepared to proceed to this trial in that calm and temperate state of mind to enable them to administer justice with perfect satisfaction to their own minds, as well as to their country. It was of great importance to society that a criminal should be punished, in order that crime should be repressed; but there was one thing of more importance, and that was, the protection of innocence. That was the great salutary principle consecrated by the laws of England, which was its distinguishing feature above the code of other nations; for of little interest would it be to any man to say he belonged to a country invested with every charm which could make life and property agreeable, if his safety and his property were not shielded by the powerful barriers of the law. In England they had happily those great securities. They had in the first instance the preliminary inquiry before a magistracy (such a magistracy as no other country enjoyed.) They had next the inquiry before a grand jury; and lastly, the assistance, in a court like the present, of the highest legal authorities, to hear the evidence on the one part and the other, and, with the assistance of a jury composed as they were, to pronounce finally upon the guilt or innocence of the accused. It was the peculiar province of the jury to decide upon the question of guilt or innocence; and they were bound to forget, if ever they had heard, statements probably erroneous, certainly unauthentic. Above all, they were bound to come to the question with the most dispassionate feeling. The crime with which the prisoners stood charged, was, undoubtedly, one of the most enormous magnitude; its perpetration had been attended with no common ferocity. It was imputed to one of the parties, that he had actually committed the murder; and to the other, that he had assisted with his previous counsel and concert, and co-operated in the promotion of the premeditated act. But in proportion to the great enormity of the crime ought to be the strength of the proof; and he did not mean to ask of them to pronounce a verdict of guilty, unless on such evidence as left no rational doubt on their minds of the fact. He repeated, that when they considered the nature of the case, and the violent aggravation with which it was attended, they were bound to call for very strong proof to convince them that any man was capable of so dreadful an atrocity; for if the evidence he had to adduce were substantiated and believed, one of the prisoners at the bar had been guilty, not only of the crime of murder in all its naked atrocity, but of the murder of a man with whom he had been living in habits of acquaintance, if not of intimacy. It was said, (whether true or not, he knew not), that the deceased had provoked one of the prisoners, by doing him some wrong at play, and that the other had never been injured by the man whose death he had concerted to aid in inflicting. These persons, under the specious pretences of friendship, had invited the deceased to accompany them upon a short country excursion; but they had invited him into their company to deprive him on the same night of his life. It was emphatically said, that murder was a crime to be perpetrated in darkness. The hour of night was mostly chosen as the opportune time for its infliction; because it was in that moment of solitude thought that no human eye could see, no ear hear the struggles of the dying: darkness rendered detection more difficult. It was therefore the peculiar feature of crimes of this kind, that their proof often depended upon circumstantial evidence, which, however, was frequently found to convey by its character and combination, a demonstration as conclusive as any which could arise from the operation of positive testimony. There was another species of evidence, which was sometimes of necessity resorted to in cases of this nature—he meant the evidence of accomplices in the crime. It was not always within the power of a prosecutor to forego the evidence of an accomplice, nor even to get that species of testimony, without compounding in some measure with acknowledged guilt. Upon a very full and anxious consideration of the whole case, those who conducted the prosecution had maturely decided upon the admission of an accomplice into their evidence. The deceased, whose murder was the subject of the present inquiry, was the late Mr. Wm. Weare—a man, it was said, addicted to play, and, as had been suggested, connected with gaming-houses. Whether he was the best, or the least estimable individual in society, was no part of their present consideration. The prisoner at the bar, John Thurtell, had been his acquaintance, and in some practices of play, had, it was said, been wronged by him, and deprived of a large sum of money. The other prisoner, Hunt, was described as being a public singer, and also known to Mr. Weare, but not, as he believed, in habits of friendship. Probert, who was admitted as an accomplice, had been in trade as a spirit-dealer, and rented a cottage in Gill's-hill-lane, near Elstree. It was situate in a bye-lane, going out of the London-road to St. Albans, and two or three miles beyond Elstree. This cottage of Probert's was, it would appear, selected, from its seclusion, as the fit spot for the perpetration of the murder. Probert was himself much engaged in London, and his wife generally resided at the cottage, which was a small one, and pretty fully occupied in the accommodation of Mrs. Probert, her sister, (Miss Noyes), some children of Thomas Thurtell's, (the prisoner's brother) and a maid and boy servant. It should seem, from what had taken place, that the deceased had been invited by John Thurtell, to this place, to enjoy a day or two's shooting. It would be proved that the prisoner Thurtell met the deceased at a billiard room, kept by one Rexworthy, on the Thursday night (that previous to the murder). They were joined there by Hunt. On the forenoon of the Friday, he (deceased) was with Rexworthy at the the same place, and said he was going for a day's shooting into the country. Weare went from the billiard rooms between 3 and 4 o'clock to his chambers in Lyon's-inn, where he partook of a chop dinner, and afterwards packed up, in a green carpet-bag, some clothes, and a mere change of linen, such as a journey for the time he had specified might require. He also took with him when he left his chambers in a hackney coach, which the laundress had called, a double-barrelled gun, and a backgammon-box, dice, &c. He left his chambers in this manner before four o'clock, and drove first to Charing-cross, and afterwards to Maddox-street, Hanover-square; from thence he proceeded to the New Road, where he went out of the coach, and returned, after some time, accompanied by another person, and took his things away. Undoubtedly the deceased left town on that evening, with the expectation of reaching Gill's-hill cottage; but it had been previously determined by his companions, that he should never reach that spot alive. He would here beg to state a few of the circumstances which had occurred antecedent to the commission of the crime. Thomas and John Thurtell were desirous of some temporary concealment, owing to their inability to provide the bail requisite to meet some charge of a misdemeanour, and Probert had procured for them a retreat at Tetsall's, at the sign of the Coach and Horses, in Conduit-street, where they remained for two or three weeks previous to the murder. On the morning of Friday, October 24, two men, answering in every respect to the description of John Thurtell and Hunt, went to a pawnbroker's in Marylebone, and purchased a pair of pocket-pistols. In the middle of the same day, Hunt hired a gig, and afterwards a horse, under the pretence of going to Dartford in Kent; he also inquired where he could purchase a sack and a rope, and was directed to a place over Westminster-bridge, which he was told was on his road into Kent. Somewhere, however, it would be found that he did procure a sack and cord, and he met the same afternoon, at Tetsall's, Thomas Thurtell and Noyes. They were all assembled together at the Coach and Horses in Conduit Street. When he made use of the names of the two last individuals, he begged distinctly to be understood as saying, that he had no reason to believe that either Thomas Thurtell or Noyes were privy to the guilty purpose of the prisoners. Some conversation took place at the time between the parties, and Hunt was heard to ask Probert if he would be in what they (Hunt and John Thurtell) were about. Thurtell drove off from Tetsall's between four and five o'clock to take up a friend, as he said to Probert, "to be killed as he travelled with him," an expression which Probert said at the time, he believed to have been a piece of idle bravado. He requested Probert to bring down Hunt in his own gig. In the course of that evening, the prisoner Thurtell is seen in that gig, with a horse of a very remarkable colour. He was a sort of iron gray, with a white face and white legs—very particular marks for identity. He was first seen by a patrol near Edgeware; beyond that part of the road he was seen by the landlord; but from that time of the evening, until his arrival at Probert's cottage on the same night, they had no direct evidence to trace him. Probert, according to Thurtell's request, drove Hunt down in his gig, and having a better horse, on the road they overtook Thurtell and Weare in the gig, and passed them without notice. They stopped afterwards at some public-house on the road to drink grog, where they believe Thurtell must have passed them unperceived. Probert drove Hunt until they reached Phillimore-lodge, where he (Hunt) got out, as he said by Thurtell's desire, to wait for him. Probert from thence drove alone to Gill's-hill cottage, in the lane near which he met Thurtell, on foot, alone. Thurtell inquired where was Hunt, had he been left behind? he then added, that he had done the business without his assistance, and had killed his man. At his desire, Probert returned to bring Hunt to the spot, when he (Probert) went to Hunt for that purpose. When they met, he told Hunt what had happened. "Why it was to be done here," said Hunt (pointing to nearer Phillimore-lodge), admitting his privity, and that he had got out to assist in the commission of the deed. When Thurtell rebuked Hunt for his absence, "Why, (said the latter) you had the tools'" They were no good, replied Thurtell, the pistols were no better than pop-guns. I fired at his cheek, and it glanced off—that Weare ran out of the gig, cried for mercy, and offered to return the money he had robbed him of—that he (Thurtell) pursued him up the lane, when he jumped out of the gig. Finding the pistol unavailing, he attempted to reach him by cutting the penknife across his throat, and ultimately finished him by driving the barrel of the pistol into his head, and turning it in his brains, after he had penetrated the forehead. Such was the manner in which Thurtell described he had disposed of the deceased, and they would hear from Probert what he said on the occasion. A gig was, about that time, heard to drive very quickly past Probert's cottage. The servants expected their master, and thought he had arrived, but he did not make his appearance. Five minutes after that period, certain persons, who would be called in evidence, and who happened to be in the road, distinctly heard the report of a gun or pistol, which was followed by voices, as if in contention. Violent groans were next heard, which, however, became fainter and fainter, and then died away altogether. The spot where the report of the pistol and the sound of groans were heard, was Gill's-hill-lane, and near it was situated the cottage of Probert. They had now, therefore, to keep in mind, that Thurtell arrived at about nine o'clock in the evening at Probert's cottage, having set off from Conduit-street at five o'clock; and though he had been seen on the road in company with another person in the gig, yet it appeared that he arrived at the cottage alone, having in his possession the double-barrelled gun, the green carpet-bag, and the back-gammon-board, which Mr. Weare took away with him. He gave his horse to the boy, and the horse appeared in a cool state, which corroborated the fact that he had stopped a good while on his way. He left Conduit-street, it should be observed, at five, and arrived at the cottage at nine—a distance which, under ordinary circumstances, would not have occupied much more than an hour. The boy inquired after Probert and Hunt, and was told that they would soon be at the cottage. At length a second gig arrived, and those two persons were in it. They rode, while Thurtell went to meet them, walked with them. The boy having cleaned his master's horse, then performed the same office for the horse of Thurtell, which occupied a good deal of time. Probert went into the house. Neither Thurtell nor Hunt were expected by Mrs. Probert. With Thurtell she was acquainted, but Hunt was a stranger, and was formally introduced to her. They then supped on some pork-chops, which Hunt had brought down with him from London They then went out, as Probert said, to visit Mr Nicholls, a neighbour of his, but their real object was to go down to the place where the body of Weare was deposited. Thurtell took them to the spot down the lane, and the body was dragged through the hedge into the adjoining field. The body was, as he has previously described it to be, enclosed in a sack. They then effectually rifled the deceased man, Thurtell having informed his companions that he had, in the first instance, taken the fourth part of his property. They then went back to the cottage. It ought to be stated, that Thurtell, before he went out, placed a large sponge in the gig; and when he returned from this expedition, he went to the stable and sponged himself with great care. He endeavoured to remove the spots of blood, many of which was distinctly seen by Probert's boy; and certainly such marks would be observable on the person of any one who had been engaged in such a transaction. In the course of the evening Thurtell produced a gold watch, without a chain, which occasioned several remarks. He also displayed a gold curb chain, which might be used for a watch, when doubled; or, when singled, might be worn round a lady's neck On producing the chain, it was remarked that it was more fit for a lady than a gentleman; on which Thurtell pressed it on Mrs. Probert, and made her accept of it. An offer was afterwards made that a bed should be given to Thurtell and Hunt, which was to be accomplished by Miss Noyes giving up her bed, and sleeping with the children. This was refused, Thurtell and Hunt observing that they would rather sit up. Miss Noyes therefore retired to her own bed. Something, however, occurred, which raised suspicion in the mind of Mrs. Probert; and, indeed, it was scarcely possible, if it were at all possible, for persons who had been engaged in a transaction of this kind, to avoid some disorder of mind—some absence of thought that was calculated to excite suspicion. In consequence of observing those feelings, Mrs. Probert did not go to bed, or undress herself. She went to the window and looked out, and saw that Probert, Hunt, and Thurtell were in the garden. It would be proved that they went down to the body, and finding it too heavy to be removed, one of the horses was taken from the stable. The body was then thrown across the horse; and stones having been put into the sack, the body, with the sack thus rendered weighty by the stones, was thrown into the pond. Mrs. Probert distinctly saw something heavy drawn across the garden where Thurtell was. The parties then returned to the house; and Mrs. Probert, whose fears and suspicions were now most powerfully excited, went down stairs and listened behind the parlour-door. The parties now proceeded to share the booty, and Thurtell divided with them to the amount of 6l each. The purse, the pocket-book, and certain papers which might lead to detection, were carefully burned. They remained up late, and Probert, when he went to bed, was surprised to find that his wife was not asleep. Hunt and Thurtell still continued to sit up in the parlour. The next morning, as early as six o'clock, Hunt and Thurtell were both seen out, and in the lane together. Some men who were at work there, observed them, as they called it, "grabbing" for something in the hedge. They were spoken to by these men, and as persons thus accosted must say something, Thurtell observed, " that it was a very bad road, and that he had nearly been capsized there last night." The men said, " I hope you were not hurt." Thurtell answered, " Oh no, the gig was not upset," and then they went away. These men thinking something might have been lost on the spot, searched, after Hunt and Thurtell were gone. In one place they found a quantity of blood, farther on they discovered a bloody knife, and next they found a bloody pistol—one of the identical pair which he would show were purchased by Hunt. That pistol bore upon it the marks of blood and of human brains. The spot was afterwards still farther examined, and more blood was discovered, which had been concealed by branches and leaves, so that no doubt could be entertained that the murder had been committed in this particular place. On the following morning, Saturday, the 25th of October, Thurtell and Hunt left Probert's cottage in the gig which Hunt had come down in, carrying away with them the gun, the carpet bag, and the backgammon board, belonging to Mr. Weare. These articles were taken to Hunt's lodgings, where they were afterwards found. When Hunt arrived in town on Saturday, he appeared to be unusually gay. He said, " We Turpin lads, can do the trick. I am able to drink wine now, and I will drink nothing but wine." He seemed to be very much elevated at the recollection of some successful exploit. It was observed, that Thurtell's hands were very much scratched, and some remark having been made on the subject, he stated, " that they had been out netting partridges, and that his hands got scratched in that occupation." On some other points, he gave similarly evasive answers. On Sunday, John Thurtell, Thomas Thurtell, Noyes and Hunt, spent the day at Probert's cottage. Hunt went down dressed in a manner so very shabby, as to excite observation. But in the course of the day he went up stairs, and attired himself in very handsome clothes. There was very little doubt that those were the clothes of the deceased Mr. Weare. He had now to call the attention of the jury to a very remarkable circumstance. On the Saturday Hunt had a new spade sent to his lodgings, which he took down to the cottage on Sunday. When he got near Probert's garden, he told that individual, "that he had brought it down to dig a hole to bury the body in." On that evening, Probert did really visit Mr. Nicholls; and the latter said to him, "that some persons had heard the report of a gun or pistol in the lane on Friday evening; but he supposed it was some foolish joke." Probert on his return, stated this to Thurtell and Hunt, and the information appeared to alarm the former, who said "he feared he should be hanged." The intelligence, however, inspired them all with a strong desire to conceal the body more effectually. Probert wished it to be removed from his pond; for had it been found there, he knew it would be important evidence against himself. He declared that he would not suffer it to remain there; and Thurtell and Hunt promised to come down on the Monday and remove it. On Monday Thurtell and Hunt went out in the gig, and in furtherance of that scene of villainy which they meditated, they took with them Probert's boy. They carried him to various places, and finally lodged the boy at Mr. Tetsall's in Conduit street. On the evening of that same Monday, Hunt and Thurtell came down to the cottage. Hunt engaged Mrs. Probert in conversation, while Thurtell and Probert took the body out of the pond, put it into Thurtell's gig, and then gave notice to Hunt that the gig was ready. In this manner they carried away the body that night; but where they took it to Probert did not know. It appeared, however, that the body was carried to a pond near Elstree, at a considerable distance from Probert's cottage, and there sunk, as it had before been in Probert's pond, in a sack containing a considerable quantity of stones. Hunt and Thurtell then went to London; and the appearance of the gig next morning clearly told the way in which it had been used over night, a quantity of blood and mud being quite perceptible at the bottom. The parties heard that the report of the pistol in the lane on the Friday evening, and the discovery of the blood in the field, had led to great alarm among the Magistracy. Inquiry was set on foot, and Thurtell, Hunt, and Probert were at length apprehended. It was found that Hunt had adopted a peculiar mode for the purpose of concealing his identity; for when he was hiring the gig, and doing various other acts connected with this atrocious proceeding, he wore very long whiskers; but on the Monday after the murder, he had them taken off; and they all knew that nothing could possibly alter the appearance of a man more than the taking away of large bushy whiskers. Strict inquiries were made by the Magistrates, but nothing was ascertained to prove to a certainty who was murdered. The body was, however, found on the Thursday, Hunt having given evidence as to the place where the body was deposited. The evidence which Hunt gave, and which led to the finding of the body, he would use: but no other fact coming out of his mouth, save that, would he advert to. He was entitled, in point of law, to make use of that. "If a person tells me, under any promise of mercy, where stolen goods are to be found, and on searching I find them, I am entitled to adduce the fact of finding against the criminal party: and for this reason—because persons may from hope or fear, be induced to state what is not true. But the finding proves the truth, and on that point I have a right to proceed." The fact only of the disclosure by Hunt, in consequence of which the body was discovered, was he permitted to make use of; and to that alone, so far as Hunt's confession went, he would confine himself. But by reference to his conversations with others, and to various circumstances not adverted to by him, he was convinced that he should be enabled to establish a perfect and complete chain of evidence. He had now stated the principal part of the facts which it would be his duty to lay before the jury. Some of them, they must observe, would depend on the evidence of an accomplice; for Probert, though not an accomplice *before* the murder, was confessedly privy to a certain part of the transaction—to the concealment of the body—to the concealment consequently, of the murder.

He must be looked upon as a bad, a very bad man. He was presented to the jury in that character. What good man could ever lend himself, in the remotest degree, to so revolting a transaction? An accomplice must always be, in a greater or less extent, a base man. The Jury would therefore receive the evidence of Probert with extreme caution; and they would mark, with peculiar attention, how far his evidence was confirmed by testimony that could not be impeached. But he would adduce such witnesses in confirmation of Probert's statement—he would so confirm him in every point, as to build up his testimony with a degree of strength and consistency which could not be shaken, much less overturned. He would prove by other witnesses besides Probert, that Thurtell set out with a companion from London who did not arrive at the ostensible end of his journey; he would prove that he had brought the property of that companion to Probert's house, the double-barrelled gun, backgammon board, and the green carpet-bag, he would prove, that some time before he arrived at the cottage, the report of a gun or pistol was heard in Gill's-hill-lane, not far from the cottage, he would prove that his clothes were in a bloody state; and that, when he was apprehended, even on the Wednesday after the murder, he had not been able to efface all the marks from his apparel. Besides all this, they would find, that in his pocket, when apprehended, there was a penknife which was positively sworn to as having belonged to Mr. Weare, and also the fellow-pistol of that which was found adjoining the place where the murder was committed,—the pair having been purchased in Marylebone-street by Hunt. These circumstances brought the case clearly home to Thurtell. Next as to Hunt. He was charged as an accomplice before the fact. It was evident that he advised this proceeding. For what purpose, but to advise, did he proceed to the cottage? He was a stranger to Mrs. Probert and her family; he was not expected at the cottage. There was not for him, as there was for Thurtell, an apology for his visit. He hired a gig, and he procured a sack—the jury knew to what end and purpose. They would also bear in mind, that the gun, travelling-bag, and backgammon-board, were found in his lodging. These constituted a part of the plunder of Mr. Weare, and could only be possessed by a person participating in this crime. Besides, there was placed about the neck of Probert's wife, a chain, which had belonged to Mr. Weare, and round the neck of the murdered man there was found a shawl which belonged to Thurtell, but which had been seen in the hands of Hunt. In giving this summary of the case, he had not stated every circumstance connected with it. His great anxiety was, not to state that which he did not firmly believe would be borne out by evidence. One circumstance he had omitted, which he felt it necessary to lay before the jury. It was, that a watch was seen in the possession of Thurtell, which he would show belonged to Mr. Weare. After Thurtell was apprehended, and Hunt had said something on the subject of this transaction, an officer asked Thurtell what he had done with the watch? He answered, that, "when he was taken into custody, he put his hand behind him, and chucked it away." Thurtell also made another disclosure. He said, when questioned, "that other persons, near the spot, were concerned in it, whom he forbore to mention. As to Thurtell, the evidence would, he believed, clearly prove him to have been the perpetrator of the murder; and with respect to Hunt, it was equally clear that he was an accessary before the fact. If, however, the jury felt any conscientious doubt, the prisoner ought certainly to receive the benefit of it, but where a case was clearly and satisfactorily made out, they would perform fearlessly that duty which they owed to heaven, and to the due administration of justice.

EVIDENCE FOR THE PROSECUTION.

JOHN BEESON examined by Mr. Holland: I live in the parish of Aldenham; I went in search of a body with Ruthven and Upson, two Bow street officers; the prisoner Hunt was with us, we went to Aldenham and found the body in a brook, called Hill Slough, near Elstree; Hunt pointed it out; the body was concealed in a sack; the head was downwards in the sack; there was a rope fastened round the sack; the length of the rope was two or three yards; there was a stone tied to the end; I was not present when the sack was opened, it was carried to the Artichoke public-house, at Elstree, the pond was a quarter of a mile from Elstree; it was to the right hand side of the road coming from Elstree towards Radlett. I am acquainted with the roads about Gill's Hill. There is a road branching off towards Watford, with a finger-post direction pointing that way. Pursuing that road, you pass a cottage, where a person of the name of Hunt lives; the road divides, one leading to Radlett and the other to Mr. Probert's cottage, at Gill's Hill. A man ignorant of the road might mistake his way. He might, however, return again on the road to Probert's cottage, though he went by mistake to High Cross. It would be a circuitous passage. Even if a person went to Radlett, he might turn to the right and get to Probert's cottage. The roads are very bad and very narrow. If a person met any thing in his way, while driving, he must back out. Travelling on from Radlett, he might get by Menbourne to Gill' Hill. A man, not knowing the road, might mistake. These roads are hilly, and a person, ordinarily speaking, must drive slow.

Cross-examined by Mr. Thessiger for Hunt It was on Thursday, the 30th of October, four persons with the coachman, went to find the body. the place where it was found, was two miles from Gill's Hill. They searched in a body, he meant all together. They searched nearly for five minutes. It was about two minutes after the place had been pointed out. The body was nearly in the centre of the pond It was possible for any person to place the body in the pond without walking in Two men might have swung the body in. One man could not have done it. The weather was wet, and the pond was consequently full. None of those who found the body went into the water, because they had a ladder. I saw Mr. Hunt point out that pond as the place where the body was. The pond altogether was as large as the table of the Court There was a short piece of the rope round the sack, loose. The rope was twisted round the sack in a careless manner. The handkerchief was outside of the sack, and the stones were concealed in it.

ROBERT FIELD sworn and examined by Mr. Broderick: I keep the Artichoke public house at Elstree; I remember a dead body being brought to my house on a Thursday. I saw the body drawn out of the pond; it was covered with a sack, and that was fastened by cords. The rope was bound round the neck, the middle and the feet, with a handkerchief tied to the end full of stones, there were two or three yards of the rope superabundant, that body was afterwards shewn to Mr. Rexworthy, and he said it was the body of William Weare.

JOHN UPSON, examined by Mr. Gurney—I am an officer of Bow-street; I was present at the examination of the prisoners at Watford, it was on a Wednesday or Thursday, I had a conversation with Thurtell after the body was found, I went in search of the body. I went to the place where it was found by the direction of Hunt. We went first to one spot, and Hunt said, "that is not the place." We went to another. We had a pole, and tried without success. A man passed with a ladder, and Beeson went on the ladder to drag, Hunt pointed with his finger, and said the body was further out. The body was found, and taken on the ladder to the Artichoke. I was not present when the body was examined.

WILLIAM REXWORTHY, examined by Mr. Bolland.—I keep a billiard room, at Spring-gardens, and knew the deceased (Mr. Weare) very well.

I saw the body at the Artichoke, at Elstree, it was the body of Mr. Weare. There was a mark of the muzzle of a pistol on the left side of the head, as if it had been driven several times against it.

Cross examined by Mr. Andrews: Mr Rexworthy, could you, in the state in which the body was, say positively that it was the body of Mr Weare?—I knew him as perfectly as if he were living, and I had known him for fourteen years.

Did you see any blood on the body?—I did not.

Now was it in a state to enable you to speak with certainty? I could speak with certainty that it was the body of Mr. Weare.

Did you ever express yourself with any doubt as to its being the body of Mr. Weare?—I have no doubt at all; I have not the least doubt about it.

I do not say what your present opinion is; but did you never express yourself with doubt?—I did not.

You were always as confident as you are now?—I was.

Mr. RICHARD WEARE was then called and sworn —[The witness was a thin, short, pale-looking man, having the appearance of a mechanic.]—Examined by Mr. Bolland: I had a brother, named William, he had no other christian name. I saw a corpse at the Artichoke, at Elstree, before the Coroner; it was on the day Mr. Rexworthy saw it; it was the body of my brother William.—This witness was not cross-examined.

THOMAS ABEL WARD called and sworn—Examined by Mr Brodrick: I am a surgeon at Watford; I examined a dead body lying at the Artichoke, at Elstree. On the day of the inquest I examined the head of the body; there were many marks of violence about the left temple, which had been occasioned by some round blunt instrument; they might have been occasioned by the muzzle of a pistol driven with force against it. A pistol was produced before the Coroner, and the marks in the scalp corresponded with the muzzle; the wounds had penetrated the scalp of the skull. Near these wounds was a fracture of the skull, with several portions of the bone broken off and driven into the substance of the brain, the pistol produced would have caused such injury, if not fired; but driven into the scull by force. It did appear to me that the injury had been caused by the pistol then produced; the injury to the brain would have produced death; the substance of the brain was penetrated by the bone, there was a mark on the right cheek, which appeared to be a gun-shot wound By a gun-shot wound is meant any wound produced by a shot fired, whether from gun or pistol, &c. I could not trace this wound deep. It only penetrated through the integuments to the bone of the cheek, it could not have occasioned instant death, nor indeed death at all. There was an incised wound on each side of the neck. There were two on the left side, and one on the right side. Of those on the left side, one was immediately under the ear; the other further back. The incised wound had been made by some sharp instrument. A knife would have produced them, certainly. On the left side, the jugular vein was divided by one of the incised wounds.

Cross-examined by Mr. PLATT. On the left side of the head, you saw a wound and fracture, which must have been effected by a blunt instrument? Yes.

If the instrument had not been driven by force into the skull, the mark of the instrument must have been more apparent on the surface? Yes.

What was the position of the wound? The fracture was above the temple, just above the anterior angle of the bone of the skull. The marks where there were not fractures were above that. There were several of them.

Now is it possible that an instrument with a larger end than that pistol that was produced, could have been introduced into the fracture? Yes

And produced the same result?—The same result, as far as the fracture goes, could have been produced by a larger instrument; the marks which I have said were above the fracture could not have been produced, except by such an instrument as the pistol; they corresponded to the end of the muzzle.

Was the skin forced into the wound?—The skin was not forced into the wound, though it was depressed by the blow that occasioned the fracture; that is to say, it was wounded, but not detached.

What was the size of the wound?—The orifice of the

fracture was an inch and an eighth or a quarter in length, and 7-8ths of an inch in width. I can show how it was by drawing it.

Mr. Justice PARK: Then do, Sir.

Mr. WARD then drew on a sheet of paper a representation of the wound, and produced from a small box the pieces of the skull which had been forced into the wound, and which he had extracted and preserved. The drawing and the pieces of bone were handed to the bench, and then to the jury. The bones were returned to Mr. Ward, but he left the drawing.

Does this (the drawing) describe the external appearance of the wound?

Mr. Justice PARK: Mr. Ward has made it plain; this is the fracture of the skull. You mean the fracture Mr. Ward, and not the wound, do you not?—Yes, my Lord.

Mr. PLATT continued his cross-examination.

Then the fleshy orifice was not cut out?—The external skin was broken, but not detached; it was a contused wound.

What was the size of the orifice of this contused wound?—I really do not understand you. There was no interval; I could have brought up the integuments, and closed them entirely, for no part had been detached.

But before it was so stretched?—There was no stretching; the integuments which covered the skull, a solid substance, had been bruised, when forced upon that solid substance which had been broken beneath it by the violence of the blow. The integuments of the skull were not torn away, but were rent in halves, as it were.

Would that drawing you have made denote the size of the aperture if it had been drawn out?—It would have been of considerable size. I could have put my finger into it.

Mr. Justice PARK. Mr. Platt, I think the case is very clear. The skull was fractured; the bone produced to us was driven into the brain, and the skin or scalp was rent; I think, Mr. Ward, you have given your evidence very clearly.

Mr. Platt; Was the rent of the integuments made in that kind of way, that a larger instrument could have been forced through? Certainly.

The jugular vein was divided, which, if not stopped, would produce death, was it not.?—Yes.

Was any artery divided?—No.

You could have judged that great hemorrhage had taken place?—No.

Was there an appearance as if the wound that divided the jugular vein had been inflicted on the living person?—There was every appearance as if it had, and nothing to shew that it had not been inflicted on the living person.

Could you say on your oath, that that wound could have been inflicted after death?—I think it possible.

Have you not the means of judging whether a wound that appears on a dead body has been inflicted during life or after death?—Not after a body has been soaked in water three or four days; the indicia are not such that I would trust them in such a case.

Then the body must have been altered by lying in the water?—Yes.

Are not the features more altered in persons dying of hemorrhage, so as to make it more difficult to recognize them?—Yes, when the hemorrhage is protracted.

Is the hemorrhage from the jugular vein protracted?—The bleeding, in the case of a wound of the jugular vein, is uncertain; sometimes it is protracted, sometimes not.

In this case the jugular vein was divided?—Not entirely divided; but the wound was very considerable.

Suppose an individual had been bled to death, and laid for a week in a pond, would it not in such a case have been more difficult for persons to ascertain who that individual was?—It would; but I conceive, from the appearance of the body I saw at Elstree, that if I had known the person in his lifetime, I should have recognized him then.

Re-examined by Mr. Broderick: What, in your opinion, was the cause of death?—The injury to the brain by the pistol.

Mr. RUTHVEN, the officer, called. He brought into the Court with him a large bag of carpeting full of various articles, a hat in a handkerchief, and a dressing-case. Sworn and examined by Mr. Bolland. I am an officer of Bow-street; I apprehended the prisoner, John Thurtell, the Wednesday after the Friday of the supposed murder (the 29th Oct.), at Tetsall's, the sign of the Coach and Horses, in Conduit-street, Bond-street, London. I found in his coat pocket a pistol not loaded. I found a pistol, key and a knife in his waistcoat pocket, and a key which belonged to an air gun. I found a muslin-handkerchief in a drawer, close to the bed side; it appeared to be marked with blood; the marks were just the same then as they are now. In a drawer I found a shirt, stained with blood in each corner of the collar, where they project above the neckcloth. I found a black kerseymere waistcoat, with marks of blood on each pocket. I found this on his bed. I found also a black coat, with marks of blood on both cuffs, and a mark on the left shoulder, I found this coat on his bed, I found a hat [produced]; there is a mark of blood now, there was one small mark on another part I arrested Hunt at his lodgings, 19, King-street, Golden Square, the same day (Oct 29). I took no articles out of his lodgings on the Wednesday,. On the Thursday night I went again to his lodgings, and found a dressing box and a double-barrelled gun, with the name of the maker, Manton [the gun was produced]. Under the bed I found this sponge [a large sponge was produced] I found a carpet bag [produced]; it was empty I found a shooting jacket, a pair of drab breeches, a pair of gaiters or leggings; one pair of half and one pair of Hessian boots, a cord, two waistcoats, two coloured handkerchiefs, three shirts, (two of the shirts were marked, one of them W. W., No 1, the other W.), one neckcloth, one collar, nightcap, clothes bag, powder flask, clothes brush, turnscrew, bullet mould, and a comb. I have had all these things in my possession ever since.

Cross-examined by Mr. Chitty. The door of Thurtell's room was open; at least it was not fastened.

Q. Any persons could have come into the room? A. Yes.

Q. The drawers in which you found the things were not locked? A. No.

Q. So that any maid-servant or person about the house might have seen them? A. The things were tied up

Q There were many people in the house were there not? A. I do not know; it was a public house. There was another person in the same room when I apprehended Thurtell, Thurtell was in bed; the person was sleeping in another bed; Thurtell made no resistance.

In answer to Mr Thessiger: I did not search Hunt's room on the Wednesday, when I apprehended him; I did not obtain these things by getting a letter to his wife; his wife was not at home; I broke the door open.

HENRY SIMMONS, sworn.—I am the constable of Watford. [He produced a pocket-pistol] It was given me by Mr. Nicholls of Battler's Green. It was stained as it is now, with the pan down. Besides the blood, there was hair upon it. there is now. There was a piece of tow in the muzzle, as there is now. I have a small knife. [He produced it.] He had it from Mr. Nicholls. I have a red shawl handkerchief. [He produced it] I received it from Dr. Pidcock, the younger, on the 31st of October I have a gold curb watch chain. [He produced it in a box.] I received it from Mrs. Probert, on the 15th Nov in the evening. I received a sack from Robert Field, landlord of the Artichoke. [Produces it.] On the 24th November, I received another from William Bulmer; a piece of a shirt I have, I received from Mr. Thos Bates, I received these various articles in the presence of the Magistrates, and have kept them ever since.

The various articles mentioned by this witness, were handed by him to the officer The greatest anxiety was shewn by the Learned Judge, that the hair and blood on the fatal pistol should not be disturbed, before they were shown to the Jury. I received also, on the 30th of Nov., a part of a coat and handkerchief from George Jones.

WILLIAM PROBERT was now called, and came from the Dock into the box and was sworn. He deposed as follows: I occupied a cottage in Gill's-hill-lane six months before October last; my family consisted of Mrs. Probert, her two sisters (Misses Noyes), part of the summer a servant maid, and a boy: in the month of October only one Miss Noyes lived with us. In October also I had some children of Thomas Thurtell's, two—none of my own. T. Thurtell is a brother of the prisoner's. I have been for some time past acquainted with the prisoner John Thurtell, he had been down to my cottage often, sporting with me; he knew the road to my cottage, and all the roads thereabouts well. Gill's-hill-lane, in which my cottage was, was out of the high road to St. Albans, at Radlett; my cottage was about a quarter of a mile from the high road. My regular way to my cottage would be to go along the high road through Radlett; there was a nearer way, but that was my usual way. My cottage was fourteen miles and a quarter from Tyburn turnpike. In the latter end of October, the week in which this happened, the prisoner John Thurtell lodged at Tetsall's, the Coach and Horses, in Conduit-street; Thos. Thurtell lodged there also. They were there every day that week. On Friday the 24th, I dined at Tetsall's with John Thurtell and Hunt, Thomas Thurtell and Noyes were there also. After dinner, Thurtell said something to me about money. Four days previous to the 24th, I borrowed 10*l*. from John Thurtell; he then said, you must let me have it back on the Thursday or Friday; on the Thursday I saw him at Mr. Tetsall's, and he asked me if I had got the 10l.; I told him I had not; I had not collected any money. He said, I told you I should want it to-day or to-morrow, else it will be 300l. out of my pocket, but if you will let me have it to-morrow, it will answer the same purpose. On the next day (Friday) I paid him 5l. I borrowed 5l. of Mr Tetsall; that was after dinner. He then said I think I shall go down to your cottage to-night; are you going down? and asked me if I could drive Hunt down? I said, "yes." He said, I expect a friend to meet me this evening a little after five, and if he comes I shall go down. If I have an opportunity I mean to do him, for he is a man that has robbed me of several hundreds. He added, I have told Hunt where to stop. I shall want him about a mile and a half beyond Elstree. If I should not go down give Hunt a pound—which I did. Hunt had just come in, and Thurtell said—"There, Joe, there's a pound; if Probert don't come, hire a horse, you know where to stop for me." I do not know that Hunt made any answer, I gave him 20 shillings in silver. Thurtell left the Coach and Horses almost immediately, in a horse and chaise; it was a grey horse; I believe Hunt brought the horse and chaise; Thurtell left a little after five. I afterwards set off to go in my own gig; I took Hunt with me. When I came to the middle of Oxford-street, Hunt got out of the gig to purchase a loin of pork, by my request, for supper. When we came to the top of Oxford-street, Hunt said, "This is the place Jack is to take up his friend at." In our way down we overtook Thurtell, about 4 miles from London. Hunt said to me, "There they are; drive by, and take no notice." He added, "It's all right, Jack has got him." There were two persons in the gig—Thurtell and another; I passed them and said nothing. I stopped at a public-house called the Bald-faced Stag, about seven miles from London, two miles short of Edgeware. It was then, perhaps, a quarter to seven. When Hunt said "It's all right," I asked him what was his name? Hunt replied, "You are not to know his name, you never saw him; you know nothing of him." I got out at the Bald-faced Stag; I supplied the house with spirits. Hunt walked on, and said, "I'll not go in, because I have not returned the horse-cloth I borrowed." I stopped about twenty minutes; I then drove on, and overtook Hunt about a quarter of a mile from Edgeware. I took him up; and we drove on to Mr. Clarke's at Edgeware. We had a glass of brandy and water, I should think we did not stop ten minutes; we went into the bar. We stopped a little farther in Edgeware, and bought half a bushel of corn; I was out of corn at home; I put it in the gig. Hunt said, "I wonder where Thurtell is, he can't have passed us." We then drove on to the Artichoke, kept by Mr. Field. We got there within about eight minutes of eight. Neither I nor Hunt got out. We had four or five glasses of brandy and water, waiting for the express purpose of Thurtell coming up; we thought we heard a horse and chaise, and started; I think we stopped more than three quarters of an hour at Elstree. We went about a mile and a half, to Mr. Phillimore's Lodge, to wait for Thurtell. Hunt said, I shall wait here for John Thurtell, and he got out on the road. I drove on through Radlett, towards my own cottage; when I came near my own cottage, within about a hundred yards, I met John Thurtell, he was on foot; he says "Hallo! where's Hunt?" I said I had left him waiting near Phillimore's Lodge for him; John Thurtell said to that, "Oh, I don't want him now, for I have done the trick;" he said he had killed his friend that he had brought down with him; he had ridded the country of a villain who had robbed him of three or four hundred pounds?" I said, "Good God! I hope you have not killed the man?" and he said "It's of no consequence to you, you don't know him, nor you never saw him; do you go back and fetch Hunt, you know best where you left him!" I returned to the place where I left Hunt, and found him near the spot where I left him. Thurtell did not go. I said to Hunt when I took him up, "John Thurtell is at my house—he has killed his friend;" and Hunt said, "Thank God, I am out of it; I am glad he has done it without me; I can't think where the devil he could have passed us, I never saw him pass anywhere, but I'm glad I'm out of it." He said, "This is the place we was to have done it." (meaning near Phillimore's lodge); I asked him who the man was, and he said, "You don't know him, and I shall not tell you," he said it was a man that had robbed Jack of several hundred pounds, and they meant to have it back again; by that time I had reached my own house; John Thurtell stood at the gate; we drove into the yard, Hunt says, "Thurtell, where could you pass me?" Thurtell replied, "It don't matter where I passed you, I've done the trick—I have done it;" Thurtell said, "What the devil did you let Probert stop drinking at his c—— d public houses for, when you knew what was to be done?" Hunt said, "I made sure you were behind, or else we should not have stopped;" I then took the loin of pork into the kitchen and gave it to the servant to cook for supper. I then went into the parlour and introduced Hunt to Mrs. Probert; he had never been there before. Thurtell followed immediately, we had stopped in the yard a little time before we went in. I returned to the parlour and told Mrs. Probert we were going to Mr. Nicholson's to get leave for a day's shooting, before we went out Thurtell took a sack and a cord with him. We then went down the lane, I carried the lantern, as we went along Thurtell said, " I began to think, Hunt, you would not come." Hunt said, " We made sure you were behind." I walked foremost; Thurtell said, " Probert, he is just beyond the second turning " When he came to the second turning he said, " It's a little further on." He at last said, " This is the place." We then looked about for a pistol and knife, but could not find either; we got over the hedge and there found the body lying; the head was bound up in a shawl, I think a red one [here the shawl already produced, was shown to witness], I can't say that is the shawl. Thurtell searched the deceased's pockets, and found a pocket-book, containing three five pound notes, a memorandum book, and some silver. John Thurtell said, " This is all he has got, I took the watch and purse when I killed him." The body was then put into a sack, head foremost, the sack came to the knees, and was tied with a cord, it was the sack John Thurtell had taken out of the gig, we then left the body there, and went towards home. Thurtell said, " When I first shot him, he jumped out of the gig and ran like the devil, singing out that " he would deliver all he had, if I'd only spare his life."

Mr. Justice PARK. Do you know if John Thurtell has been in the sea service?

Witness. I don't know, I think I have heard him say so.

Mr. Justice PARK. We know that singing out means crying out.

Witness proceeded: J. Thurtell said " I jumped out of the gig and ran after him, I got him down, and began to cut his throat, as I thought, close to the jugular vein, but I could not stop his singing out; I then jammed the pistol into his head, I gave it a turn round, and then I knew that I had done him." He then said to Hunt, " Joe, you ought to have been with me, for I thought at one time he would have got the better of me. These d—d pistols are like spits, they are of no use." Hunt said, " I should have thought one of those pistols would have killed him dead, but you had plenty of tools with you," we then returned to the house and supped. In the course of the evening, after supper, John Thurtell produced a handsome gold watch; I think double cased; it had a gold chain.

Mr. Justice PARK: was the chain attached to it?

Probert. It was, my Lord. He took off the chain and offered to make Mrs. Probert a present of it, saying it was more fit for a lady than a gentleman. Mrs. P. refused for some time, but at length accepted of it. He put the watch and seal in his pocket, we had no spare bed that night, I asked when they would go to bed. I said my sister would sleep with Thomas Thurtell's children, and that they could have her bed. They answered they would sleep on the sofa. Hunt sang two or three songs after supper; he is a professional singer. Mrs. Probert and Miss Noyes went to bed between twelve and one. When they were gone, John Thurtell took out a pocket-book, a purse, and a memorandum-book; the purse contained sovereigns, I can't say how many. He took 15*l.* in notes from the pocket-book, and gave Hunt and myself a 5*l.* note and a sovereign each, saying—"that's your share of the blunt." There were several papers in the books; they and the purse and books were burnt, a carpet bag was opened. Thurtell said it had belonged to the man he had murdered; it contained wearing apparel and shooting materials, they were examined and put in again, I think two or three silk handkerchiefs were left out, there was also a back-gammon board, containing dice and cards; I also saw a double-barrelled gun, it was taken out of a case and looked at; all the things were taken away next day in a gig, by Thurtell and Hunt. After this, Thurtell said, "I mean to have Barber Beaumont and Woods; Barber Beaumont is a Director of a Fire Office with which J. Thurtell had some dispute, Woods is a young man in London who keeps company with Miss Noyes. It was a general conversation, and I cannot recollect the particulars; he might have mentioned other names, but I can't recollect them. Thurtell said to Hunt, "We must now go out and fetch the body, and put it in the pond." I said, "By G—d you shan't put it in the pond, you'll be my ruin else." There is a pond in my ground. Thurtell said, "Had it not been for the mistake of Hunt I should have killed him in the other lane, and returned to town and enquired of his friends why he had not come." First, only Thurtell and Hunt went out; when they came back, Hunt said, "Probert, he is too heavy, we can't carry him, we have only brought him a little way." Thurtell said, "Will you go with us? I'll put the bridle on my horse and fetch him." I went out to the stable with him, and left Hunt waiting near the gate. Thurtell's horse was brought out, and Thurtell and I went down and brought the body on the horse; Hunt did not go with us. We took the body to Mr. Wardle's field, near my gate Hunt took the horse back to the stable, and came back to the garden, and we dragged the body down the garden to the pond, we put some stones in the sack, and threw the body into the pond. The man's feet were perhaps half a foot above the water, John Thurtell got a cord, threw it round the feet, and gave me the other end, and I dragged it into the centre of the pond, and it sunk. We all three returned to the cottage, and I went to bed almost immediately. I found my wife up, next morning I came down about nine o'clock. Thurtell said, in presence of Hunt, that they had been down the lane, to look for the pistol and knife, but neither could be found. They asked me to go down the lane and seek them, in the course of the day, which I promised to do. When I went down the lane, I saw a man at work near the spot, so I took no notice. That morning they went away after breakfast. On Sunday they came down again, and Thos. Thurtell and Mr. Noyes came also. T. Thurtell and Hunt came in a gig. Hunt brought a new spade with him. He said it was to dig a grave for the deceased that he brought it. Hunt returned with the gig after setting down T. Thurtell, and brought J. Thurtell and Noyes in the chaise. Hunt was very dirtily dressed when he came down, and went up stairs to change. When he came down he was well dressed —in almost new clothes. Hunt said the clothes belonged to the deceased, he told me he had thrown a new spade over the hedge into my garden. I saw it afterwards, it was a new spade. J. Thurtell and I walked to the pond. He asked me if the body had rose? I said, no, and he said it would lay there for a month. In the afternoon Hewart called, and I went with him to Mr Nicholls's. On my return, I told Thurtell and Hunt that Mr Nicholls had told me that some one had fired a pistol or gun off in Gill's-hill-lane on Friday night, and that there were cries of murder, as though some one had been killed. He said it was about eight o'clock, and added, "I suppose it was done by some of your friends to frighten each other." J. Thurtell said, "Then I am baked." I said, "I am afraid it's a bad job, as Mr. Nicholls seems to know all about it, I am very sorry it ever happened here, as I fear it will be my ruin." Thurtell said, "Never mind, Probert, they can do nothing with you." I said the body must be immediately taken out of my pond again. Thurtell said, "I'll tell you what I'll do, Probert; after you are all gone to bed, Joe and I will take the body up and bury it." Hunt was present at this. I told them that would be as bad if they buried it in the garden. John Thurtell said, "I'll bury him where you or no one else can find him." As John Thurtell was going into the parlour, Hunt said, 'Probert, they can do nothing with you or me, even if they do find it out, as we were neither of us at the murder." Thurtell and Hunt sat up all that night, I, Noyes, and Thomas Thurtell, went to bed. Thos. Thurtell slept with his children In the morning John Thurtell and Hunt said they went to dig a grave, but the dogs were barking all night, and they thought some one was about the ground J Thurtell said, "Joe and I will come down to-night and take him quite away, and that will be better for you altogether." Thomas Thurtell and Hunt, and my boy Addis, went away in one chaise after breakfast, and John Thurtell, T. Noyes, and Miss Noyes, in another. The boy was sent to town to be out of the way. That evening J. Thurtell and Hunt came again in a gig about nine, they took supper, after supper, J.Thurtell and I went to the stable, leaving Hunt talking to Mrs. Probert. Thurtell said, "Come, let's get the body up, while Hunt is talking to Mrs. Probert, she will not suspect." We went to the pond, and got the body up, we took it out of the sack, and cut the clothes all off it. We left the body naked on the grass, and returned to the parlour; we then went to the stables, and John Thurtell went to his gig, and took out a new sack and some cord, we all three returned to the pond, and put the body head-foremost into the sack, we all three carried it to the lower garden gate, we left Hunt waiting with the body, while Thurtell and I went round the pond. I carried the bundle of clothes, and threw it into the gig, we then put the horse to, and Thurtell said, "we had better leave the clothes here, Probert, there is no room for them. The clothes were left and the body was put into the gig. I refused to assist them in settling the body in the gig. They went away. I, next morning, burnt some of the clothes, and threw the rest away in different places. I was taken into custody on the Tuesday evening after they went away.

Cross-examined by Mr Andrews. I do not know who apprehended me. When I was taken, I did not express any desire to become a witness, I cannot say when I first expressed a desire to become a witness It was after Hunt had made a confession. I can't say whether I was asked to become a witness before or after Hunt's confession. I heard that Hunt had made a confession, but I don't recollect from whom The first I heard of my becoming a witness was when I was taken before the Grand Jury by Mr. Williams, to the best of my recollection. Before that, I expected that we were all to be tried; I did not know what was to become of us; I did not know what was to be done to me. I took no pains to become a witness before being taken before the Grand Jury. I have never seen Mrs Probert since I left my own house, when I was arrested. I don't know of my own knowledge that Mrs Probert is now here: I was told so by Mr Williams, my Solicitor

Mr ANDREWS Has not a Mr Noel been your Solicitor? I am sorry to say that he has

Mr. ANDREWS. How long did he act in that capacity? For a few months in the year 1819.

Mr ANDREWS Has he not acted as your Solicitor since that period? Not that I recollect

Mr. ANDREWS Had you no communication with him in 1823? Not that I recollect; but I cannot swear that I have not.

Mr ANDREWS. You say you heard that some injury was intended to certain persons, and yet you gave no alarm? I did hear that at my cottage, but I did not believe it

Mr ANDREWS You must have believed it when you heard of the murder; and when you saw the dead body brought to your house, did not you give any alarm then? I did not.

Mr ANDREWS You received the parties into your house after the transaction? I did

Mr. ANDREWS. You supped with them and breakfasted with them, in company with your wife, on the following morning? I did.

Mr ANDREWS Were you sober then? I was

Mr. ANDREWS. And yet you did not spurn them, and kick them from your house? I did not.

Mr. ANDREWS Did you tell Mrs Probert what had happened? I did not

Mr. ANDREWS Did not Mrs Probert appear disturbed at what was going on? She did.

Mr ANDREWS. Did she not ask you any questions as to what was passing? She did.

Mr. ANDREWS Did you not tell her? I am not certain

Mr ANDREWS By virtue of your oath, Sir, did you not tell her what occurred on Friday night? I can't swear positively, but I might have told her something.

Mr. ANDREWS. Did not Mrs Probert express uneasiness on the Saturday? She did.

Mr. ANDREWS. Did she not inquire who Hunt was? No, she had heard of him often, though she had not seen him.

Mr ANDREWS. At what time did you come down on the Saturday? Between eight and nine

Mr Andrews. Will you swear, upon your oath, that you did not come down at six o'clock on that morning? Certainly, I can swear that I did not.

Mr Andrews Will you swear it was after eight when you came down? I will not· but to the best of my recollection it was between eight and nine.

Mr Andrews. What did you do when you came down? I went to the stable, or perhaps into the garden.

Mr Andrews. Did you go down the lane? I did not.

Mr Andrews What sort of hat did you wear on that occasion? I think a black hat, such as I generally wear.

Mr Andrews. Did you not wear a white hat? I can't say. I have two or three hats, and I sometimes wear a white one when at home.

Mr. Andrews. Did you see your wife receive a gold chain from J. Thurtell? I did.

Mr Andrews Did she wear it on the Saturday? I did not see her wear it on the Saturday.

Mr. Andrews Did she, when she received it, put it on herself, or did Thurtell put it on? I can't state that, but I think she put it on herself; I saw Thurtell rise when he presented it to her.

Mr. Andrews. Did Mrs. Probert express any uneasiness on the Sunday? I think she did.

Mr. Andrews. When Thurtell produced the sack and the cord, on Friday night, where was the boy? I think in the kitchen.

Mr. Andrews. Where was the sack before Thurtell produced it? I don't know, I never saw it before.

Mr. Andrews. Will you swear you had not seen it before J. Thurtell said, "I'll go and fetch the sack and cord?" I will.

Mr. Andrews. Did not the boy tell you where it was? No.

Mr. Andrews. Who was in the stable when the horse was taken out to fetch the body? I do not recollect.

Mr. Andrews. Where was the boy then? I think in bed; he slept in the room over mine.

Mr. Andrews. Were you ever in difficulties before this? I have.

Mr. Andrews. Were you ever in such a scrape as this before? Never.

Mr. Andrews. Had you never a charge of felony preferred against you before this? I had.

Mr. Andrews. Where was that? In the King's Bench prison.

Mr. Andrews. What was the nature of that charge? I was accused of taking some silver from the till of the man who kept the coffee-house, and who owed me 100*l.* at the time.

Mr. Andrews. What was the consequence of that charge? I was sent for six months to the house of correction.

Mr. Andrews. Was that the only charge of felony ever made against you? Yes, the only one.

Mr. Andrews. Were you never in Hereford? Yes, I was born there.

Mr. Andrews. Were you never charged with sheep-stealing there? Never.

Mr. Andrews. Well, perhaps it was lamb-stealing? No, I was never charged with either.

Mr. Andrews. Come, Sir, you know what I mean by charged, were you never accused of such a crime there?— Never.

Mr. Andrews. Then the accusation is quite new to you? It is.

Mr. Andrews. Then what was the charge against you? I had bought some skins, which were afterwards owned.

Mr. Andrews. Oh, then you were accused as a receiver of stolen goods? I was not.

Mr. Andrews. Were you not taken before a Magistrate? No.

Mr. Andrews. Were the goods not taken away?— They were not.

Mr. Andrews. I understand you have passed much of your time in prison? I have been in the King's Bench prison, and in the Rules, between two and three years.

Mr. Justice Park. Were you imprisoned in the King's Bench on civil suits? Yes, my lord.

Mr. Andrews. Well, you have been in the House of Correction and in the King's Bench prison; are these all? Yes.

Mr. Andrews. Do you know Mr. Framstone? I do.

Mr. Andrews. Now, sir, having given you that name, I ask you, on your oath, were you not committed by that gentleman for refusing to answer certain questions before the Commissioners of Bankrupts? Yes; I was committed to the King's Bench prison.

Mr. Justice Park. I thought you were going to establish a new imprisonment. he has already told us he has been in the King's Bench Prison.

In answer to further questions he deposed as follows.—
I have been a bankrupt. No dividend has been paid out of
my estate. I was frequently remanded by the Commissioners. I have lived only six months at the cottage. I
lived with my brother-in law in the Strand. We were not
partners, but did business together. It was a large
grey horse that was employed the night of the murder. It
was in my stable a night. Mr. Hunt had a white hat and
black handkerchief on the Friday night. Had heard of the
transaction of the Insurance Office; and yet subsequently
introduced Thurtell to my wife. Thurtell was making
love to Mrs. Probert's sister also a love, however, that
would come to nothing. I thought John Thurtell's saying
it was mere idle bravado. I do not know Mr. Beaumont,
to my knowledge. Never mentioned it to any person. No
one was present, save Hunt and Thurtell, when the money
taken from the body was distributed. I did not see any
cards played at my house, either on the Friday, Saturday,
or Sunday nights. I do not believe my wife played cards
on Sunday. I never, to my knowledge, saw my wife play
at cards. I never heard any person say it was a bad example to children. I have lived in London eleven years, I
transacted business in Herefordshire also

Cross-examined by Mr. Thessiger. I had known Hunt
12 months, I have been in his company several times;
I was the person who introduced Hunt to Thurtell, about
six or seven months ago at the Cock; I do not recollect inviting Hunt to Gill's Hill Cottage, I believe Thurtell
asked me to drive Hunt down to Gill's Hill Cottage; I did
not say there was no spare bed at my house; I expressed
no surprise at Hunt's going down uninvited to Gill's Hill
Cottage, he not having been personally introduced to Mrs.
Probert; Hunt paid for the pork in Oxford street: I have
never paid him for it since, it was only 18d.; I had 3 or 4
pounds in my pocket when I borrowed the 5*l*. from Tetsall.
I am not certain what I might have said, when Hunt said
at the gate, "Take no notice, and drive on." Hunt had
never been at Gill's Hill Cottage before. Phillimore Lodge
is in the high road, a mile and a half beyond Elstree, towards
St. Albans. Hunt paid for four or 5 five glasses of brandy
and water, and I paid for the one I had at Edgeware, there
were two or three handkerchiefs, and I burnt the mark out of
one of them. Up to the day I went before the Grand Jury, I
said to Mr. Franklin, the Chaplain, myself and Hunt were
innocent of the murder. The exact words were, very

likely, that neither of us knew any thing about the murder till after it was done. I was convicted of a felony before I was sent to Brixton.

By Mr. Gurney. On the Sunday evening that I went to Mr. Nicholson's, I remained out two hours and a half; Hunt and I were prisoners when I had the conversation with Mr. Franklin.

By the Court. When I spoke to my wife about netting, it was to satisfy her, as she was in a passion, and asked, "What have you been doing, you three? You have been counting money, burning papers, and dragging something heavy across the ground."

Mrs. PROBERT, was then called. By desire of his Lordship, she was accommodated with a seat. She spoke in a low tone, but Mr. Gurney kindly repeated her answers aloud. Her testimony was as follows:—I remember the night of 24th of October, when Mr. John Thurtell and Mr. Hunt came to Gill's Hill Cottage, to have heard the sound of a gig passing my cottage. It was about 8 o'clock, I think, the bell of our cottage was rung nearly an hour after. After that ring nobody came into our house. My husband came home that night nearly at ten. I came down stairs, found Mr. Probert, John Thurtell, and a stranger in the parlour. My husband introduced that stranger as Mr. Hunt to me. I saw John Thurtell take out a gold chain, which he shewed to me. It was a gold watch chain, with a great deal of work about it, is was such a chain as this, I think [the chain was shewn her]. He offered to make it a present to me; I refused it for some time, and at last he gave it me [she was shewn the box and chain produced by the constable of Watford]. I recollect giving that box and the chain to the constable, in the presence of the magistrates. When I and Miss Noyes went up stairs, we left John Thurtell, Hunt, and Mr. Probert in the room. I did not go to bed immediately; I went from my room to the stairs to listen; I leaned over the banisters. What I heard in leaning over the banisters, was all in a whisper. What I heard at first was, I thought, about trying on clothes. The first I heard was, "This, I think, will fit you very well." I heard a noise, like a rustling of paper on the table; I heard also something like the noise of papers thrown into the fire. I afterwards went up to my own chamber. Out of doors I saw something, I looked from my window, and saw two gentlemen go from the parlour to the stable; they led a horse out of the stable, and opened the yard gate, and let the horse out. Some time after that,

I heard something in the garden; I heard something dragged as it seemed very heavily; it appeared to me to come from the stable to the garden, the garden is near the back gate, it was dragged along the dark walk, I had a view of it when they dragged it out of the dark walk, it seemed very large and heavy; it was in a sack. It was after this I heard the rustling of papers, and the conversation I have described. After the sack was dragged out of the dark walk, I had a view of it until it was half way down the walk to the pond. I had a good view of it so far. After this, I heard a noise like a heap of stones thrown into a pit, I can't describe it in any other way; it was a hollow sound. I heard, besides what I have before mentioned, some further conversation. The first I heard was, I think, Hunt's voice; he said " let us take a 5*l*. note each." I did not hear Thurtell say any thing, then—I am trying to recollect—I heard another voice say, " we must say there was a hare thrown up in the gig on the cushion—we must tell the boy so in the morning." I next heard a voice, I can't exactly say whose, " we had better be off to town by four or five o'clock in the morning;" and then I think John Thurtell it was, who said " we had better not go before eight or nine o'clock;" and the parlor door then shut. I heard John Thurtell say also (I think it was his voice), " Holding shall be next." I rather think it was Hunt who next spoke; he asked, " has he (Holding) got money," John Thurtell replied, " it is not money I want, it is revenge; it is," said J. Thurtell, " Holding who has ruined my friend here." I did not at first understand who this friend was, I believe it meant Mr. Probert my husband. I cannot say whether Holding had anything to do in the transactions of my husband's bankruptcy. " It was Holding," said J. Thurtell, " who ruined my friend here, and destroyed my peace of mind." My husband came to bed about half-past one or two o'clock; I believe it was, I did not know exactly the hour.

A short conversation then took place in a low tone, which was not heard in the Reporter's box, between the Counsel for the prisoners and the Learned Judge and Mr. Gurney, as to whether it was proper to ask Mrs. Probert concerning any conversation that passed between her and her husband.

Mr. Justice PARK said to Mr Gurney, " All that you can ask, is, whether a conversation took place, in which witness communicated to her husband what she had seen and heard. You cannot ask what her husband said."

Mr. Gurney then asked the witness—"When your husband came to bed, did you mention to him what you had seen and heard, according to the evidence you have given?"

The witness, Mrs Probert, became apparently excessively agitated and faintly articulated, "Must I answer?"

Mr. Gurney. I do not want you to tell us what was said.

Mr Justice Park. Pray compose yourself, good woman; you need not be alarmed

Mrs. Probert. Must I answer questions concerning my husband? These were, we believe, her words, but the law and faultering and hysterical manner in which they were pronounced, rendered it difficult to catch them.

Mr Gurney. No evidence you now give, can prejudice your husband. He has been this day put before a jury of his countrymen, and acquitted of this murder

Mrs. Probert, in a sobbing hysterical shriek, "Oh, has he! has he!"

Mr Gurney repeated his question.

Mrs. Probert. Oh, I'll answer anything! but has he been acquitted? [The agitation of the witness for some time was so excessive, that she was unable to attend to the questions. She ejaculated at times a few unconnected words, in a low sobbing tone.]

Mr. Justice Park. Pray compose yourself, pray, good woman, don't be alarmed, we are not wanting you to say anything against your husband. Nothing will be drawn from you against your husband. Pray compose yourself; pray do not be alarmed.

During this scene, Hunt turned round to the persons standing by him in the dock, and smiled, as if in incredulity of Mrs. Probert's appearance of feeling.

Thurtell did not change his countenance, but bent down a little, and took snuff, drawing up his brows, and closing his lips firmly, with the expression of face habitual to him.

Mr Gurney then repeated his question, and Mrs. Probert answered—Yes, I did mention to him (my husband) what I had seen and heard.

The next morning Hunt and Thurtell came and dined with us, and on the Sunday, Thos. Noyes and T. Thurtell then also came. On the Monday night, J Thurtell and Hunt came again; it was past nine, I think, when they came. They staid to supper, and went away soon after.

Cross examined by Mr. Platt: You affected surprise to hear that your husband was acquitted. Now did you not know that he was to be acquitted previously to his giving evidence? No [in a low tone].

Did you not hear that he was to be acquitted of the charge, provided he gave his testimony here truly? I don't recollect that I was told so

Can you say on your oath that you were not told so? I don't know that I was.

There were two garden gates on the left-hand side of the road, going along the lane, one as you passed out of the lane into the stable yard; another gate, leading to the garden, forms part of a high fence; my bed-room window looked towards the fence. I could look over the fence, so as to see the horse come out of the door, and I think I could see the door-way of the stable itself; it was a fine moon-light night. There was but one sitting-room in the cottage over the parlor, the window of which looks to the garden, I rather think the short man whom I saw dragging something heavy was Hunt, it was at the landing-place of the floor where I slept that I listened, all the conversation was carried on in whispers; there was a great deal of whispering, which I did not hear; I could not distinctly hear the whole of the conversation, I thought I could distinguish the different voices, but cannot be positive; my husband whispered so low that I could not hear him, cannot take upon myself to say positively that he did whisper, my husband gave me no money just before he was apprehended; he did not give me 23*l*., did not tell me what to say if any body should come; never saw Holding in John Thurtell's company, it was my husband who was acquainted with Holding; I and Miss Noyes retired to bed about twelve, I was in my room a little time before I went to the window, a few minutes after I got up stairs, I saw the horse coming from the stable; I heard the parlor door opened a few minutes after, I saw a short man with a light, and another go out from the parlor to the stable; heard no noise in the stable; cannot say whether the light continued in the stable till I saw the horse, I heard no one go out before that, but I think I heard some one go into the kitchen before; we kept a store of potatoes in the garden, there was a hole made for them, and they were covered over. I went out into the garden on Saturday; I did not go near the pond; cannot say whether the pond is so shallow, that you may see the bottom, seldom went to look at the fish in the pond, did not go out on Sunday or Monday, the walk on entering the garden, is what I called the dark walk, and is surrounded by shrubs. I heard the noise first in the dark walk, it seemed as if something heavy was being dragged along the dark part of the path. After I heard this noise in the dark walk, I saw something dragged along the path leading to the pond, I know the part where the apple tree stands, and I know the part opposite to it, this is the part of the pond farthest removed from the cottage; I think it is a continuation of the path where I saw something heavy dragged along, I did not see my husband in the garden when I looked out of the window.

By Mr. THESSIGER: I did not expect my husband home on the 24th October; I was not prepared to receive the persons he brought. My husband went away on the preceding Monday morning; I never saw Hunt before, he was introduced by my husband, my husband did not say he was the gentleman of whom I had often heard him speak; there was singing on the Friday night, Hunt sung two songs, nobody else sung, it was not by my husband's desire or request that Hunt sung; John Thurtell asked him to sing once, and I asked him myself the second time, I pressed him to sing, we did not play cards on that night; Thurtell gave me the chain after supper, before the singing, I did not attempt to return the chain to him on Sunday, after I had seen all that passed from the window; there were cards on Sunday night, I did not introduce them; cannot exactly say who played, Probert was gone at the time, I did not play; do not know whose cards they were; I will swear my husband did not join in the play; it is possible he might have come in before the play was over; I did not hear either of the Thurtells remonstrate against it, and say it was a bad example for the children, Mr. Noyes came down on Sunday, and stayd till Monday morning; I did not communicate to him what I had seen and heard, did not shew him the gold chain at that time.

THOMAS THURTELL was next called and examined by Mr Gurney; On Friday, the 24th of October, I was at Tetsall's, in Conduit-street, Hunt and my brother dined there; some time after dinner Hunt went out and returned; when he came again I rather think he brought a sack with him; I rather think he brought a gig to the door; he did not say any thing to my knowledge when he brought the sack, I think it was a grey horse, my brother went away in that gig.—The witness here implored the Court to think of his situation, and the relation in which he stood to the prisoner at the bar.

Mr. Justice PARK said the witness had a duty to discharge to God and his conscience, but that he had no doubt the questions would be put to him with all possible kindness and consideration for his feelings

Hunt and Probert afterwards went away; my brother alone, as far as I know; I heard Hunt say something to Probert before dinner; I saw two large pistols on the table; some conversation took place. I asked one of them, what they were going to do with the pistols, I think I heard Hunt say to Probert, " Bill, will you be in it?" or something to that effect, on the next day I saw Hunt, who asked me if I wanted any money. He named £20, or something of that sort He did not say how he came by the money. I expressed my surprise at seeing him with so much money. He said they had been netting game. I can't call to mind what led to this

Mr Justice PARK here admonished the witness to be cautious what he was about, he had his previous testimony before him, and must have the truth

Thomas Thurtell said he could not remember every thing

Examination continued. Hunt said, we Turpin lads can do the trick, or something of that sort There was something said about a bag, Hunt said he had been killing game, and Probert held the bag. (The witness shewed considerable reluctance in giving this testimony) Hunt used the word murder in joke. Hunt said we have been committing murder, or something of that sort in joke He said " we have been committing murder to be sure." This was in answer to a question from me; of course, I asked them what they had been doing; I went to Probert's cottage on Sunday; I walked as far as Maida Hill, Hunt and my brother then took me up in a gig, I saw a spade in the gig, when I came to Probert's, Hunt asked me to throw the spade over the garden gate; my brother had got down and was walking with Noyes, whom we overtook. I said, with regard to the spade, " had you not better take it as far as the stable?" and he said, No, I know what I am about, and by his desire, I threw it over. He said, he did not wish Probert's wife to know it, or something of that kind.

[The moment he appeared in the witness box every eye was turned towards his brother in the dock The prisoner Thurtell looked upon him with the same apparent indifference with which he had viewed the other witnesses He took up his pen, and began to make arrangements for continuing to take notes as before The witness at first seemed somewhat agitated, but after a few minutes he regained his composure.]

THOMAS NOYES I am a wine merchant; I know Mr. Tetsall, Thomas Thurtell, and the prisoners On Friday the 24th of October, I dined with them at Tetsall's; Mr.

Probert borrowed some money of Mr Tetsall, for the purpose of paying it over to John Thurtell. John Thurtell went away in a gig, it was an iron grey horse; he was alone, Hunt and Mr. Probert also went away in Probert's gig, I saw some of them again on the Saturday morning at Tetsall's, I saw John Thurtell, Hunt, and Thomas Thurtell, I went down to my brother-in-law's cottage on Sunday, I walked, and the two Thurtell's and Hunt overtook me in a gig, John Thurtell alighted, and walked with me, Thomas Thurtell went on with Hunt. I was afterwards met by Thomas Thurtell in a gig at Brockley Hill. He came to meet us in a gig. On the Sunday evening in question, at Gill's Hill, cards were introduced, John Thurtell, Thomas Thurtell, Hunt, and myself played at Whist. Probert went out. We did not play the game out. Probert was absent about a quarter of an hour. On that Night Thurtell and Hunt sat up. I left the cottage on Monday, at past two, my sister and John Thurtell were of the party. The others went away in the morning.

Miss ANN NOYES. She was at first a good deal agitated, and was accommodated with a chair. I was at Probert's cottage on Friday the 24th of October. About eight o'clock I heard a gig passing. I heard a ring at the bell about half-past nine; during the evening Mr. John Thurtell, Hunt, and Mr Probert came into the room, Thurtell had a black coat on.---[Here there was a tremendous outcry outside the Court.---Mr. Justice Park, observing that no person moved to stop this noise, said he would fine Mr. Hawkins 50l. if he heard the noise repeated.]---I knew that Mr Probert had a white hat, which was kept in the hall. None of the three had a white hat that evening. They had a little brandy, and I rather think that John Thurtell proposed to go to Mr Nicholls's, to ask for a day's shooting. They all went out and returned about eleven; when they came back, they mentioned that Mr Nicholls was not at home. They had supper, I did not sup with them. I saw a gold watch that Mr Thurtell had, he took it out of his pocket, it had a chain. It was a hunting-watch. Mr. Thurtell took the chain off, and gave it to Mrs. Probert, he proposed that Mr. Probert should give it to her first, but on Mr. Probert declining, he put it round her neck himself. The chain produced she believed to be the same: there was some singing that night, Mr Hunt sung; soon after I went to bed. I did not come down the next morning till after breakfast. I saw Hunt and Thurtell go out at half-past nine. On the Sunday morning, Mr John Thurtell, Thomas Thurtell, and Hunt came down. I believe Hunt's dress was changed after he came to our house.

When the dress was changed he had on a black coat and waistcoat, and, I rather think, a white handkerchief. Mr. John Thurtell said, "How smart Mr Hunt is dressed to-day." Hunt had rather large whiskers. During the day the word "Turpin" was used. John Thurtell said that Probert would not do for a Turpin. There were cards played that evening. I saw Mr Hewart on Sunday. Mr. Probert went out on the Sunday evening. I went up with Mr. Thurtell the next day. I saw a knife in John Thurtell's possession [The knife produced by the constable was handed to the witness; it was the same found in the lane.] The knife she saw with John Thurtell was very like this.

Cross-examined by Mr. ANDREWS. I slept in a room very near where Probert slept, I did not hear him get up that morning. I have seen Mr Probert in a white hat and a black hat: the hall was the passage leading into the parlor from the kitchen: I did not see Mr Probert go out on the Saturday. John Thurtell had been often at the cottage before. he slept there several times, and did not always sleep on the sofa. I can swear he once slept nearly a week at the cottage: he slept alone.

Cross-examined by Mr THESSIGER. I was present when Mr. Hunt was introduced to Mrs Probert. Mr. Probert did not say he was the singer he had often talked about. Mr Probert did say that Mr. Hunt was a good singer: this was before he sung after supper.

THOMAS TETSALL. I keep the Coach and Horses, in Conduit-street. John Thurtell, Thomas Thurtell, and Probert frequented my house for a short time. I recollect the 24th October: four of them dined there on that day---J and T. Thurtell, Mr. Hunt and Mr Probert: I was on that day asked to lend Probert 5*l*. I gave it to him. I don't know exactly what he did with it. I don't know when they went away.

Cross-examined by Mr. Thessiger. The Thurtells lodged at my house; they were introduced to me by Probert, who said they were anxious to keep out of the way for a short time.

Re-examined: Hunt wore very large whiskers at first on the Monday after the 24th they were off. I can't say if either of the Thurtells were at my house on the 25th. I saw both on Sunday the 26th. John Thurtell wore leather breeches, long gaiters and a drab waistcoat. he went across the road to get shaved. I never saw him so dressed before. he went away in a gig with Hunt, who was indifferently dressed. they went at half-past ten: I saw a new shovel in the gig. There was also a piece of beef put in by their order. Hunt was shabbily dressed.

Cross-examined. Probert told me there was a warrant out against them he introduced them to me. he wanted me to be a bondsman for them.

WM REXWORTHY. I have known the late Mr. Weare about sixteen years: I always considered him a man of property he has generally carried money in his flannel shirt. I have seen him take large sums from thence. I have seen him with the Thurtells. I do not know that they were intimate I saw them several times before the murder: I saw them on the Thursday before the murder. the last time I saw them the Thurtells and Hunt were together, they asked for Mr. Weare, and I said he was not there, I was shewing them a new billiard table which I had just set up, and then Mr. Weare came in, I saw John Thurtell and Weare together on the Thursday before the murder, I saw Mr. Weare at No. 6, Spring-gardens, between one and two on the day of the murder He went away, and I saw no more of him.

Cross-examined, I keep two billiard rooms, I see the same faces come again and again to my rooms, I saw the body of the man I supposed to be Mr Weare, when it was taken out of the water, and in the sack, I saw it again in the coffin [A knife was shewn to witness] I know this knife, it belonged to Mr. Weare; I saw it with him the day of the murder.

Cross-examined. I know it, because Mr. Weare once forgot it at my house, and I had it for a month before I saw him again, I know it by a mark, as well as by the wear of it; it is a remarkable knife

Mr ANDREWS Were I to give my opinion, I should say not, but the Jury shall see it.

MARY MOLONEY. I was laundress to the late Mr Weare, he lived at No 2, Lyon's-inn. I was in his rooms on Friday, the 24th of October, I saw his clothes and linen on the drawers, Mr. Weare put them in his carpet bag.— [A bag was shewn to witness]—That was Mr Weare's carpet bag. There were five linen shirts, six pair of socks, a shooting jacket and leggings, a pair of breeches, a pair of laced-up boots, a pair of Wellington boots, and a backgammon board and things in it, put into the bag.

[A backgammon board was here shewn to witness]

That is the board, and these are the things that were in it. I saw Mr Weare put it in himself He dined at his chambers; he had two chops between two and three o'clock. I did not expect him home that night. he said he was going out of town, he was expected back on the Tuesday following; about three o'clock, I got a hackney-coach for him from the Strand, at the Spotted Dog in the Strand, it came up Holywell-street, with the horses heads towards Charing-cross, by his orders: he went away about three o'clock, or a quarter after; a carpet bag, a double-barrelled gun in a case, and a box-coat, were put into the coach, Mr. Weare had a buff waistcoat, and a new olive coloured coat on, he pulled his watch out before he went, I knew it, I had seen it before, it was a gold watch with a gold chain [here a chain was shewn to the witness], it was exactly like this; [a knife was shewn to witness] this is Mr Weare's knife; the watch had a double case, and was worked; he also wore a steel chain round the neck to secure it; the coach drove off towards Charing-cross [Here the shooting jacket, waistcoat, shirt, &c. were identified by witness.]

THOMAS CAVE. I drive a hackney-chariot. I remember taking up a gentleman at Lyon's Inn, in the month of October, I did not take any person up there for three weeks before; I was called from opposite the Spotted Dog, a shortish man got into my coach, a carpet bag and a gun were put into the coach also. The gentleman brought the gun and the girl the bag. I think it was in the week the murder was committed in Hertfordshire. I drove to Charing-cross, then up to Maddox-street, and there the gentleman got out and went to a house; on his return he ordered me to drive him to Quebec-street, and thence to the corner of Cumberland-street, in the New-road. He got out, and on his return in ten minutes there was a tall gentleman with him, dressed in a rough coat; they took away the things. I heard nothing pass between them. They went down Cumberland-street. This was about half-past four. Some lamps were lighted and some not.

THOMAS WILSON. I am one of the horse patrole, I was in the Edgeware-road on the 24th of October. I don't know John Thurtell; I met two persons in a gig about half-past six on that night. The horse was a roan grey. I met them between the five and six mile stones. They were driving at a furious rate. I could not identify the men, but I knew the horse again. I saw him at a Mr. Probatt's stables, I am sure it was the very same; it had a very white face.

Cross-examined by Mr. ANDREWS. They passed me quickly, but it was light enough to distinguish between a roan and a grey horse. I always described the horse as a roan grey.

Mr. ANDREWS. Will you swear that?

Witness. Yes. I told Mr Clutterbuck and Mr Stafford so.

Mr ANDREWS. That you mean to swear? I do. The gig was a dark one; I never described it in any other way; I saw the horse again in something more than a week. I knew it at Mr. Probatt's stables; I was ordered there to look at it. I met a man driving it up to be shewn. I said that was the horse that passed me that night. I knew it was the horse that was to be viewed by me. I never said to any one "I thought that was a grey, but I find it to be a roan."

JAMES SHEPHERD. I am an ostler to Mr. Cross's stables, Whitcomb-street, the prisoner Hunt came to hire a gig, on a Friday; the Friday before I heard of Mr. Weare's murder; it was a dark green gig; Hunt said it was going to Dartford; it was a roan horse, with a whiter face than the body, I saw the horse to-day; it is the same I saw on the Friday and Saturday in October; it is Mr. Probatt's, the livery-stable-keeper, Hunt asked for a sack; and where he could get one; I told him, as he was going to Dartford he would get one by Westminster Bridge; the gig he only hired from him, and the horse from Probatt; he came back on the Saturday, but he hired no gig on the Sunday.

STEPHEN MARCH was next examined. I lived as ostler to Mr. Probatt, the livery-stable-keeper at Charing-cross, I know Hunt the prisoner; I see him now, he hired the horse on a Friday; three days before he heard of Mr. Weare's murder; the horse was a dark roan, it was to go to Dartford. I took the horse to Cross's Livery Stables; it was to be put to a gig; I hired him another on a Sunday; a bay horse, and yellow gig. Hunt did not say where it was going, he brought it back on Monday, about twelve o'clock; he said he should want one about half-past three in the afternoon; he asked for the same horse, the roan that he had on the Friday. He went away in the yellow gig about half-past three. He returned about half-past two o'clock in the morning; I looked at the gig, and found it and the horse very dirty; there was a little blood at the bottom of the gig; the horse was a good deal distressed, and the thong of the whip was three parts unravelled.

BENJAMIN COXWELL. I am shopman to Mr. Bow, Pawnbroker, High-street, Mary-le-bone; I sold a pair of pistols similar to those presented to me on the 24th of October last; I sold also a key and a mould; I sold them to two strangers. One was tall and the other short, I asked 1l 17s. for them, and received 1l 15s. I should not know the persons again.

JOHN BUTLER was next called. I am ostler at the Bald Faced Stag, half a mile from Edgeware, on the London Road. On Friday night, the 24th of October, between six and seven, Mr. Probert came to the house in a horse and chaise; he stopped a very few minutes and went on towards Edgeware.

WM. CLERK I was landlord at the White Lion, Edgeware, in October last. I know John Thurtell; on the day of the 24th, I saw him about thirty yards beyond the nine mile stone on the Edgeware-road, he was travelling in a horse and gig; I observed the gig, because it was on the wrong side of the road. There was a person of short stature in the gig with him; it was a white-faced horse; I saw it last night come into Hertford; I returned from Langley to Edgeware; it is a mile from my house to where I met Thurtell; Mr. Probert and Hunt came to my house that evening, and drank brandy and water; we talked of Thurtell; Mr. Hunt took out of his pocket a newspaper, and said, " read that" I did so, and Hunt came to my bar; Hunt had then very large whiskers on. I saw John Thurtell on the Sunday on the top of Edgeware, walking with Mr. Noyes; I remarked that Thurtell looked very ill, he said he was so; he was not able to get bail; he saw both prisoners afterwards in custody; Hunt had not then whiskers on.

Cross-examined by Mr ANDREWS. The night was not very dark; the carriage he met had lamps lighted. All that passed between Thurtell and me was what I have stated. They stood at my house till twenty minutes after seven; they were a quarter of an hour at his house Mr. Probert did not enter the house, and was impatient for Mr. Hunt to come off. They must be nearly three miles behind John Thurtell and his companion.

D WHITE, a young boy, was next sworn. My father keeps a corn-chandler's shop at Edgeware. I know Mr. Probert by sight; he came to my father's with another gentleman. he bought a sack of oats and some beans: it was about 20 minutes after seven.

Cross-examined by Mr. THESSIGER. He did not seem to be in a hurry to get away.

S PROBATT. I keep the White Lion-inn at Charing Cross; Hunt hired a horse from my Son on the 25th. of October. he had a bay horse also on the Sunday and a fresh horse on the Monday; the same as is now in Hertford. On the Saturday Hunt said he should want a horse to go to Dartford. He produced the money, a five pound note and two sovereigns. I took the money for the hire out of the sovereigns. There was a Mr Reece in the Coffee-room, and Mr. Hunt remarked that he was an opulent sort of man, and it would do him good to take some money from him. He then put his hand in his pocket, and produced a pistol, saying, "that was the fellow to do business with." It was like the pistol now produced in Court.

Cross-examined by Mr THESSIGER· The conversation took place on the Saturday, the horse had a white face; it might be in a joking sort of way that Hunt spoke of Mr. Reece.

ROBERT FIELD was again produced: I knew Mr Probert before October last, he came to my house in a one-horse chaise, with another person; the stranger was nearly the size of the prisoner Hunt, they had five glasses of brandy in the gig; Probert said Hunt could sing, he did not sing, though asked even for a verse, they stopped a half hour, or thirty-five minutes. Probert's horse was a good one. My house is about two hundred yards from Elstree, I saw the singing man on Monday, he was with another man; that man was the prisoner, John Thurtell, they came to my house at half-past five on the Monday; they remained a quarter of an hour smoking a pipe the horse was put to the gig near half an hour; I saw Hunt on the Tuesday, at half-past three; he came from the direction of London, I gave the constable a sack and shirt on the 5th of November, which were in my possession from the time of the inquest.

Cross-examined by Mr. Platt: I knew the hour they were at my house, from people who were also there, breaking up early. By my watch, it was eleven minutes before nine.—After five o'clock, two coaches go down of an evening, to that part of the country; one from Smithfield, and the other from Holborn.

RICHARD BINGHAM, ostler at the White Lion-inn, Edgeware, examined· On the evening of the 24th Oct. last, about seven o'clock, a gig stopped at the White Lion, at Edgeware, with two gentlemen in it; one was short, and the other was tall; the short man had large dark whiskers, with a sallow complexion; he was rather high in the cheek bones, and about thirty-four or thirty-five years old. They had a glass of rum and water The tall gentleman had a light-coloured great coat, the short, a dark one. They had a bald-face horse, my master is Mr. Clarke, who had just then come home, another gig came up, but I do not know who were in it.

Cross-examined by Mr. Andrews. The first gig had time to get on a mile or two before the other came up. It was a dark night. Whilst the first gig was there, I was baiting the horse; neither of the men got out of the gig.

MARY MALONEY said, the description given of the short person, corresponded with that of Mr. Weare.

JAMES FREEMAN. I am a labourer, living at a place called "The Folly," near Gill's Hill cottage. I had occasion to go out on the 28th of October, into the Gill's Hill lane, about eight o'clock, to meet my wife and take her home; I had a gate to go through from my house; the gate was about thirty poles from Probert's cottage; when I got into the lane, I saw two gentlemen in a gig, going from Probert's cottage towards Batler's green. I heard the gig before I saw it, coming in a direction from Radlett, which would be past Probert's cottage. It stopped at an elbow of the lane, and one of the gentlemen got out. I spoke to one of them. The horse had a very white face I have seen the horse in this town; it was shewn to me by Mr Probatt. I am sure that is the very same horse I saw in the lane that night. When I left my cottage the moon was not up, but it was a star-light night. The moon rose afterwards, between eight and nine. I did not see enough of either of the men to be able to identify them The one who jumped out had a light long great coat on I afterwards met my wife, and we went home together.

PHILIP SMITH: I am a farmer, living at Aldenham.—On the 24th of October I was on a visit at Mr Nicholls's, at Batler's Green; I left Mr. Nicholls's about ten minutes before eight o'clock; I had my wife and child with me; my wife and child were in a donkey chaise, and I was walking; I was going to a place called High Cross, I passed the corner of a lane leading to Gill's Hill; I know the spot where a person was supposed to be killed; in crossing the road that night, the nearest part I went to the spot was about two hundred and fifty yards; in going along I heard the wheels of some sort of a carriage, and then I heard the report of a pistol, or a gun. This attracted my attention, and I remarked upon it to my wife. In about a minute or two afterwards I heard groaning. I then stopped the donkey chaise. The groaning lasted about a minute or two. I did not go up to the spot from whence the sound proceeded, as my wife was alarmed.

Mrs. SMITH, wife of the last witness, and the nurse were then tendered, but not called, as their evidence went to the same facts

RICHARD ADDIS. I lived as servant to Mr. Probert at

Gill's-hill, in October last; I looked after his horse and gig; he had the horse about two months before the 24th of October last; it was a powerful horse; I remember the evening of the 24th of October, about a quarter before eight, I heard the wheels of a gig; it was going by my master's house, I thought it was my master's gig; I went out, but I found it had passed on in a direction, very fast, towards Batler's-green. About nine o'clock there was a ring at the gate bell; I went to answer it, and found Mr. J. Thurtell there, he was standing by the side of the horse, and desired me to take the horse and gig in. I have seen the horse since in London, Mr. Probatt shewed it to me; the colour was a kind of an iron grey, or strawberry; I took the horse in and rubbed him down; the horse and gig seemed as if it had come from Batler's-green, in a direction from London. Mr. J. Thurtell said he was going down to see if he could meet Mr. Probert. I put the horse in, took the harness off, and did what was necessary. Mr J. Thurtell returned soon afterwards alone to the stable door, and asked me if I had rubbed the horse down? I told him I had. When I saw the gig, it was very heavy; there was a kind of a gun in a case poking out at each end, between the folds of the leather apron. I did not observe any thing else in the gig that night, but next morning I saw a carpet bag and a backgammon box. (Box produced.) That is the box. Either Mr. Probert or Mr. Thurtell told me to fetch the box and the bag out of the gig. Mr. Thurtell had a light great coat on that night. My master came home in about three quarters of an hour afterwards. His gig came in the direction from Radlett. Mr. Probert and Mr. Hunt were in the gig, and Mr. Thurtell was hanging behind. Mr. Thurtell had gone out again to look for my master. I took my master's horse and gig in and cleaned it. I observed some spots of blood on Mr. Thurtell's great coat on that night. I saw Mr. Thurtell sponging his coat; I am most confident he had a sponge; he seemed to be sponging the collar of his coat. This was about three quarters of an hour after my master came home; I saw a pail of water in the stable; Mr. Thurtell asked for some water; he was grabbling about in the water with the sponge; I afterwards saw my master; he came to the stable door and asked for a candle and lantern; I gave it to him, and he, and Mr. Thurtell, and Mr. Hunt, went out together at the gate; they were going in a direction towards Batler's-green; my master said he was going as far as Mr. Nicholls's house;

they were gone about three quarters of an hour, I was then in the kitchen. Mr. Probert told Susan to put the pork chops on. I stopped in the kitchen a little while, and then went into the stable to do the horses. Whilst I was there, Thurtell and Hunt came to the stable. I think that was the time when Thurtell sponged his coat, Hunt remained outside. They were there only a few minutes, and went away in a direction towards the house. When I had rubbed the horses down, I went into the kitchen. Mr. Probert came out for a bottle of rum, I believe, from the pantry in the kitchen. He then sent me to ask Mr. Thurtell what a clock it was, I went and asked him, he pulled his watch out of his pocket, it had no chain. Mrs. Probert observed that it was awkward to have a watch without a chain, he said it was. I went to bed at 12 o'clock. I saw no more of them that night. I rose at seven to clean the horses and fetch the cow up. As soon as I had done my work I went into the kitchen. I saw Thurtell and Hunt at the gate going into the garden. This was a little while after I got up. After I got the cow up, I saw Thurtell and Hunt in the kitchen. Hunt was sponging Thurtell's coat all over. Thurtell asked me if I had time to clean his boots. I said, I had. The soles of the boots were damp. I cleaned them; the dirt was very hard on, they went away next morning; the gun, the bag, and the box, were put into the gig; they asked for a sponge and went away, and turned as if they were going towards Batler's-green. My master seemed in rather low spirits that day, walking about the garden; he went out with a double-barrelled gun, about the middle of the day, shooting. On Sunday morning, I saw Hunt come into my master's garden; he was dressed in dark-coloured clothes; he went up stairs to dress himself, and he came down very decent; in the afternoon of that day I was sent to Mr. Nicholls's; I went down Gill's-Hill Lane, in consequence of something that Harrington said. When I went down I saw some blood in the rut of a wheel. On the Monday morning, I went to town along with Mr. Thomas Thurtell and Mr. Hunt. Mr. Thomas Thurtell was put down, and I was dropt at the Angel-inn, St Clements. I had no business in London.

Cross-examined by Mr. Andrews. The lane where I saw the blood is so narrow, that a gig cannot turn in it. I had been often up and down Gill's Hill-lane when I lived at Mr. Probert's; it is impossible for a carriage to turn in it or a gig either, except in a corner, where there is a heap of mud, and there it would be likely to be overturned.

If, then, a gig passed your master's house when you heard the noise, it must have gone on to Lechmoor Heath before it turned?—No, it might have turned before it came to Batler's-green. It could have turned before it came to Mr. Nicholls's house; two or three hundred yards before that, there is a place where a gig might turn. He had been asked half a dozen times about the sponging by the different persons. He had always said that he was not very certain about it, whether Mr. Thurtell had sponged his coat or no. He saw his master on Saturday morning, about seven o'clock, before breakfast; he was sure it was before breakfast, and thought it was seven; they had a clock in the house. he did not know that his master had gone down the lane in the morning; he had remembered Mr. Thurtell sleeping before at the cottage; he slept on the sofa before the fire.

By Mr. Thessiger. It was Mr. Probert who told him to go to town, he told me he had no more occasion for me, and that he would look out for a situation for me.

By Mr. Justice PARK. I knew where the persons slept who were at my master's house, and who slept on the sofa, and who in the bed; Mr. J. Thurtell once slept there a fortnight before, he then slept on the sofa, and not in a bed.

SUSANNAH WOODRUFF having been called and sworn—and it being nine o'clock,—

Mr. Justice PARK interposed and addressed the Jury. In the suggestion he was to make, he considered not his own convenience, but that of the Gentlemen of the Jury. By the Law of England, he was not allowed to discharge the Jury in criminal cases, and he was not enabled to allow them to return to their families until the case was finished. He was obliged to keep them together, though, no doubt, proper accommodation would be afforded them. But he was, for himself, perfectly willing to go on to finish the case before they separated. If, however, it was more agreeable to the Jury to retire to what he hoped would be their night's rest, he had no doubt they would be furnished with proper accommodation. He had no personal wish on the subject. He had been accustomed to bear fatigue of this kind. The Foreman would consult with his brethren, and collect their wishes before they proceeded to the examination of another witness.

The FOREMAN of the Jury.—My Lord, it is the wish of my brothers, as well as myself, to be allowed to retire, in order to take half an hour's refreshment, after which we hope to be able to proceed to a conclusion.

Mr. Justice PARK.—Why, Sir, ever since I have been in the profession, I confess that I have a great objection to these applications. Since I was a young man I have seen, too often, the miserable consequences of them, and I have made up my mind not to accede to them. On these occasions I never take any refreshment myself. I know the consequences of such interruptions to be injurious to the prisoner, to the interests of justice, and to those of the public.

The FOREMAN of the Jury.—Could we, my Lord, be permitted to take some refreshment in the box?

The JUDGE —Yes, undoubtedly; sandwiches, for instance, but nothing more, unless it be a little wine and water But in the mean time, in order that we may lose no time, we will proceed to examine this witness.

SUSAN WOODRUFF.—In October last I was servant to Mr. Probert at Gill's Hill Cottage; about half-past eight on the 24th of October, Friday, a gig came to the cottage, there came two gentlemen; one was in a blue coat (Mr. Thurtell), he came into the kitchen; he took out a watch and laid it on the table, and took off the chain, but what sort of a chain it was I do not know; he rolled it up; I went to stir the fire, and something was in it rolled up like a bit of wire; I could not tell what it was; I had orders to cook a supper; it was pork; it was afterwards put off; I received orders not to dress the supper so soon; they were going out, they staid out for an hour; they supped; Thurtell and Hunt did not go to bed, they staid up. I went to bed; I got up on Saturday at six o'clock; and as I came down I met Hunt and Thurtell coming up the steps from the garden. I observed their shoes and boots were both very dirty. I went afterwards to fetch some water; I went into the parlor; I saw Thurtell lying on the sofa; he had a white hat on, the white hat was my master's; I observed in the parlor there was a bag, not that (which was shewn her on the table of the Court), and some bundles besides; they went off about ten, they had then both black hats on; they came again on Sunday night; I saw them both—Thurtell and Hunt. On the Tuesday morning I went into the chaise house, and saw a sack hanging on a nail; it seemed very wet.

JOHN HARRINGTON. — I am a labourer, living at Aldenham, I was at work with a man named Richard Hunt, in Gill's-hill-lane, on the day after the murder. Two gentlemen came past ten minutes after six; one of them I should know; that gentleman there is one of them (pointing to the prisoner Thurtell); the other was a shorter man with black whiskers; the tall gentleman had a white hat on at the time; they passed me about ten poles and seemed to be grabbling about, and looking for something in the hedge; they returned and passed us again; the tall man spoke to my comrade Hunt, and told him he was capsized out of a gig last night, and had lost his pen-knife and a handkerchief; I don't know what my partner said to him; did not pay attention to what further passed, I went on with my work. At eight o'clock, when I went to breakfast, I went to the place where I saw them grabbling; I there found a pen-knife. The place was in the road toward Batler's Green. I gave the knife to Mr. C. Nicholls. (The knife produced by the constable was shewn to witness.) That is it. It was then covered with blood. I found a pistol after, about ten o'clock. I found the knife in the cart-rut, and the pistol in the brambles of the bushes; that too is covered with blood. I observed nothing else in it. It was a two-bladed knife; one blade is broken.—I think the pistol had been fired off, the pan was down, as it is now [pistol shewn him]. Mr. Nicholls was with me when I found that pistol; when I went to Mr. Nicholls's I saw much blood, and the marks in the lane as if of two men stumbling about. There was a large hole in the hedge, and much blood. A gig could not have turned at the place where the blood was, it could not have turned without going to the end of the lane, fifty poles further on. On the same day, about eleven o'clock, the same two persons passed me in a gig. The horse was to the best of my knowledge an iron grey. I am certain they were the same persons. I did not then know Probert, I do now. He came through the lane about 12 o'clock. He had a large dog.

The prisoner Thurtell then addressed the Court.—My Lord, I must pray you again to speak to the gentlemen of the Jury on the subject which you just now mentioned— the propriety of postponing further proceedings till to-morrow. I would beg them to consider the situation in which I stand. I have been up this day at 6 o'clock; and when the other witnesses have been gone through, there are twenty more of them, I understand, ["Oh no," from the Crown Counsel], I shall be too much exhausted to do justice to my defence.

Mr. Justice PARK: By the law of the land, a case ought to go on till it is closed, and I am ready to go on with it. I am willing, however, to do what I can to accommodate either the Gentlemen of the Jury or yourself. It is with the Jury however, that the matter must rest.

THURTELL. I hope the Jury will take my situation into consideration.

Mr. Justice PARK I cannot order the Court to be adjourned, unless the Jury desire it—it is for them to say.

THURTELL: My Lord you are very good, I hope the Jury will take into consideration the situation in which I stand. Gentlemen, I have been up so early, and so much of the case yet remains, that I shall be exhausted before I begin my defence

Mr. Justice PARK Gentlemen of the Jury, the Counsel for the Crown say that the remainder of the case will be very short.

THURTELL—But after that my Lord there are two of us, Hunt and myself, who have to enter on the defence separately.

Mr. Justice PARK: Let us then at any rate go on with the remainder of the case for the prosecution; I see many reasons why we should; and then if you state that you cannot conveniently go on with your defence, I will take it on myself to adjourn the Court.

In the whole of his conversation with the Learned Judge, the conduct of Thurtell was perfectly firm, temperate and respectful. He seemed at the same time persevering in his request, and rational and attentive to the objections urged.

RICHARD HUNT, labourer. I was with Harrington in Gill's-hill-lane, on Saturday, October 25; I know no more than he does; I saw the two men passing down the lane; I should know them; the two gentlemen sitting there are they, I think, (pointing to the two prisoners). One of them entered into a conversation, and said he was capsized out of a gig. One of them had a white hat, the side bulged in; another a black one.

WILLIAM BULMER. I am a labourer; I was walking in Probert's garden in October last, on the morning after the murder, about 6 o'clock, I saw two persons in that garden; the tallest of the two had a white hat; they went towards the house.

GEORGE NICHOLLS. I know Mr. Probert; neither Probert nor any of his friends came to me on the night of the murder; on Monday a labourer delivered a knife and a pistol to me, which I afterwards handed over to Simmons, the officer; it was bloody; on Monday evening I observed what appeared like brains about the barrel of the pistol. Mr. Probert came to my house on Monday; something passed between us respecting what happened in the lane.

JOHN PIDCOCK. I am a surgeon; I was at the Artichoke, at Elstree, when the body of Mr Weare was there; I took the shawl from off the neck, saw a sack over the shawl: I saw the body first at the Artichoke, when the sack was taken from the body I found a handkerchief, which I delivered to Simmons, the officer, the body was quite naked when the sack was taken off, with the exception of the shawl, [a large red handkerchief, having a great cut or hole in the centre, was here produced to the witness, who immediately identified it.]

JOHN FLEET I am assistant to Mr Johnson the messenger On the 24th of October, I was at the Cock public-house in the Haymarket, acting officially under a commission; Hunt came in a gig there, about half-past 4 in the afternoon; he delivered a note to me, which I have destroyed; John Thurtell lived at the Cock; I have seen him living there I knew the room he occupied; it was No. 10 The contents of the note were---"Have the goodness to give Mr Hunt my great coat and red shawl, which you will find in a closet at No. 10." I went to the room, and took the things out, and brought them down, and gave them to Hunt The shawl produced is something like the shawl I gave to Hunt. I do not know the hand-writing of the note

CAROLINE WILLIAMS. I was servant at the Cock; which was kept by Thomas Thurtell; his brother, John Thurtell lodged there; he had a shawl like the one produced.

LUCY SLATER I was servant at the Cock; John Thurtell lodged there; I have seen him use a shawl similar to the shawl produced.

JOHN MARSHALL. I am a gunsmith in London; I know the gun produced; I saw it last a twelvemonth ago, I saw it at Mr. Weare's chambers in Lyons' Inn.

W. BLAKESLEY. In October I, lodged at No. 9, King-street, Golden-square, the residence of the prisoner Hunt and his wife; remembered Hunt coming home on the 27th of October, in a single horse chaise; I saw him take out a carpet bag filled with things, a gun, with a dark case, similar to that produced; a dressing case, similar to that on the table; they were carried into his apartments; there were also some coats.

JOHN UPSON. I am an officer. I took the prisoners from London to Watford; we came in two gigs; at Watford, the next morning, a conversation took place between me and Thurtell, about Hunt's confession; I made use of no previous promise or threat; in the course of the conversation about Hunt's confession, I asked Thurtell what he did with the watch, and he told me that he threw it away in a place among some trees where there were some pailings.

By Mr. THESSIGER. When we were at Watford, Hunt gave me an order for the things to be given up, and told me where they were to be found.

J. FOSTER I am a constable at Rickmansworth; on the 30th October, I had Thurtell in my custody at the Plough; he made a communication to me; I made use of no previous promise or threat; he said that Hunt was a rascal for *nosing* him so; that he (Thurtell) would not do so to him (Hunt), particularly after he (Thurtell) had offered the watch for sale in his (Hunt's) name, and as his property. He said he was offered no more than 25*l* for it, though it was worth 60*l*.

T Thurtell was again called, but he did not answer.

Mr. Justice PARK. Gentlemen of the Jury, you have relieved me from a great difficulty; I should not have acceded to the wish of the prisoners, had not you also expressed your concurrence in that course; one advantage arising from which, will be, that we shall have given the case the fullest and most patient attention; I shall now adjourn the Court until to-morrow morning. Let two of the most steady constables be sworn according to the form which I shall direct.

Two constables were then sworn " To keep the Jurors in some safe and convenient place until the sitting of the Court to-morrow; to furnish them with every proper and convenient accommodation, and not to speak to them themselves, or to allow others to speak to them, touching the matter in issue, without the leave of the Court."

The Court was then adjourned to 9 o'clock to-morrow morning.

SECOND DAY.——WEDNESDAY, JAN. 7.

Upon the removal of Thurtell and Hunt from the Dock last night, they were agreeably surprised to find that their irons were not to be replaced. On arriving at the prison, Thurtell at once relaxed that contemptuous reserve which from the first he had observed towards Hunt. He seemed to recognise him as a fellow-sufferer, and all his feelings of anger appeared to be transferred to Probert. He asked Hunt how he felt himself, and a sort of friendly conversation followed. They both had some cold meat, tea, and coffee, and Thurtell ate heartily. He called for his pipe, as usual, and enjoyed himself with great comfort.

This morning the prisoners were called soon after seven, and were conducted to Mr. Wilson's room, where they had a comfortable breakfast. Shortly after 8, a carriage was brought to the gate, and at half-past 8, a lane was formed through the crowd which was assembled, for the prisoners to pass. Two of the turnkeys then mounted the box, and the prisoners came forth. Thurtell was first, and looked well; on getting into the carriage, he laughed at the curiosity of the multitude; Hunt followed, and took his seat beside Thurtell, with whom he began a conversation, and they both smiled; but the smile of Hunt was forced, and his agitation was very great. On their arrival at the gaol, they sat close to each other in the pound, and continued to speak to each other in friendly terms. Mr. Harmer remained for some time with Hunt, to whom he intimated his intention of memorializing the Crown in the event of his being found guilty.

It was anticipated by the High Sheriff yesterday, that the trial of the prisoners could not be concluded the same night; he had therefore given directions for twelve beds to be prepared for the Jury, in a large room over the Court, and to this room they were conducted; they were furnished with a good dinner from the Salisbury Arms, with wine, tea, coffee, and whatever else they thought necessary for their comfort. No person was suffered to have any communication with them, except in the presence of the officers; and at night they were locked up, and were not again visited till this morning, when they were provided with their breakfast. At half-past 8, they were conducted into Court, and took their places in the box.

At seven o'clock this morning, the doors of the Court were opened, and in a few minutes every part of the edifice was crammed almost to suffocation.

At nine o'clock Mr. Justice PARK entered the Court; an order was then made, that all the witnesses for the prisoners should go out of Court, except Mr. Waddeson, who would be the first called.

The prisoners were then conducted to the bar; Thurtell looked assured; he held in his left hand some manuscripts, and had near him a pocket-handkerchief, filled with books and papers, which he carefully assorted upon the desk near him. Hunt looked dispirited.

DEFENCE OF JOHN THURTELL.

The fact of the prisoner being about to address the Jury, being communicated to those without, the pressure for admission was renewed, and every avenue was crowded almost beyond endurance.

Mr. Justice PARK now addressed the prisoner as follows:—" John Thurtell, this is the time that it becomes your duty to make your defence."

There was a solemn pause. Thurtell, who was standing forward in the dock, bowed, and in a low tone said a few words to Mr. Jay, who stood close to him.

Mr. JAY then addressed his Lordship: My Lord, my client wishes to call his witnesses first.

Mr. Justice PARK. I cannot in my capacity attend to wishes; I must abide strictly by the rules of the Court. This, therefore, is the proper time for the prisoner making his defence.

Thurtell then retrograded a few feet in the dock, and with his face to the Jury-box, in a firm, sustained, and graceful attitude, addressed the Court as follows:—

" My Lord, and you, Gentlemen of the Jury,

"Under the pressure of greater difficulties than, perhaps, it has ever before fallen to the lot of man to sustain, I now appear before you, to vindicate my character, and preserve my life. I have been supported under the impression that the hour would arrive when I should be enabled to defend myself before that tribunal, which the institutions of my country have awarded to the accused ; namely, an enlightened Court, and a Jury of Twelve fellow-subjects, uninfluenced by prejudice; I have been represented by that public Press, which carries on its rapid wings to the extremity of the land, either benefits or curses, as a man, the most depraved, the most profligate, the most cruel ' I have been represented as a murderer, who had perpetrated his crime with greater atrocity, and under circumstances of more premeditated malice than any that has hitherto been heard of in the sad catalogue of criminals. I have been stigmatised as a callous, cruel, heartless, remorseless, prayerless villain, who had seduced his friend into a sequestered path, in order the more securely to dispatch him. I have been described as a viper, who had nestled in the bosom of my victim, with the preconcerted intention of striking a surer blow—as a monster, who, having committed a deed of horror, at which our common nature recoils, and humanity stands aghast, endeavoured to extinguish the upbraidings of conscience, in the tumults of debauchery. These have been the descriptions given of me, not alone daily, but hourly by the public Journals, and communicated from one extremity of the kingdom to the other. You, Gentlemen, have no doubt read them; I will not say that you have been influenced by them, but it would exact too much from the common virtue of human nature to suppose that men could entirely divest themselves of impressions so successively repeated, or that they could dispossess themselves of those feelings— which such statements are calculated to excite But I feel satisfied, Gentlemen, that as far as it is possible, you come to this investigation with minds unbiassed, and judgments unaffected by the atrocious slanders which have been published against me I feel assured that you will decide as becomes the character of that sacred office with which you are invested. Guilt, of such a complexion as that imputed to me, must have grown with my growth, and strengthened with my strength ; but you shall hear from men of the most unblemished reputation, that at least there was a period of my life, when the bosom of him who now stands before you as an accused murderer, flowed with the most kindly feelings of affection, and that my faults were those of an improvident generosity, and an unsuspecting confidence. Beware then, Gentlemen, of preconceived opinions. Believe not, that the years of no very lengthened existence have perverted those natural feelings of benevolence; and indeed Nature must have taken a refluent course in my heart, if these qualities of early life were succeeded by vices which only demons could feel; rather do me the justice to believe, that they are the slanderous imputations, disseminated by that press which was wont to be the shield of innocence, but which, in my case, and in the want of other intelligence, has pandered to the worst feelings of our nature Gentlemen, my entrance into life was under circumstances the most auspicious. I was reared by a kind, affectionate, and religious mother, who first taught my lips to utter their first accents in praise of that Being, who guides the conduct of your hearts, and of the Learned Judge upon the Bench. My youthful steps were directed by a father, conspicuous for the possession of every good quality, but above all, for his unaffected piety. On leaving my parental home I entered the service of our late revered Monarch, who was emphatically styled the father of his people For years I had the honor of holding his commission and served under his colours, and I may justly take the credit to assert, that I never disgraced the one, nor tarnished the other. I have done my country some service. I have fought and bled— I never feared to draw the steel against my open foe— against my country's enemy—but to raise the assassin's arm, and against an unsuspecting friend, believe it not—it it is horrid, monstrous, and incompatible with every feeling of my heart, and every habit of my life. Amongst the numerous other vices attributed to me, it has been said that I have been what is termed a sporting man—a gambler. To that accusation, with a true penitence of heart, I plead guilty. I was a gambler some time past, but three years have now elapsed since I entered a gaming-house, or was present at a horse-race or other sporting exhibition, but even had the charge been true, had I continued the practice, I am yet to learn why such a vice is unpardonable in me. Why I am to be thrust out of the pale of society for the practice, when half the nobility of this scale set the example, and the most enlightened Statesmen have been my apologists. True, too true, I have been a gambler—but an unfortunate one. My afflicted family have been the only sufferers, and myself the only victim. It has been the remark of one of the sages of antiquity, that no man starts decidedly wicked; and though I fear it will be too long a trespass on your attention, yet I am compelled, by the circumstances in which I am placed, to lay before you the details of my past life, calling upon you to extend to my conduct the benefit of such a truth.

When you, who are to decide on my fate, carry in your mind the great hazard in which I stand—when you reflect upon the state of feeling which must accompany a mind for a long time ill at ease—when it is recollected that I have been grossly injured by those from whom I had a right to expect kindness, you will, I am sure, feel disposed to pity the sufferer, and forgive his ramblings. The close of the last war, which shed a brighter lustre than ever before beamed on our glories, cast a shadow on my fortunes, Having ceased to be actively employed in military service. I unhappily was induced to enter into the commercial world, I entered it under the influence of all those romantic feelings which the habits of a soldier's life had strengthened, but which were as hostile to my commercial pursuits as they were congenial with my military attachments. I considered my commercial connexion in the same light as I was wont to view a military mess, and my fellow dealers as brother officers I laid myself bare to the claims of the avaricious and the unfortunate—I relieved the distresses of the one, and was injured by the designs of the other. I became a bankrupt. My solicitor, who had been my earliest friend—the friend of my bosom—became a traitor, and I found him, in the hour of my embarrassment, in the ranks of my bitterest enemies. From the examination of my affairs, I had reasons to form the most confident ground of re-establishment. I had hoped to be again restored to the respect of my connexions—but a baleful influence intervened. Too frequently, alas, does the over-reaching avarice of one, running counter to the feelings and interests of the other creditors, destroy for ever the prospects of the unhappy debtor. Such was my misfortune. Thomas Osborn Springfield was my assignee. I had obtained the signature of some creditors, and the promises of almost the whole, to obtain a supersedeas of the Commission of Bankruptcy; but when I thought the winter of my fortune had passed away, and that the blossoms of hope were ripening, a chilling frost came to blight them. My principal creditor demanded a bonus of 300l for his signature, in this demand he was backed by my own solicitor, who was also his. I spurned the dishonourable offer, and in so doing was cut off from the prospect of retrieving my fortune, and cast upon the world the dupe of many, and despised by all. My brother Thomas, shortly after arrived in London; and availing himself of my assistance, embarked in the silk trade. His warehouse was accidentally destroyed by fire—accidentally, I repeat, as has been proved by the decision of a Jury, at a trial at which the Learned Judge who sits on the Bench, presided, and yet this calamity was made the occasion of an attempt to fix on me the crime of removing fraudulently the goods—those goods which the verdict of a Jury had decided to have been destroyed by an accidental fire, and of the truth and justice of which decision the most unexceptionable evidence and most unequivocal corroboration will be given in the approaching trial on the alleged conspiracy. I have, my Lord, perhaps, given too free an expression to my feelings, but borne down, as I have been, by calumny and falsehood, the victim of accumulated slanders, it is impossible to confine myself to very measured language—

"The flesh will quiver, where the pincers tear,
The blood will follow where the knife is driven."

You have been told, Gentlemen, amongst its other unfounded calumnies, by the public press, that a Mr.

Woods has asserted that he was inveigled into a house in Manchester-buildings, where he supposed it was intended to murder him, and that he saw me standing in the passage. Happily, I am enabled, if such a charge were this day at issue, to prove, from the unquestionable testimony of some of the most respectable individuals, that I was, at the time when I am thus described to be in Manchester-buildings, in the city of Norwich. Of Mr. Woods I shall say no more at present, I abstain from doing so from feelings of delicacy towards a most worthy female. In proof of my respect for her, I grant to him the mercy of my silence. When, I ask, Gentlemen, did it ever before happen to a British subject to be called to answer for his life under such an accumulation of unfounded calumnies—such a mass of commented obloquy? When has it ever before occurred that the very actions of a man's life, which, if truly known, would have redounded to his credit, have been, by a strange perversion, construed into proofs of guilt? and by that Press too, which ought to be the shield of innocence, the avenger of oppression, the detector of falsehood, and above all, the strongest support of that best security of English liberty, Trial by Jury, by that Press, I say, all these slanders have been heaped upon me before trial; nay, it has whetted the public appetite for slanders still more atrocious. That engine which, in other cases, would have operated to refute the imputed falsehood, has been employed to give a deeper dye to my supposed guilt. One would have thought that the claims of an honourable service, spent in the army, would have protected me at least until the day of trial from such a persecution. Towards me the very order of nature has been reversed. The few days of my late misfortunes have thrown a livid shadow over the glories of days long past. The actions of my life have been misrepresented—every kind of connexion and engagement which I might have formed, has been ransacked to supply the magazine of slander. You have been told that even in the day of glory, when the battle's rage had ceased, and the peril of the conflict was over, the vanquished, unoffending, yielding, nay, supplicating foe—

[Here the prisoner was affected, and shed tears.—Mr. Justice Park Sit down for a moment; sit down.—The prisoner felt for some moments the struggle of his feelings, but soon reassumed his firmness.]

You have been told, I say, that the yielding, vanquished, supplicating foe, has fallen in cool blood beneath my cowardly steel, that, not satisfied with the blood of my victim, I coolly set to plunder his person. Nay, more—that, with a folly only to be equalled by the atrocity of such an act, I subsequently boasted of the ruffianly barbarity as the exploit of a soldier.* Is there an English officer, is there an English soldier, or an Englishman, whose heart would not revolt at such a dastardly deed of cold-blooded cruelty? Far better had it been, ere I had seen this day, that I had fallen in honourable conflict, surrounded by my brave companions, than thus to be borne down, the object of unrelenting malignity. I should have been covered with honourable dust. My family might then, while mourning for my loss, have blessed my memory, and the glory of such a death would have rolled its fires into the fountain of their sorrows. Before, my Lord, I proceed to read the remarks on the evidence which has been offered in support of the conspiracy against me, I take the liberty to return my sincere thanks to the High Sheriff and Magistrates. I cannot allow the opportunity to pass without expressing my regret that any misunderstanding should have arisen between the Rev. Mr. Lloyd and one of my solicitors. I hope that all angry feelings between them are done away, and that the bonds of amity are ratified. To the Rev. Mr. Franklin, the Chaplain of the prison, I owe my acknowledgments for his virtuous exertions to inspire me with the awful truths of religion. His exertions to awaken me to such considerations have trebly armed me to meet with firmness the trial of this day. Though last, not least, allow me to mention the Governor of the prison, his fatherly conduct I can never forget. (He then opened a paper, containing written remarks, which he read as follows)—I will now, Gentlemen, call your attention to the evidence in this case, which you will remark, instead of being clear and consistent, is so far unlike the evidence usually adduced in support of so awful a charge, that it is contradictory, inconsistent, and derived from the mouths of persons who have been willing to save their own lives by any sort of falsehood. The first witness is Beeson, he has told you that there are several roads to Probert's cottage, so that

---

*It must have been curious to see the looks of RUTHVEN and UPSON, the Bow Street Officers, during the acting of this solemn appeal, and pretended horror of this murder. When these Officers took Thurtell and Hunt to gaol, handcuffed and ironed as they were, Thurtell amused the company, by recounting many of his successful villainies, and amongst them this very exploit he described how he stabbed the unfortunate foreigner, and stripping him, discovered a belt round his body, containing 240 doubloons. "No bad morning's work—was it Joe?" said Thurtell to Hunt.

the inference of the gig being seen with the head, from Batler's-green, is now done away. He also mentions, that he went out to search for the body, and that those who sought were utterly at a loss for it till they were told where it was by Hunt. Hunt could inform them where the body was, and why could he do so, but because he had deposited it himself? Beeson also told you that one person could not have thrown the body into the pond where it was found. Now what proof, I shall ask you, is there, that the body ever was, as has been alleged, in Probert's pond? None but the evidence of Probert. I shall lay before you, at the proper time, what appears to me to be a view of the probabilities of this part of the case. There was also, Beeson tells you, a large pond, near the small one, in which the body was found. Who could have chosen the smaller pond, but a person acquainted with the country—who could have known that the larger pond was sometimes dry, and the small one not? Who but Probert, himself? It appeared, in answer to a judicious question of the Learned Judge, that both the sack in which the body was enveloped, and the cord with which it was tied, were bought by Hunt. I pass over the evidence of Field and Upson as immaterial. The next evidence is that of Rexworthy. Rexworthy, you must recollect, is, from his own account, a gambler, and a supporter of gamblers; but his evidence, if worthy any thing, has no fact that is material against me. The next witness who bears upon the case is Ruthven, who produces some of the articles found in the room at Tetsall's when I was apprehended; but there is no proof that these articles are mine. I never wear white neckcloths; I have not worn a white neckcloth for two years till this day. You have been told there was another person in the same room with me. Now, let me ask you whether it was prudent on my part, if I had done the act with which I am charged, to suffer another person to be in my room, and have thus allowed him an opportunity of discovering my guilt? Mr. Simmons produced a red shawl handkerchief, which was proved to have been worn by Hunt, and which proved nothing against me. I now come to the only evidence which at all connects me with the crime committed—the evidence of the only man whose testimony points at me. And who is he? What is he? He is himself the murderer. Is it credible that he would have introduced me, just hot from slaughtering, to his wife? Where was the murder committed? A quarter of a mile from his own house. Where was the body found? In his own pond. Who took it there? Himself. Who took me to Tetsall's? Probert. He gives here the true account respecting the 10*l*., but he gave a different one before the Coroner and the Magistrates. Is such a man to be believed? Before you doom a fellow-creature to an ignominious death, I conjure you to weigh well the statements of Hunt and Probert.

Gentlemen, are you to doom me to an ignominious death upon such evidence as this? Can you reconcile the difference between the statements of Hunt and Probert? And yet these men have been running a race to be admitted as approvers—these men have put up their evidence to auction, hoping to find a bribe in proportion to the length of their consciences. The evidence of Probert throughout clearly tends to shew that the proposal of murdering Mr. Weare was familiar to him. He tells you I informed him that I was going "to do" for Mr. Weare, "for he had robbed me of several hundreds." Can you believe that I was so egregious a fool as to make such a declaration to a person who was a previous stranger to such a transaction? Probert says, I told Mr. Weare to stop at certain places on the road; he was a stranger to that part of the country; and Mr. and Mrs. Probert both say, he never was at their cottage before. Mr. Weare was to be put down at an appointed place. Why? because Hunt and Probert thought that it was the most proper place to commit the murder. Look at Hunt's confession before the Magistrates, and Probert's evidence yesterday, and see whether they do not both say that this was the particular spot intended for the sanguinary deed. Is it credible that Probert would have induced a stranger to visit him at a house were he had no accommodation for company, unless he had some unfair design towards him? It is in evidence that Probert advanced twenty shillings to enable Hunt to go down by himself. He clearly did not take him in his gig, and in going down Hunt was allowed to purchase a loin of pork, and pay for it with Probert's money. Is not this the conduct of men who were going on a joint business? He said, I passed him four miles on the road, and he describes Hunt as having used some ambiguous remarks; and therefore I believe that Hunt and Probert enticed Mr. Weare near the fatal spot, and that I too was intended as their victim. I think it is clear that they had prepared themselves for this bloody business, by the quantity of brandy and water which they got on the road. Probert tells you that Hunt and I were to sleep at his house.—

According to Mrs. Probert's account, there was not sufficient accommodation for us. Why did he then invite me down? The motive is plain—why, in order to cast upon me the odium and the consequences of the guilty deed which he and Hunt had meditated. It must not be forgotten, that there was no spare bed without depriving Miss Noyes of her's Would you have done otherwise than he did? Is it not manifest that the object of bringing me there was to throw all suspicion from himself upon me? The conversation which Probert attributes to me on the night in question is utterly inconsistent with his own innocence Is it possible that I should have introduced matters of such great and awful danger to a man like Mr Probert, if he himself had no previous intimation on the subject? Mr. Probert, in his evidence, has not failed to press into the service the most gratuitous odium upon my character, and has invented things which could never have been said by me. He says I told him that I would murder Mr Barber Beaumont and Mr Woods—the latter being on the eve of marrying Mrs. Probert's sister, and then keeping company with her. If such had been my intention, is it credible that I should have mentioned such a subject to Mr. Probert, above all other persons? Observe now the difference between the evidence of Probert and that of his wife He says that I and Hunt went for the body and took it over Mr. Wardle's field near to the gate, and that we then dragged it to the bank of the pond. Mrs. P says that we took it into the stable and dragged it down the park walk from the stable to the pond. Probert said that we had no lantern; but Mrs Probert winds up this part of the story by saying that it was a fine moonlight night These are manifest contradictions, but they are still more obvious when you come to consider the local situation of the garden in which they lay this scene. The garden, as described by Probert, had a house on one side, and a stable on the other, which last was in such a situation that it was impossible for him to have seen what he describes Probert says that after this he went to bed immediately, and I beg you will bear it in mind that he also states that he did not get up till next morning at nine o'clock—a fact which is flatly contradicted by his servant boy. Probert states that he told me on Sunday that Mr. Nicholls knew all about this business, and that I then said, "I am baked," and yet after this warning I returned to town, to the place where I usually lived, and where I was well known, and could easily have been found at any time, and where, in fact, I was found. Mrs. Probert says that Hunt came down in dirty clothes, and that those very clothes, were seen on him on the Friday night, although, previously to his leaving London, I had lent him some of my brother's clothes, which he did not return to me till Tuesday, the day before my apprehension. Mr P has told you, in order to add weight to his testimony, that on the Monday I took his servant out of the way, that he might not answer questions, but the truth is, that the very next day Probert was to quit his cottage, having received a regular notice to quit from his landlord. Gentlemen, I will not disgust you by many more remarks upon this cold-blooded act. I cannot help persuading myself that the discrepancies I have already pointed out are quite sufficient to discredit such witnesses in your judgment; and I am sure at least you will receive with great caution the testimony of such a man as Probert. Between him and Hunt you will bear in mind that there has been a struggle who should obtain the mercy of the Crown. He has been admitted as an approver, and therefore every word of his testimony must be regarded with the strongest suspicion. You will observe, that after much prevarication, and after swearing in his examination in chief that he did not come down stairs on the Saturday morning till after nine o'clock, he refused to swear that it was so late as eight, although his servant boy swears it was seven when he came down. You will not fail to have remarked on the character of this witness. It was wrung from him by Mr. Andrews, that he had six or seven times been committed by the Commissioners under his bankruptcy, for perjury; you will not forget that he introduced Hunt to me, with an intention which is now too manifest. The disgusting affectation with which Mrs Probert gave her evidence is quite sufficient to lay her credit under the strongest suspicion; what faith can you put in the testimony of a female who confesses that she put round her neck the gold chain which had been plundered from the murdered man; and that after the sanguinary tragedy had been perpetrated, she called upon the blood-stained Hunt to sing her a song? You will recollect that this is the conduct of a *woman*—knowing that a murder had just been committed, and that the hand of the assassin, whom she called upon to sing, was still reeking with his victim's blood. The bare statement of this fact is sufficient to overwhelm her as a witness, and render her utterly unworthy of her sex. I must, however, call your attention to some of the facts which she has stated. She says she saw two men bring a horse to take the body out of the back gate; that some digging took place on the spot, and that she saw the body carried out. She also details a long conversation in whispers between herself and her husband, which, she says, took place at the distance of a flight of stairs from one door to another. In answer to a question put by the learned Judge, she says that this long conversation was after she had seen the digging, and yet her husband says that immediately after leaving the body he went to bed. Is it not clear, Gentlemen, that this whispering, pretended to have been overheard, was a scheme settled between Mr. and Mrs. Probert? I know not, but I believe most firmly, that the body never was in Probert's pond. From Mrs. Probert's description of what is called the garden and yard-gate, you will see that my statement is confirmed, as well also by the difference between her and her husband's statement, as to the bringing in of the body. I may here explain the circumstance of the supposed grave, by telling you that it was a potatoe field, and that the potatoes were taken away previously to Mr. Probert's leaving the cottage. Mr. Probert said that the body was stripped by the side of the pond, but I could not learn from the evidence on which side it was. In the print in *The Observer* Newspaper, of Nov. 9, it is represented to have been on the opposite side to where Mrs. Probert says she saw it dragging. From the evidence of Mr. Probert and others, it is clearly proved that Hunt hired the horse and gig, and got every thing ready on the occasion; and from the evidence of Fleet, it is found that Hunt took the shovel, which has been produced. Probert supplied the sovereign to pay Hunt's expences. I beg to call your serious consideration to the evidence of Mr. Clarke, the landlord of the White Lion at Edgeware. You will remember he states, that as he was returning home, he met a gig on the wrong side the road, and that at the same time a coach was passing, by the lamps of which he was enabled to distinguish my person. Does not your own experience prove this to be false? And I now hereby declare most solemnly, that it is utterly false. Is it possible that on a wide road, in a dark night, a man passing at a quick rate, being 30 yards off, could be able to distinguish the countenance of another in an opposite gig, by the lamps of a coach? Would not the lamps in such a case hinder, rather than assist the view? Does not every night's experience prove this? But the circumstance of my being on the off side, and having, as he says, a gentleman with me, is, I submit to you, the strongest proof that he could not catch a glimpse of my countenance. We all know, according to general principles, that when a witness tries to prove too much he fails in every particular. The testimony of Mr. Clarke is therefore not to be depended upon, and I shall be able to prove that he is a man on whom no reliance can be placed. I beg also, to draw your attention to the evidence of the hackney coachman who set Mr. Weare down at a quarter past four o'clock. You will please to recollect, that he said positively it was half-past four when the deceased left his coach—that he met him and assisted in carrying his bag. Now all the other witnesses say that I did not leave Mr Tetsall's till five. These facts prove that I could not be the man who met him, and establish the fact that some other person must have met the deceased. It is obvious, therefore, that this coachman is also introduced to assist in the conspiracy against me, and I have no doubt that, if he had been allowed to see me in prison, and I had been pointed out, he too, like the other witnesses, would have identified me. The witness, Freeman, says he met a gig in Gill's-Hill-Lane; before the Magistrates he said it was a yellow gig, but now he says he never did say so, although to my perfect recollection he did. The evidence of Mr Clarke's ostler proves that the night was so dark that it was impossible to distinguish any thing. Probert, who I am sure you will think unworthy of credit, says, if my recollection be correct—

Mr Justice PARK here interposed, and said, "Prisoner, I don't wish to interrupt you, but I don't wish you to deceive yourself by stating a fact which is not well founded. In the depositions taken before the Magistrates, which I have before me, it does not appear that the witness, Freeman asserted that it was a yellow gig, you have asserted that he did say so, but I cannot allow that to be said. Go on with your observations; I interrupted you for your own sake.

The Prisoner resumed—That is the strong impression on my mind, I assure your Lordship. The evidence of Probert is, that he left the Artichoke public-house 11 minutes before nine, but Mr Field says, that he left at a quarter-past seven. Taking this statement to be true, it is clear that Probert and Hunt had time enough to go to the top of

Gill's Hill-lane, and return to the Artichoke after they had perpetrated the murder, so as to enable them to throw the guilt upon the shoulders of any other person than their own Can you believe, or can any body believe, that Probert, without some enquiry, would have left his companion Hunt, on a dark night, at nine o'clock, half a mile from his own cottage? Is that possible, or can you be so much imposed upon as to believe it? No—I am satisfied you will not. I am satisfied you will consider this circumstance as sufficient to overrule Probert's statement, and without that there is no evidence to support the charge against me I must avert to the testimony of Mr. Clark's ostler. He stated, that two gentlemen arrived at his master's house, at a quarter past seven, that it was dark, and that he could not distinguish the countenances of either, and yet he takes upon himself to distinguish the countenance of one of the gentlemen, who the laundry maid said she believed was Mr Weare But, Gentlemen, there is no other person to prove this fact, there is no other person to prove that the gig did stop at his master's house. And, let me ask you, when this unhappy business was agitated, why did not the ostler come forward to offer his evidence at the Coroner's Inquest, or before the Magistrates? He certainly did not, and now he comes forward for the first time. I now declare, that, looking at Mr Clarke's evidence and the ostler's, it was impossible for me to have been seen by them. As to the evidence of the man who sold the pistols, I am sure you must be quite satisfied it does not at all identify me with this transaction. With respect to the evidence given by Upson and Forster, as to the conversation they have mentioned, certainly something of the kind did occur, but they have entirely mistaken the purport and nature of it I am quite certain, that the real meaning of any thing I might say, was no more than to express my disapprobation of the persons suspected, and to designate them by the word "scoundrel" If I had been in this horrible affair, I certainly would never have betrayed my companions. As to the watch, it might have been found, and if so, why did they not produce it?

My Lord and Gentlemen of the Jury,—I ought to rejoice that the circumstance alone on which the prosecutors rely in support of their case, afford the strongest evidence of my innocence. The case for the prosecution is founded entirely on circumstantial evidence. I have demonstrated to you that the circumstances proved do not point at me, as being concerned in the perpetration of this murder. But, Gentlemen, circumstantial evidence is at best but a fearful guide to human judgment. If human judgment is to be guided by circumstantial evidence alone, the greatest errors may be committed. Nothing can be more frail, more liable to deception and false conclusions than mere circumstances, which are at all times equivocal. In the annals of foreign and domestic jurisprudence, some of the most melancholy and dreadful instances are to be found of a too fatal adherence to the supposed infallability of circumstantial evidence. Among the former we find a father condemned to death, upon mere circumstances, for the supposed murder of a child, and a poor servant girl convicted of a theft, of which she was wholly guiltless, and among the latter, the instances are many. My Lord Hale, in his Pleas of the Crown, vol 2, p. 290, says—" I could never convict any person of murder or manslaughter unless the fact be proved to have been done, or at least the body of the dead man be found." The Learned Judge then mentions instances in illustration of the wisdom and humanity of this rule. One is from the authority of Lord Coke, who related a case as having occurred in Staffordshire, of a man charged with the murder of another, whose body was consumed to ashes in an oven, and the body not being found, the party was acquitted of the murder.—Another, from the same authority, was that of an uncle, charged with the murder of a niece, under suspicious circumstances, the child being missing, time was given to the accused to produce her at a given time, but having produced a supposititious child, he was convicted and executed, but it was afterwards proved that the real niece, upon her attaining the age of 21, had come forward and claimed her land. The truth was, that the child having been beaten by her uncle had run away, and at the period mentioned she came forward. This was a strong instance in verification of the principle laid down by the learned writer I have quoted. In the " Percy Anecdotes," the following instances are recorded :—

" In the reign of Elizabeth, a person was arraigned before Sir James Dyer, upon an indictment for the murder of a man who dwelt in the same parish with the prisoner. The first witness against him deposed, that on a certain day, as he was going through a close, which he particularly described at some distance from the path, he saw a person lying dead, and that two wounds appeared in his breast and his shirt and clothes were much stained with blood; that the wounds appeared to the witness to have been made with by the puncture of a fork, or some such instrument, and looking about, he discovered a fork lying near the corpse, which he took up, and observed it to be marked with the initials of the prisoner's name, here the witness produced the fork in court, which the prisoner owned to be his.—The prisoner waived asking the witness any questions.—A second witness deposed, that on the morning of the day on which the deceased was killed, the witness had risen very early with an intention of going to a neighbouring market-town, that as he was standing in the entry of his own dwelling-house, the street door being open, he saw the prisoner come by, dressed in a suit of clothes, the colour of which he described; that he, the witness, was prevented from going to market, and, that afterwards the first witness brought notice to the town, of the death and wounds of the deceased, and of the prisoner's fork being found near the corpse, that upon this report the prisoner was apprehended, and carried before a Justice; that he, this witness followed the prisoner to the Justice's house, and attended his examination, during which, he observed the exchange of clothes the prisoner had made, since the time he had seen him in the morning; that on the witness charging him with having changed his clothes, he gave several shuffling answers, and would have denied it, that upon witness mentioning this circumstance of change of dress, the Justice granted a warrant to search the prisoner's house for the clothes described by the witness, as having been put off since the morning; that this witness attended and assisted at the search, that after a nice search of two hours and upwards, the very clothes the witness had described, were discovered concealed in a straw bed. He then produced the bloody clothes in Court, which the prisoner owned to be his clothes, and to have been thrust in the straw bed with the intention to conceal them, on the account of their being bloody.—The prisoner also waived asking this second witness any questions.—A third witness deposed to his having heard the prisoner deliver certain menaces against the deceased, whence the prosecutor intended to infer a proof of *malice prepense* In answer to this, the prisoner proposed certain questions to the Court, leading to a discovery of the occasion of the menacing expressions deposed to, and from the witness's answer to those questions it appeared that the deceased had first menaced the prisoner.—The prisoner being called upon for his defence, addressed the following narration to the Court, as containing all he knew concerning the manner and circumstances of the death of the deceased; 'He rented a close in the same parish with the deceased, and the deceased rented another close adjoining to it; the only way to his own close was through that of the deceased, and on the day the murder in the indictment was said to be committed, he rose early in the morning, in order to go to work in his close with his fork in his hand, and passing through the deceased's ground, he observed a man at some distance from the path, lying down as if dead or drunk? he thought himself bound to see what condition the person was in, and on getting up to him he found him at the last extremity, with two wounds in his breast, from which much blood had issued. In order to relieve him, he raised him up, and with great difficulty set him on his lap; he told the deceased he was greatly concerned at his unhappy fate, and the more so as there appeared reason to think he had been murdered. He intreated the deceased to discover, if possible, who it was, assuring him he would do his best endeavours to bring him to justice. The deceased seemed to be sensible of what he said, and in the midst of his agonies attempted to speak to him, but was seized with a rattling in his throat, gave a hard struggle, then a dreadful groan, and vomiting a deal of blood, some of which fell on his (the prisoner's) clothes, he expired in his arms. The shock he felt on account of this accident was not to be expressed, and the rather, as it was well known that there had been a difference between the deceased and himself, on which account he might possibly be suspected of the murder. He therefore thought it adviseable to leave the deceased in the condition he was, and take no further notice of the matter; in the confusion he was in when he left the place, he took the deceased's fork away instead of his own which was by the side of the corpse. Being obliged to go to his work, he thought it best to shift his clothes, and that they might not be seen, he confessed that he had hid them in the place where they were found. It was true, he had denied before the justice that he had changed his clothes, being conscious that this was an ugly circumstance that might be urged against him, being unwilling to be brought into trouble if he could help it. He concluded his story with a most solemn declaration, that he had related nothing but the exact truth, without adding or diminishing one tittle, as he should answer for it to God Almighty '—Being then called upon to produce his witnesses, the prisoner answered with a steady, composed countenance, and resolution of voice, ' He had no witnesses but God and his own conscience '—The Judge then proceeded to deliver his charge, in which he pathetically enlarged on the heniousness of the crime, and laid great stress on the force of the evidence, which, although circumstantial only, he declared he thought to be irresistible, and little inferior to the most positive proof The prisoner had indeed cooked up a very plausible story, but if such or the like allegations were to be admitted in a case of this kind, no murderer would be ever brought to justice, such deeds being generally perpetrated in the dark, and with the greatest secrecy. The present case was exempted in his opinion from all possibility of doubt, and they ought not to hesitate one moment about finding the prisoner guilty. The foreman begged of his Lordship, as this was a case of life and death, that the Jury might withdraw; and upon this motion, an officer was sworn to keep the Jury locked up. The trial came on the first in the morning, and the Judge having sat till nine at night expecting the return of the Jury, at last sent an officer to enquire if they were agreed on their verdict. Some of them returned for answer, that 11 of their body had been of the same mind from the first, but that it was their misfortune to have a foreman, who, having taken up a different opinion from them, was unalterably fixed in it. The messenger had no sooner gone, than the complaining members, alarmed at the thought of being kept under confinement all night, and despairing of bringing their dissenting brother over to their own way of thinking, agreed to accede to his opinion, and having acquainted him with their resolution, they sent an officer to detain his Lordship a few minutes, and then went into Court, and by their foreman brought in the prisoner *Not-Guilty*. His Lordship could not help expressing the greatest surprise and indignation at this unexpected verdict; and after giving the Jury a severe admonition, he refused to record the verdict, and sent them back again, with directions that they should be locked up all night without *fire or candle*. The whole blame was publicly laid on the foreman by the rest of the members, and they spent the night in loading him with reflections, and bewailing their unhappy fate in being associated with so hardened a wretch. But he remained inflexible, constantly declaring he would rather suffer death, than change his opinion. As soon as his Lordship came into Court next morning, he sent again to the Jury, on which the eleven members joined in requesting their foreman to go into court, assuring him they would abide by their former verdict, whatever was the consequence; and on being reproached with their former inconstancy, they promised never to desert or recriminate upon their foreman any more. Upon these assurances they proceeded again into court, and again brought in the prisoner Not Guilty. The Judge, unable to conceal his rage at a verdict which appeared to him in the most iniquitous light, reproached them severely, and dismissed them with the cutting reflection *'That the blood of the deceased lay at their doors.'* The prisoner on his part fell down on his knees, and with uplifted eyes and hands to God, thanked him most devoutly for his deliverance; and addressing himself to the Judge, cried out *'You see my Lord that God and a good conscience are the best witnesses.'* The circumstance made a deep impression on the mind of the Judge, and as soon as he had retired from Court, he entered into conversation with the High Sheriff upon what had passed, and particularly examined him as to his knowledge of the foreman of the Jury. The High Sheriff answered his Lordship, that he had been acquainted with him many years; that he had a freehold estate of his own of above fifty pounds a year; and that he rented a very considerable farm besides; that he never knew him charged with an ill action, and that he was universally beloved and esteemed in his neighbourhood. For further information, his Lordship sent for the minister of the parish, who gave the same favourable account of his parishioner, with this addition, that he was a constant churchman and a devout communicant. These accounts increased his Lordship's perplexity, from which he could think of no expedient to deliver himself, but by having a conference in private with the only person who could give him satisfaction; this he requested the Sheriff to procure, who readily offered his service, and without delay brought about the desired interview. Upon the foreman of the Jury being introduced to the Judge, his Lordship retired with him into a closet, where his Lordship opened his reasons for desiring that visit, making no scruple of acknowledging the uneasiness he was under on account of the verdict, and conjuring his visitor frankly to discover his reasons for acquitting the prisoner. The Juryman returned for answer, that he had sufficient reasons to justify his conduct, and that he was neither ashamed nor afraid to reveal them; but as he had hitherto locked them up in his own breast, and was under no compulsion to disclose them, he expected his Lordship would engage upon his honour to keep what he was about to unfold to him a secret, as he himself had done. His Lordship having done so, the Juryman proceeded to give his Lordship the following account. The deceased being the titheman where he (the Juryman) lived, he had the morning of his decease been in his (the Juryman's) grounds, amongst his corn, and had done him great injustice by taking more than his due, and by acting otherwise in a most arbitrary manner. When he complained of this treatment he had not only been abused with scurrilous language, but the deceased had struck at him several times with his fork, and had actually wounded him in two places, the scars of which wounds he then shewed his Lordship. The deceased seemed bent on mischief, and the farmer, having no weapon to defend himself, had no other way to preserve his own life but by closing in with the deceased, and wrenching the fork out of his hands; which having effected, the deceased attempted to recover the fork, and in the scuffle received the two wounds which had occasioned his death. The farmer was inexpressibly concerned at the accident which occasioned the man's death, and especially when the prisoner was taken up on suspicion of the murder. But the Assizes being just over, he was unwilling to surrender himself and confess the matter, because his farm and affairs would have been ruined by his lying so long in gaol. He was sure to have been acquitted on his trial, for he had consulted the ablest lawyers upon the case, who all agreed that, at the deceased had been the aggressor, he could only have been guilty of manslaughter at most. It was true he had suffered greatly in his own mind on the prisoner's account; but, being well assured that imprisonment would be of less consequence to the prisoner than to himself, he had suffered the law to take its course. In order, however, to render the prisoner's confinement as easy to him as possible, he had given him every kind of assistance, and had wholly supported his family ever since. And, to get him clear of the charge laid against him, he had procured himself to be summoned on the Jury, and sat at the head of them; having all along determined in his own breast rather to die himself, than to suffer any harm to be done to the prisoner.' His Lordship expressed great satis-

P

faction on that account; and after thanking the farmer for it, and making this farther stipulation, that in case his Lordship should survive him, he might then be at liberty to to relate this fact, that it might be delivered down to posterity, the conference broke up. The Juryman lived, fifteen years afterwards, the Judge inquired after him every year, and happening to survive him, delivered the above relation."

"An upholsterer of the name of Shaw, who was residing at Edinburgh in 1721, had a daughter Catherine who lived with him, and who encouraged the addresses of Lawson, a jeweller, contrary to the wishes of her father, who urged his daughter to receive the addresses of a son of Robertson, a friend and neighbour. The girl refused most peremptorily. The father grew enraged, passionate expressions arose on both sides, and the words 'barbarity, cruelty, and death,' were frequently pronounced by the daughter. At length her father left her, locking the door after him. The apartment of Shaw was only divided by a slight partition from that of one Morrison, who had indistinctly heard the conversation and quarrel between Catherine and her father, and was particularly struck with the words she had pronounced so emphatically. For some time after the father had gone out, all was silent, but presently Morrison heard several groans from the daughter. He called in some of the neighbours, and these listening attentively, not only heard her groan, but also faintly exclaim—'*cruel father, thou art the cause of my death!*' Struck with the expression, they got a constable, and forced the door of Shaw's apartment, where they found the daughter weltering in her blood, and a knife by her side. She was alive, and speechless, but on questioning her as to owing her death to her father, she was just able to make a motion with her head, apparently in the affirmative, and then expired. At this moment, Shaw enters the room. All eyes are upon him. He sees his neighbours, and a constable in his apartment, and seems much disordered, but at the sight of his daughter, he turns pale, trembles, and is ready to sink. The first surprise, and the succeeding horror, leave little doubt of his guilt in the breasts of the beholders; and even that little is done away, on the constable discovering that the shirt of William Shaw is bloody. He was instantly hurried before a Magistrate, and, upon the deposition of the parties, committed for trial. In vain did he protest his innocence, and declare that the blood on his shirt was occasioned by his having blooded himself some days before, and the bandage having become untied. The circumstances appeared so strong against him, that he was found guilty, was executed, and hung in chains at Leith. His last words were, '*I am innocent of my daughter's murder*' There was scarcely a person in Edinburgh who thought the father innocent; but, in the following year, a man who had become the occupant of Shaw's apartment, accidentally discovered a paper which had fallen into a cavity on one side of the chimney. It was folded as a letter, and on opening it, was found to contain as follows:—" Barbarous father, your cruelty in having put it out of my power ever to join my fate to that of the only man I could love, and tyrannically insisting upon my marrying one whom I always hated, has made me form a resolution to put an end to an existence which is become a burthen to me." This letter was signed, " Catherine Shaw," and on being shown to her relations and friends, it was recognised as her writing. The Magistracy of Edinburgh examined it, and, on being satisfied of its authenticity, they ordered the body of William Shaw to be taken from the gibbet, and given to his family for interment; and, as the only reparation to his memory, and the honor of his surviving relations, they caused a pair of colours to be waved over his grave, in token of his innocence."

In the year 1736, Mr. Hayes in travelling, stopped at an inn in Oxfordshire, kept by one Bradford He there met with two gentlemen with whom he supped, and in conversation unguardedly mentioned that he had then with him a considerable sum of money. Having retired to rest, the two gentlemen, who slept in a double-bedded room, were awakened by deep groans in the adjoining chamber They instantly rose and proceeded silently to the room The door was half open, and on entering they perceived a person weltering in his blood, in the bed, and a man standing over him, with a dark lantern in one hand and a knife in the other. They soon discovered that the gentleman murdered was the one with whom they had supped, and that the man who was standing over him was their host. They instantly seized him, and charged him with being the murderer. He positively denied the crime, and stated that he came there with the same intentions as themselves; for that hearing a noise which was succeeded by groans, he got up, struck a light, and armed himself with a knife in his defence, and had but that minute entered the room before them. These assertions were of no avail, he was taken before a neighbouring Justice, to whom the evidence appeared so decisive, that on writing out his mittimus, he hesitated not to say, 'Mr. Bradford, either you or myself committed this murder.' At the ensuing assizes at Oxford, Bradford was tried, convicted, and shortly after executed; still, however, declaring that he was not guilty of the murder. This afterwards proved to be true; the murder was actually committed by Mr. Hayes's footman, who immediately on stabbing his master, rifled his pockets, and escaped to his own room, which was scarcely two seconds before Bradford entered the chamber. The world owes this knowledge to a remorse of conscience of the footman on his death-bed, eighteen months after the murder; and, dying almost immediately after he had made the declaration, justice lost its victim. It is however, remarkable, that Bradford, though innocent and not at all privy to the murder, was nevertheless a murderer in design. He confessed to the clergyman who attended him after his sentence, that having heard that Mr. Hayes had a large sum of money about him, he went to the chamber with the same diabolical intention as the servant. He was struck with amazement, he could not believe his senses; and in turning back the bed clothes to assure himself of the fact, he, in his agitation, dropped the knife on the bleeding body, by which both his hand and the knife became stained, and thus increased the suspicious circumstances in which he was found."

"In the year 1742, a gentleman was stopped by a highwayman in a mask, within about seven miles of Hull, and robbed of a purse, containing twenty guineas. The gentleman proceeded about two miles further, and stopped at the Bull Inn, kept by Mr. Brunell. He related the circumstance of the robbery, adding, that as all his gold was marked, he thought it probable that the robber would be detected. After he had supped, his host entered the room, and told him a circumstance had arisen which led him to think that he could point out the robber. He then informed the gentleman that he had a waiter, one John Jennings, whose conduct had long been very suspicious; he had long before dark sent him out to change a guinea for him, and that he had only come back since he (the gentleman) was in the house, saying he could not get change; that Jennings, being in liquor, he sent him to bed, resolving to discharge him in the morning; that at the time he returned him the guinea, he discovered it was not the same he had given him, but was marked, of which he took no further notice until he heard the particulars of the robbery, and that the guineas which the highwayman had taken were all marked. He added, that he unluckily had paid away the marked guinea, to a man who lived at some distance. Mr. Brunell was thanked for his information, and it was resolved to go softly to the room of Jennings, whom they found fast asleep; his pockets were searched, and from one of them was drawn a purse containing exactly 19 guineas, which the gentleman identified. Jennings was dragged out of bed, and charged with the robbery He denied it most solemnly; but the facts having been deposed to on oath, by the gentleman and Mr. Brunell, he was committed for trial So strong did the circumstances appear against Jennings, that several of his friends advised him to plead guilty, and throw himself on the mercy of the court. This advice he rejected; he was tried at the ensuing assizes, and the jury, without going out of court, found him guilty. He was executed at Hull a short time after, but declared his innocence to the very last. In less than twelve months after this event occurred, Brunell, the master of Jennings, was himself taken up for a robbery committed on a guest in his house, and the fact being proved on his trial, he was convicted and ordered for execution. The approach of death brought on repentance, and repentance confession Brunell not only acknowledged having committed many highway robberies, but also the very one for which poor Jennings suffered. The account he gave was, that after robbing the gentleman, he arrived at home some time before him. That he found a man at home waiting, to whom he owed a small bill, and not having quite enough of money, he took out of the purse one guinea from the twenty which he had just possessed himself of, to make up the sum, which he paid to the man who then went away. Soon after, the gentleman came to his house, and relating the account of the robbery, and that the guineas were marked, he became thunderstruck! Having paid one of them away, and not daring to apply for it again, as the affair of the robbery, and the marked guineas, would soon become publicly known, detection, disgrace, and ruin, appeared inevitable. Turning in his mind every way to escape, the thought of accusing and sacrificing poor Jennings at last struck him; and thus, to his other crimes, he added that of the murder of an innocent man."

"The case of M. de Pivardière is one of the most singular instances of criminal precipitation, that the annals of

French justice furnish Madame de Chauvelin, his second wife, was accused of having had him assassinated. Two servant maids were witnesses of the murder, his own daughter heard the cries and last words of her father—"My God! have mercy upon me!" One of the maid-servants falling dangerously ill, took the sacrament; and while she was performing this solemn act, declared before God that her mistress intended to kill her master.— Several other witnesses testified that they had seen linen stained with his blood, others declared that they heard the report of a gun, by which the assassination was supposed to have been committed. And yet, strange to relate, it turned out after all that there was no gun fired, no blood shed, nobody killed! What remains is still more extraordinary: M de la Pivardiere returned home; he appears in person before the Judges of the province, who were preparing every thing to execute vengeance on his murderer. The Judges are resolved not to lose their process, they affirm to his face that he is dead: they brand him with the accusation of imposture for saying that he is alive; they tell him that he deserves exemplary punishment for coining a lie before the tribunal of justice; and maintain that their procedure is more credible than his testimony! In a word, this criminal process continued eighteen months before the poor gentleman could obtain a declaration of the court that he was alive!

"The pen trembles in my hand," says Voltaire, "when I relate these enormities! We have seen, by the letters of several French lawyers, that not one year passes, in which one tribunal or another does not stain the gibbet or the rack with the blood of unfortunate citizens, whose innocence is afterwards ascertained when it is too late."

The prisoner next adverted to the case of Colman, who was tried for murder in 1748. He was identified by a number of witnesses, as having been seen in a cross-road, where a servant girl was murdered, the girl herself lived nine or ten weeks after the murder, and she herself swore positively to Coleman, who was tried and executed.

This case was to be found in the "Newgate Calender" In 1751, Welsh and Jones, were tried for this same woman, Sarah Green, and they both acknowledged that Colman was innocent of the murder The account was too tedious to read, and some of the details too disgusting, he should not therefore trouble the Jury with it. And now, Gentleman, continued the prisoner, having brought these cases under your view, am I not justified in solemnly warning you against giving to circumstances, a weight to which they are not entitled? Though circumstances may be considered and balanced, am I not justified in submitting to you, that unless they are entirely irreconcileable with my innocence, their weight ought to be small against me? Am I not justified in saying, that in justice to me, and with a due regard to your own consciences, that you may discharge your duty with satisfaction to yourselves, you are bound to consider whether all the circumstances which have been brought forward in evidence, might not exist, and yet the individual who is now addressing you, be innocent of the murder? These circumstances are consistent with—I might almost say they prove my innocence of this detested crime. Have I not a right then to call upon you, not only to confer upon me the benefit of a doubt, or of that presumption of law, which supposes every man to be innocent, until he is proved to be guilty; but under the guidance of an unbiassed and candid judgment, to do an act of justice to yourselves, to the public, and to myself, by dismissing me from this bar, by your verdict of acquital? Remember, Gentlemen, my existence hangs upon your breath. If you should not feel fully assured of my innocence, if you should even have a doubt of my guilt, the law gives me, and your own hearts will give me the benefit of that doubt. Cut me not off—I implore it of your justice, of your humanity—in the very summer of my youth. I implore it not for myself, but for the sake of those whose memory is unsullied; for the sake of those whose character accusation never stained; for the sake of their home, a happy home, which my death will render desolate. However, I look forward, whatever may be the result of this solemn inquiry, with a sweet complacency of mind, arising from a conscience void of guilt. Assisted by the Divine Power, I feel supported by the consciousness of having ever acted on humane, just, and honourable principles. I know myself incapable of committing an ill action, much less such a dreadful crime as that which is laid to my charge. I trust there is not a spectator in Court who does not believe these emotions to be the genuine inmates of my breast. If there be any, I would address them in the language of the Apostle, "Would to God they were altogether such as I am, save these bonds." Gentlemen of the Jury, in your hands, I repeat it, are placed my honour and my existence—the hopes and fears of my family—all that is most dear to man. I feel sensible, that those sacred interests can be no where so safely reposed, as in the breasts of a free and independent British Jury, the pride and boast of our country, and the envy of the world. I stand before you as before my God, overwhelmed with misfortunes, but unconscious of crime; and while you decide on my future destiny, I earnestly intreat you to remember my last solemn declaration; I am innocent, so help me God!"

The prisoner delivered the conclusion of this address with an energy and apparent intensity of feeling, which made a manifest impression upon all who heard it. His manner was throughout characterised by perfect propriety. He read the extracts with considerable skill; laying particular stress upon such parts of the several narratives as were calculated to make an impression. His voice was firm, distinct, and marked by a slight provincial accent. In reading that part of one of the Percy Anecdotes, in which the party accused is said to have thrown himself upon his knees, when he heard the verdict of acquittal, and to have thanked God for his deliverance, Thurtell appeared to be considerably affected. He wiped away a few 'natural drops' from his eyes, and soon resumed his characteristic firmness and self-possession

EVIDENCE FOR THE PRISONER, JOHN THURTELL.

SAMUEL WADESON was then called, and examined by Mr. ANDREWS. I am a solicitor; in the course of my professional practice I became acquainted with Mr. Probert in July 1818; I was concerned for his creditors; he was examined by me before the Commissioners of Bankruptcy, he underwent six or seven examinations, and on each occasion was committed; I have no hesitation in saying, that I would not believe him on his oath, unless supported by additional testimony.

LANGDON HAYDON examined by Mr. PLATT; I am a land surveyor and auctioneer; I have known J. Thurtell for some years; I never heard any thing against his character for humanity; I have always thought him a liberal, kind and good hearted man.

Mr. Justice PARK. When did you cease to have any intercourse with him?—I have never lost sight of him.

Captain JOHN M'KINLAY, examined by Mr. ANDREWS. I am a Captain in the Navy; John Thurtell was under my command from the year 1812 to 1814 I was at that time

Captain of the Bellona; he was always correct in his conduct; I never saw any thing bad in it; I never heard any thing against his character for humanity.

By Mr. Justice PARK. I have known nothing of him since the year 1814.

JOSEPH WALMESLEY, examined by Mr. CHITTY. I am an officer for the Sheriff of Middlesex. I have known John Thurtell for the last three years; I have frequently been in his company; I always thought him a humane, quiet, peaceable, well-disposed man.

The Counsel for the prisoner Thurtell having intimated that they had no more witnesses to call, the prisoner Hunt was now asked whether he had any thing to say in his defence?

The Prisoner. My Lord, I have a defence to make, but from extreme anxiety of mind, I do not feel myself competent to read it.

Mr. Justice PARK. Let the officer of the Court read it.

" My Lord—Having, under a positive assurance that I should be admitted a witness for the Crown, made a full confession of all the facts within my knowledge, and having implicitly relied on the good faith of the Magistrates for the due performance of their solemn promises, made previously and subsequent to my disclosure, I forbore to make the slightest preparation for my defence; and after your Lordship shall be made acquainted with all the circumstances under which that confession was drawn from me, your Lordship's heart will be able to appreciate, although I am unable to describe, the painful emotions of surprise and disappointment by which I was overwhelmed, when, only a few days before the Assizes, it was notified to me, for the first time, that I was to be placed in my present perilous and awful situation.

" Your Lordship will perceive that the very circumstance which I was told would ensure my safety, has alone rendered me amenable to the laws—namely, my own disclosures and declarations; for although the prosecutors may not offer my confession in evidence, yet, as that confession has been published in every newspaper, and has been circulated in many thousand pamphlets, and been the subject of universal conversation, is it probable, or even possible, that any of the gentlemen who are now sitting in judgment on my case can be ignorant that such a confession has been made? How futile, then, and unavailing would be any arguments to raise a presumption of the innocence of a man, who already, to a certain extent, stands self-condemned? Feeling myself in this dilemma, I shall abstain from troubling your Lordship with any detail of facts or observations upon the main question involved in the indictment, but merely assert, that I was not present when the unfortunate deceased lost his life, and that I was ignorant of any premeditated plan to destroy him; I never knew of the murder until after it was committed, my crime consists solely in concealment; and my discovery could not bring the dead to life; my error arises, not from any guilt of my own, but from my concealment of the guilt of others I am now on my trial for having been privy to the previous design—I never was, I certainly concealed it afterwards, sooner than betray the misfortune which had been confided to me. Your Lordship, however, will, I am sure, tell the gentlemen of the Jury that no concealment or conduct of mine after the death will make out the present charge, and I hope both your Lordship and these gentlemen are too just and merciful to convict me from prejudice, and not from proof.

"I now, my Lord, most respectfully solicit your humane attention to the following statement—

"On the morning of Wednesday, 29th of October, I was apprehended in London, and directly conveyed to Watford, where an investigation was going on respecting the then supposed murder of Mr. Weare. On my arrival I found several Magistrates assembled, and Mr Noel, who was apparently conducting the prosecution, addressed me as follows:—" Mr. Hunt, for God's sake, tell the Magistrates whatever you know of this murder, and in all probability you will be admitted as an evidence It is clear that Mr Weare has been murdered, and we only want to find where the body is, and if you know, for God's sake tell us" I repeatedly denied all knowledge of the circumstance, and Mr. Noel as frequently importuned and urged me to confess. At last the Magistrates said, "Mr. Hunt, you had better retire and consider the offer made to you, and recollect your perilous situation." I was then conveyed into another room, and was presently followed by Mr Noel, who in the presence of Ruthven and Upson, repeatedly told me that if I would tell where the body was (provided I did not actually commit the murder), that I should be admitted as an evidence, and my life would be spared; and added, that the Magistrates had authorized him to make a pledge to this effect. Still, however, I was firm in my denial, and continued so until Upson, the officer, tortured my feelings, by the mention of my family. He said to me, "Hunt, you have a mother?" I answered, 'Yes, I have.' "And a wife also?" I said, 'Yes.' "And you love them dearly?" I answered, 'Yes, very dearly.' Then, said he, "For their sakes do not risk suffering an ignominious death, but tell where the body is, and give your evidence immediately, or you may be too late, for Probert or the other will disclose, and then nothing can save you."

" This address had a great effect upon me, and Noel perceiving it, again pressed me, saying, 'Do not hesitate, for you have now a chance; consider the situation you are in, and avail yourself of the offer now made you, for I am authorised by the Magistrates to say, that you will be admitted as an evidence for the Crown, and not treated as the others. You will merely be confined until the trial, to give your evidence, and then be discharged.' On receiving this assurance I consented to become a witness, and Mr. Noel then asked me if I knew where the body was? I told him yes, that I could not describe the place by name, but I could point it out; on which Mr. Noel struck his hand on the table, and exclaimed, 'That's all we want,' and shaking me by the hand, said, 'Hunt, I am very glad you have saved your own life.' We now returned into the room, where the Magistrates were, and Mr. Noel told them I was ready to make a disclosure, and said, I have made known to him, by your orders, that if he discovers where the body is, he is to be admitted as an evidence but, before he says any thing, I wish him to have that assurance in your presence, that he may be satisfied from yourselves that I was authorized to make the promise. The Magistrates, Mr. Clutterbuck and Mr. Mason, replied, that Mr. Noel had their authority for what he had done, and then Mr. Noel said, 'Now, Mr Hunt having heard the Magistrates decision as to your being a witness, I hope that you are satisfied, and I beg you will take a seat, and tell us all you know.' I then detailed every thing that occurred to my recollection, but having been apprehended early on the preceding day, conveyed into the country, and harassed and importuned throughout the night, it could hardly be expected that I should, at 4 or 5 o'clock in the morning, in making a very long statement, recollect every circumstance: indeed, the Magistrates were aware that such could not be the case, and they told me, that as in the hurry and confusion of the moment I had no doubt omitted many facts, that I should afterwards on reflection recollect, and if such should be the case, I had only to address a letter to the Magistrates, and they would immediately attend to it. Shortly after quitting the room, several particulars came to my recollection which I had not named, and I directly sent for Mr Noel and mentioned them to him. At nine o'clock the same morning, I went with the officers and pointed out the spot where the body had been deposited; I was then taken back by the Magistrates to sign my statement, and previous to my being taken to prison, Mr. Clutterbuck desired that I should be treated with kindness, and not put under any unnecessary restraint. I was accordingly conveyd to St. Albans without being ironed or handcuffed, and was there treated with every possible indulgence.

"On being taken before the Coroner, I experienced very different treatment; but still I had no intimation given me that I was not to be admitted as a witness for the Crown, until just before the present indictment was found.

"It is perfectly true, that when before the Coroner I was admonished to make no farther confession; but the admonition was a mockery; I had already, under a solemn promise, confessed every thing material; and the Coroner himself, when he thus affected to forwarn me, well knew that he and his Jury were that instant sitting in inquest on the body solely in consequence of my disclosure; no Jury could have sat—no death could have been proved—no body could have been found—no trial could have been had, but for my instrumentality. I was trepanned into a confession by the plighted faith of the Magistracy of this county. If they break it now, they will not merely make me the victim of its violation, but they will be answerable to society for every future crime against the discovery of which their conduct will be an eternal admonition. Who can confide in promises hereafter? Who can rest his life on Magisterial assurances? To no human being can they ever pledge themselves more sacredly than to me; yet here I stand to-day a proof of their sincerity—nay more than this—not only have they broken faith and violated honour, but while the press was unceasing in the excitement of prejudice—while the theatre and the painter were employed in poisoning the public mind—while every engine was at work to diminish the chances of an impartial trial, these very men, who had thus ensnared me by perfidious declarations, closed their prison door against friends and legal advisers, and opened them only to the mandate of the King's Bench. Thus was I first ensnared, and afterwards sought to be sacrificed Seduced into a confession, which was trumpeted through the world, and then cruelly secluded until the time arrived when I was to suffer,—not for my crime, but my credulity; not because I erred, but because I trusted; not because I violated the law, but because I confided in the conscience of its ministers. It is in vain to say that my confession was not complete; it was as ample as could have been expected at the moment, from an exhausted frame and agitated mind. It was subsequently amended, where it was at first deficient; and no sophistry can evade the fact, that through that confession alone the body was discovered. Thus, then, the main circumstance, that on which every thing turned, was disclosed at once; and it is absurd to attribute to aught but momentary confusion, any minor concealment, when the great, essential, and indispensable developement had taken place.

"As a proof that even the Coroner himself considered my confession so ample as to ensure my pardon, and that in his mind, notwithstanding his admonition, the promise of the Magistracy ought to be held inviolate, hear his own words to Mr. Nicholls, one of the witnesses—" The consequence of your delay has been the escape of Hunt from justice; for he has been admitted a witness for the crown, by the Magistrates, as they were afraid the body was disposed of. Now what did these words mean, if the Coroner was not convinced that I had merited and ensured my pardon?

"The prosecutors, my Lord, may affect to say, that as they refused to grant me the boon promised for the disclosure, they will decline using, or taking any advantage of the confession, and I humbly submit that such a line of conduct would alone be consistent with justice and fair dealing; for if they retract their engagement, they ought not to place me in a worse situation than I was in at the first moment, when, confiding in their integrity, I unbosomed the secret. If the prosecutors act with liberality, and forbear to offer a tittle of evidence respecting the body, and, in conducting the case, consider it as still undiscovered, I can have no cause to complain of plighted faith and broken promises, because your Lordship need not be reminded that it has been laid down as a principle that no death can be considered as proved unless the body be found, and consequently in this case no conviction can take place. But if witnesses are produced to prove the finding of the body, can it be said that my confession is not taken advantage of? and will not the prosecutors be taunting me by an affectation of candour, if they take credit for not giving in evidence any declaration made by me, while they avail themselves of the very essence and substance of the communication?

"In confirmation of the promises made to me by the Magistrates and Mr. Noel, I beg to refer to a statement which the latter gentleman has published in the newspapers; wherein he says, 'It is now incumbent on me to state, the reasons for the offer of mercy held out to Hunt,' and then he thus proceeds 'Notwithstanding the most diligent searches for the body, no discovery had been made of it as late as four o'clock past midnight of Thursday morning, the 30th of October, the sixth day after the murder, and at that hour the informations and investigations had terminated with no clue whatever to the real person murdered.' Mr Noel next describes his invitations to me to make a disclosure, with a view to my being admitted as an approver, his desiring me to retire to consider of his proposal, and after I had left the room, he says he addressed the Magistrates as follows:—" Gentlemen, if you do not approve of the offer of mercy held out to Hunt, say so, and I will go to him. Recollect, without the body is found, notwithstanding the strong evidence against one of the parties, we shall do nothing, and Mr. Clutterbuck and Mr Mason both gave unqualified approbation to my mode of examination, and of the offer of mercy held out to Hunt.'

"And in another part of Mr Noel's statement he says, 'Not only at Watford, but at the inquest, it was the general opinion of Mr. Mason and the Magistrates, that the body might have remained concealed in Hill's Slough, the place where it was found (a distance of three miles and a half from the spot where the murder was committed) until it had been decomposed, and beyond the possibility of identifying; and such was the insignificance of the slough, that persons employed to drag all pits, ponds, &c would have passed by it, and therefore they were confirmed in their opinion as to the policy and propriety of sanctioning my offer of mercy to Hunt; and previous to the offer being made, it was our united opinion that the corpse had been removed to London and probably thrown into the Thames, either entire or piecemeal,

"In addition to this statement, Mr. Noel inserts a letter from Mr. Clutterbuck to himself, in which the Magistrate observes, that as my case was then gone out of the hands of the Magistrates, all that could be done for me, was to ask of the Court, whether they would allow me to be evidence for the Crown.

"Having now, my Lord, faithfully stated the inducements by which I was led to make that disclosure, which alone rendered myself and my fellow-prisoners amenable to justice, I respectfully submit to your Lordship, whether, in being now put upon my trial, and made the victim of my own credulity, I have been fairly and candidly dealt with. I will not, my Lord, attempt to point out or discuss the mischiefs likely to arise if such engagements as were entered into with me are to be cancelled at pleasure, because they will occur much more forcibly to your Lordship's enlightened mind: indeed, so far as I am individually concerned, my fate is a subject of trifling importance. I have no desire to prolong a wretched existence, unless it be to afford the opportunity of endeavouring, by prayer and penitence, to obtain mercy and forgiveness of the Almighty, for the sins and transgressions I have committed. But in pity to the feelings of an aged and respectable mother, a virtuous and amiable wife, and my dearly beloved brother and sister, I do feel most anxious to avoid an ignominious death; and it is therefore for their sakes, more than for my own, that I fervently and earnestly entreat the performance of the solemn pledge made to me of sparing my life. I have nothing further to add, but most humbly repose my fate to the justice and humanity of your Lordship."

This paper having been read by the clerk, the prisoner, Hunt, said he wished to add another observation, which he proceeded to read from a written paper. The greatest part of Probert's evidence is false, and particularly where he endeavours to screen himself, and save his own life by inventing falsehoods to destroy mine. One circumstance which he stated must evidently be false, I mean where he pretends to point out the place at which he says I wished to be put down. I was never in that place in my life, and how is it possible that he could be acquainted with the place, especially as it was very intricate, and the light extremely bad?

The prisoner, Hunt, called no witness in his defence.

Mr. Rooke, the Coroner, was then called by Mr Justice Park, to prove that Gill's Hill Lane, the spot where the body was found, is situated in the County of Hertford.

CHARGE TO THE JURY.

Mr. Justice PARK then addressed the Jury to the following effect—

Gentlemen of the Jury, this important case has justly occupied a very considerable portion of our time. It is a case of the deepest importance both to the prisoners at the bar, and to the public. The prisoners are indicted in the following manner: John Thurtell as the principal felon, or the man who committed the murder; the other, as having aided, stirred up, moved, abetted, procured, consulted, and directed John Thurtell in the prosecution of the murder, or, in legal language, as having been an accessary before the fact. It has been properly said that if the prisoner, Joseph Hunt, were only guilty of concealment of the murder after the death of the deceased, though he would be a wicked and a despicable character, still he would be only what is termed in law an accessary after the fact, and not accessary before the fact, and he cannot be convicted under this indictment. This question, like all questions of inquiry into the death of man, is of the greatest public importance; for the law of England deems so highly of human life, that every killing of another is held to be murder, unless the person accused can prove such circumstances of alleviation as to reduce the offence from murder to manslaughter. In the present case, the question does not turn on that point at all. The single question in this case is, whether John Thurtell committed the fact; because it is not pretended, that if he killed the deceased, the act could be justified, and the defence of the prisoner is, that he did not commit the fact. There is a distinction between the cases of the two prisoners, although there is no distinction as to the legal consequences of the offence with which they are charged, because an accessary before the fact is by positive statute placed on the same footing with respect to punishment as the actual perpetrator of the murder. There is, however, this distinction between the cases of the two prisoners, that if you should think the evidence not sufficient to affect John Thurtell, you need not trouble yourselves with any further inquiry as to Joseph Hunt; for as Joseph Hunt is only indicted for having aided and counselled John Thurtell in the murder with which he is charged, if you are of opinion that John Thurtell did not commit it, you cannot of course find Joseph Hunt guilty of aiding and counselling him. There is also this difference in their cases, that though you should be of opinion that John Thurtell is guilty of the murder, it does not necessarily follow that the other is guilty of aiding and counselling him, for this must depend on distinct and independent proof. I have endeavoured to explain these distinctions to you, with as much clearness as possible, and I trust I have succeeded in making myself understood. There are some circumstances, however, and especially the defence of the prisoner Thurtell, which I wish to notice before I go into the evidence, which it is my intention to do most minutely, and at the same time, as far as my judgment goes, to give you my opinion on every point. Gentlemen, the greater part of what was said by John Thurtell in his defence, did him great credit, I must, except indeed some part of what he said, but I allude particularly to his observations at the commencement and close of his defence. This part of his defence, which I take to be his own, did him great credit. It was manly, energetic, and proper. I cannot help saying, however, (although every body who knows me, knows that I never go out of my way to say any thing harsh or severe of any body), that I did not admire the judgment or those who advised him to introduce the middle part of his address. If the first and last part of his address had any effect—and it could not fail to have an effect upon every sensible mind—that effect must have been weakened by the dreadfully long quotations which he was advised to introduce from such books as the Percy Anecdotes, and Newgate Calendar, which, for any thing I know to the contrary, may be mere books of romance. In the opinion quoted from the immortal writings of Lord Hale, I fully concur; and I have myself acted upon it since I had the last pleasure of meeting you in this Court. In fact, no Judge, who knew any thing of his profession, ever doubted about the opinion to which I allude, namely, that before a man can be convicted of murder, it is necessary to prove that the person whose death is laid to his charge, is, in point of fact, a dead man.—The opinion quoted from the immortal writings of Lord Hale, could receive no additional weight from the farrago which was put into the prisoner's hands. I do not blame the prisoner for this, but the persons who counselled and advised him to take such a course. With respect to the observations which were addressed to you on the subject of circumstantial evidence, if the doctrine for which the prisoner was advised to contend, were carried to its full extent, there would be an end of the judicature of man. The eye of omniscience can alone see the truth in all cases, circumstantial evidence is there probably out of the question, but clothed as we are with the infirmities of human nature, how are we to get at the truth without a concatenation of circumstances? Though in human judicature, imperfect, as it must necessarily be, it sometimes happens, perhaps, in the course of one hundred years, that in a few solitary instances, owing to the minute and curious circumstances which sometimes envelope human transactions, error has been committed from a reliance on circumstantial evidence; yet this species of evidence, in the opinion of all who are most conversant with the administration of justice, and most skilled in judicial proceedings, is much more satisfactory than the testimony of a single individual, who swears that he has seen a fact committed. With respect to the man Probert, I think it necessary to declare in the outset, that a more infamous character never presented himself in a Court of Justice. The testimony of the respectable Solicitor, who declared that he would not believe Probert upon his oath, unless, as he judiciously added, confirmed by other evidence, does not make Probert half so infamous as his own testimony has made himself; since it is more wicked to conceal the death of a murdered friend, than to have committed perjury before the Commissioners of Bankrupts. I will assume what was said by Thurtell in his defence, that such a man as Probert might have a bad motive for charging him with the crime, but this very circumstance ought to make us more comfortable under the necessity which is imposed upon us of resorting to circumstantial evidence. Probert and one or two more bad men might have entered into a conspiracy, but it is impossible that the 53 individuals who were witnesses in this indictment, many of whom never heard of Thurtell, or knew any thing of his person, should have entered into a conspiracy, to bring the charge home to the prisoner at the bar. If, therefore, circumstantial evidence was ever useful, it must be eminently so in a case like the present. It has been said, that circumstantial evidence should always be received with doubt; it ought undoubtedly to be received with caution, and so indeed should all human testimony. Why are you, Gentlemen, and myself, placed in the situation which we now fill, but to use all the faculties which God has given to us, to prevent the punishment of innocence, and effect the detection of guilt? You are not to reject circumstantial, any more than direct testimony, and I doubt not, that you will weigh all the evidence which has been submitted to you, and so pronounce upon it as will satisfy your own consciences, as just, honourable, and religious men. Another most distressing circumstance in this case is, the prejudice which has been raised against the prisoners through the Press, of which they have both complained, and which nobody can gainsay. It is quite painful to one's feelings to think of it. I said just now, and I repeat it, that every body who knows me, knows that I never go out of my way to say a harsh word of any human being, but I should consider myself unworthy of the seat I occupy—I should think myself open to impeachment, if I did not, whenever my duty called upon me, fearlessly and manfully discharge that duty. I hope I care not for the face of man, whether high or low. The whole artillery of libel shall never for a moment induce me to depart from what I conscientiously consider to be the line of my duty. The prisoners have been obliged in their defence to press this point on your attention; they have been compelled to appeal to you, to warn you, to beseech you, if ever you have heard or read any accounts of this painful and melancholy transaction, to dismiss them from your minds, as you would a pestilence. It is these statements of evidence before trial, which corrupt the purity of the administration of justice in its source, and if they are not checked, I tremble for the fate of our country. It is the boast, and justly the boast of the constitution of this country, that an important part of the administration of its justice is placed in such hands as yours. You have called God to witness, that as you do justice between the King and the prisoners at the bar, so you will answer to your God, and call upon him for help; but how can you adequately discharge this solemn duty, if your minds have been previously poisoned by the publication of what is, in fact, no evidence at all? If it be true, of which, however, I personally know nothing, that a supposed confession of Hunt has been published and read in all the public papers—if this be true, can any thing be conceived which is calculated to have a more dreadful effect on the administration of justice? Here is a confession published as coming from the mouth of one of the prisoners, and purporting to be a solemn declaration of the facts, which confession has not been even tendered to me by the Counsel for the Crown, and which, if it had been tendered, I should have rejected.—Is the public mind to be poisoned by the publication of what the judicial authorities of the country cannot consider as admissible in evidence? It is certainly a most grievous circumstance. It has thrown a great deal of additional labour upon me by bringing me here a second time to try this case; but my regard for justice induces me to waive that consideration. I did not think it fair, after hearing the affidavit which was read in Court, to put the prisoners upon their trial, and I have the satisfaction of knowing, that the course which I adopted has received the sanction of my brethren, whom I have since consulted. I have no doubt, from what I have seen and known of some of you, that no newspaper publications, no lampoons, libels, or calumnies, will have the least effect on your minds, either for or against the prisoners, and that you will do your duty as you are to answer for it to God. I have thought it necessary, Gentlemen, to make some observations on the point which was urged by one of the prisoners, as to the effect of circumstantial evidence. There was another point urged by the other prisoner, which has already been the subject of a motion made before me, and which is entitled to more consideration. No argument has been urged in the written defence of the prisoner Hunt, which was not as ably enforced by his Counsel in the motion to which I allude; but I have already stated, that there was no valid ground which could induce me to put off the trial, to give time for an application to the Crown; and, however powerful the arguments which might be urged as a ground for such an application, I could not consistently with my duty act upon them. If the confession of the prisoner were made under such circumstances as have been stated by his Counsel, and it had been tendered to me in evidence, I should have rejected it immediately; I could not and would not have received it. I excuse the prisoner for any erroneous vision he may entertain upon a point of law, but he has competent legal advisers, and those advisers know well enough that a confession obtained by saying to the party " you had better confess," or " it will be worse for you if you do not confess," is not legal evidence. But though such a confession is not legal evidence, it is every day's practice, that if in the course of such a confession the party state where stolen goods, or a body may be found and they are found accordingly, this evidence, because the fact of finding proves the truth of the allegation, and his evidence in this respect is not vitiated by the hope or threats which may have been held out to him. This part of the statement which Hunt is said to have made would have been legal evidence, and no greater hardship, therefore, is suffered by the young man, than by every man who has been heretofore tried The objection which has been made is one of which neither you nor I can take notice. It is a matter which rests with a higher authority than mine, high as mine is in this particular situation I have no power to entertain it, and I am bound therefore to submit his case to you. The main body of this charge rests upon the testimony of Probert and his wife, and it is necessary, therefore, that I should clearly point out to you what the law of England is on the subject of accomplices —When an accomplice is put into the box to prove any facts, he charges himself with the same crime, be it robbery, or be it murder. In the latter, he is undoubtedly a murderer in a moral point of view, but as an accessary after the fact, he would be entitled to the benefit of clergy

By the law of England, Gentlemen, an accomplice is a competent witness. When such a witness is presented, it is for the Judge to decide upon his competency, and the Jury are to consider the degree of credibility to which he is entitled. In the present instance, I admitted—I was bound to admit Probert as a competent witness, but I call upon you not to credit one word of his evidence, unless you find his testimony corroborated, I do not say it is necessary that he should be corroborated upon every statement, for in such transactions there are generally some facts which are known only to the perpetrators, and cannot be got, save through the medium of an accomplice, it is on this ground, and on this ground only, that the law makes an accomplice a competent witness. If, therefore, you find Probert corroborated upon the main points, by credible witnesses, it is my duty to tell you that you are bound to give credit to his testimony The prisoner Thurtell has in the course of his defence made some very sensible and proper observations upon the evidence, and to which, I also accede, but I cannot accede to the assertion, that because you find Probert to be a bad character. you are therefore bound to discredit his testimony altogether. Mr. Wadeson has told you, and I think in telling you so he has given a very fair definition of the law on the case, that he would not believe Probert upon his oath, unless his evidence was corroborated by respectable testimony This, Gentlemen, is exactly what I call upon you to do It is of deep importance to the well being of society, that the evidence of accomplices should be received upon certain occasions, otherwise many a dark and criminal deed would go unpunished. When evil-minded men confederate together for criminal purposes, we always find that their friendship is hollow, and of short duration. Their confederacy is a confederacy of vice, and the moment danger approaches, each seeks his own safety, reckless of the fate of his companions. Gentlemen, it is well for society that it is so, otherwise it would be difficult to check their course of iniquity. It appears from the affidavit of Hunt himself, that he was acquainted with the facts, and that in consequence of the advice of an attorney, who seems to have acted a most unwarrantable and unjustifiable part upon this occasion, he ran to tender his evidence to the Magistrates, as if from a fear that some one else would be before him. I said before, and I now repeat the assertion, that the Magistrates have no power to enter into, or make any such compact with an accused person. It is for the Counsel for the Crown to apply to the Court to have an accomplice admitted as evidence. Besides, it appears that the depositions of Hunt were not taken before the Magistrates upon oath, but only by word of mouth, and therefore it is clear that he was not accepted by them as a witness for the Crown. But even had his depositions been taken upon oath, still it would remain for the Judge to decide upon the propriety of admitting him as an evidence for the Crown. The first witness called was a man named Beeson. (Here the Learned Judge proceeded to read the evidence of the first witness, after which, he pointed out to the Jury a plan of the ground, the roads, the pond, &c.) Gentlemen, you were told that a body was found in a pond, and here I feel it necessary to refer to the inference in law, as laid down by my Lord Hale, whose steps I have ever humbly endeavoured to follow, that unless the body be found, or the fatal blow be seen to be given, it is impossible to support a charge of murder. In this case I felt it necessary to have it proved that the body found was the body of Mr. Weare. This fact you will find proved to you by Rexworthy and the brother of the deceased. You have it also proved to you by the testimony of Mr. Ward, the surgeon, who gave his evidence in a manner highly creditable to him as a professional man, and as a gentleman, that the wounds inflicted on the deceased were sufficient to cause death. In the indictment there are two counts, the first charging the prisoners with having caused the death of Mr Weare by thrusting a pistol into his head; the second with having caused his death by cutting his throat with a sharp instrument; so that, if it be proved to you, that the death was caused by the prisoners in the one way or in the other, they are equally guilty Now, Gentlemen, we come to the grand question—namely, by whom was the murder committed? And here I feel it necessary to state, that an accessary before the fact, is equally guilty with the principals. You have it in evidence that Hunt was not present at the actual murder. If two or more persons set out to do a criminal act, and if the act be performed by one only, the accomplices are equally guilty with the principal; and it is laying a most flattering unction to the soul to entertain a contrary opinion. We may, Gentlemen, come to the evidence of Probert, whom I wish you to consider as the basest of men, but whose testamony, if corroboratad, you are bound to receive. The officer who arrested Thurtell says, that he found a pistol and pistol screw in his coat pocket. Now, attend to the corroboration upon this point. The pawnbroker's boy, a disinterested witness, tells you that he sold the pistol and another like it, and a pistol screw, to the prisoner Thurtell and another, whom he described as a tall man and a short one, on the very day of the murder of Mr. Weare. He swears also to the other pistol found in Gill's-hill-lane, and having blood and hair upon it, and which perfectly corresponds with that found on Thurtell. On searching Hunt's lodgings, the officer found a backgammon-board, cards, and dice, a double-barrelled gun, some shirts, boots, stockings, and other things, all of which have been fully proved to you to have been the property of the late Mr Weare. This Gentlemen, is strong evidence to bring the prisoners Thurtell and Hunt together; and it is for you to consider whether the latter was not an accessary before the fact, and had not received these things as a douceur for the part which he took in the transaction. They went out, Probert, says under the pretence of going to Mr. Nicholls's Mrs. Probert says they went out under the same pretence, and that they never went to him. Mr. Nicholls says they never went to him. Probert again said, that they carried the lantern down the lane with them. The boy Addis so far confirms this, that he says before they went out they asked for a lantern Probert says, that they had told him the next morning, that they had been down the lane to look for the knife and pistol. Now we find, if you believe the two men, Harrington and Hunt, who were working in the lane, that two persons came down the lane at an early hour on Saturday morning, one of whom wore a white, and the other a black hat Harrington, it is to be observed, only swears to the person of one of these individuals, viz. the one with the white hat, who was, he says, the prisoner Thurtell. Thurtell, it is proved, however, had no white hat of his own, but Probert had one. Now, the question is, whether Thurtell had this hat of Probert's? On this point, a piece of evidence not immaterial, is that of Susan Woodruff the cook-maid, who, in the course of the evening, went into the parlour of the cottage, and saw John Thurtell lying on the sofa with her master's hat on his head. Now, when it was proved that Thurtell and Hunt were searching about apparently for the pistol and knife, and that afterwards a pistol and knife were found near the place where they had searched, the testimony of Hunt and Harrington becomes a very material piece of evidence, not in itself, but as corroborating and confirming the positive testimony of Probert.—[After reading in the evidence of Probert, to the part where Thurtell is represented to have produced the gold watch, the Learned Judge asked]—Is there a confirmation of this? According to Mrs Probert, Thurtell produced the chain and gave it her. Mrs Probert, too, it must be remarked, is perfectly admissible as a witness, for her husband is not included in the charge against the prisoners at the bar. Even if he had not been acquitted, I may remark, she would not have been inadmissible as an incompetent or infamous witness, but she would not have been examined, on account of that wise and humane provision of the law of England, which, for the strengthening and rendering sacred the domestic ties, would not allow the evidence of a wife to be taken as a charge against her husband. Mrs Probert, therefore, is now perfectly admissible, and no otherwise incredible, or to be distrusted, than on that account, which the prisoner Thurtell very properly gave weight to in his address—viz. the consideration that she so long kept a chain which she must have suspected to have been obtained by the medium of a crime. But what the nature or strength of the suspicion was, it is not for us to say, to say that she could have suspected such a crime as murder to have been committed, would be to go further than humanity or justice will warrant us. Thurtell, she says, gave it her, and Miss Noyes says he put the chain round her neck. Respecting the watch too, which is mentioned by Probert, there is in confirmation the evidence of Upson and Forrester. Thurtell, Upson tell us, said to him that he threw away the watch over the palings beyond Watford, in a place where there was some grass, to get rid of it To Forrester he said, that Hunt was a rascal for so nosing him, that he would on no account have done so to him. and among other things, that he had offered the watch for sale. In this particular, therefore, Probert is confirmed by these witnesses Here I have been unwillingly drawn into the mention of a conversation affecting Hunt. It has been very properly said by Mr, Thessiger, that this conversation which passed between the prisoner Thurtell and others, not in the presence of Hunt, should not be permitted to make any impression against Hunt. I therefore mention it only, as it corroborates the testimony of Probert respecting Thurtell The Learned Judge having read the part of the testimony of Probert, in which are detailed the circumstances of the murder, and where Thurtell is represented to have said, " When I first shot him he jumped out of the gig, and ran like the devil, singing out, that if I would spare his life he would deliver all he had won." He remarked, singing out is a maritime term I asked at that time whether Thurtell had not been in the navy It subsequently appeared, from the testimony of Captain M'Kinley, that he had The use of this term is a circumstance very fit to be taken into your consideration, as it gives a probability to this part of the testimony of Probert And here this brings us to the consideration of the motives of the crime. In the case of all atrocious crimes, one is naturally anxious to find a motive for the guilt It appears from this part of the testimony, that there had been previously gambling transactions between the prisoner Thurtell and the deceased The crime therefore, if it was committed, may have had its origin in that dreadful vice of gambling, which the prisoner Thurtell, in his address to you, has so properly marked with reprobation, a vice which deadens all the good feelings of our nature, which leads to the commission of crimes we should not otherwise have dreamed of, and I hope the dreadful events which have been brought before you, will be a lesson, if any such be needed, to our nobility and gentry, if it be true, as he has said, that a large proportion of them has set him an example of an attachment to the baneful vice Yes, I trust that the business of this day, whatever way it ends, will be an effectual as it is a dreadful warning against practices which lead to consequences so fatal to the peace of society The Learned Judge then remarked that the appearance of pistol corroberated Probert's evidence of the manner of the murder. As to the carpet bag and gun, he observed, these were proved both by the man and woman servants to have been at the cottage. They were also proved to have been the property of Weare. It became the Jury then to ask themselves how they could have been brought there, except on the supposition of Thurtell's guilt? If, indeed, they believed Probert to have been the man, he might have brought them there, but of that they would judge from the rest of the evidence.

The prisoner, Thurtell, here interposed· My Lord, the double-barrel gun that I carried down to Probert's cottage, was sold by auction at the levy; I beg your Lordship's pardon, but this was omitted by accident in my case.

Mr Justice PARK If you have overlooked evidence which you have now present to produce, I will hear it If you mean that you have omitted to make a statement in your address to the Jury, I will make it for you with pleasure, and the Jury will judge what weight is to be attributed to it, though they will recollect that a prisoner's statement is not to be taken as conclusive evidence of the fact.

Mr Justice PARK proceeded to read the evidence of Probert, respecting the disposal of the body and effects On this point he observed, you have the confirmation of the wife, who overheard the whispering and the talking in the parlor, and saw something dragged from the stable, along the garden towards the pond,

Thurtell here stated, that the Under Sheriff could prove that the double-barrelled gun had been sold.

Mr Hawkins, one of the Under Sheriffs, was then called and sworn Thurtell asked him whether his double-barrelled gun had not been sold at the sale of Probert's effects?

Mr HAWKINS· There was a double-barrelled gun.

Mr Justice PARK· Whose gun was it?

Witness. We understood it to be Probert's.

Mr. Justice PARK. If it were not, you would have been authorised in levying it. I am ready to listen to any suggestion of the prisoner's, but the fact he brings forward proves nothing, the identity of the gun is completely proved It came with Thurtell in his carriage, and went away with him, according to the testimony of the servant boy. That could not have been the gun sold as the gun of Probert. The Learned Judge then proceeded to read the rest of the evidence of Probert, in which he was confirmed by the testimony of Thomas Thurtell, who spoke to the change in the dress and appearance of Hunt; by Mr Nicholls, who spoke of the visit made to him, by Richard Addis, the servant boy, who said that he was sent to London without having any business to do there—a statement which agreed with Probert's testimony, that he was sent there to be out of the way. The testimony of Probert, that the body was first put into one sack, and subsequently taken out of that, and put into another, was corroborated by the testimony of Anne Woodruff, the servant maid, who saw a wet sack hanging up in the chaise-house. In his cross examination, Probert said, that up to the day when he went before the Grand Jury, he had said to Mr Franklin, the chaplain, that both he and Hunt were innocent of the murder. This might be said to be inconsistent with his present testimony: but it was not inconsistent with the notions which persons like him not unfrequently entertained. He may have considered, however unwarrantably, that a person was not guilty of a murder, when his hand was not used in the perpetration of it. The Learned Judge then read over, with a few observations, the evidence of Mrs. Probert, Thomas Noyes, Miss Noyes, and Thomas Thurtell. On the evidence of Miss Noyes, he remarked, that it was a material circumstance, that she had heard a gig pass the cottage between eight and nine o'clock. The Jury might draw an inference, as to what persons were probably then passing. She also stated, it was to be observed, that when Probert, Hunt, and Thurtell went out of the cottage, on the Friday evening, they said, that they were going to Mr. Nicholls's, that, when they returned, they said Mr. Nicholls was out, and that this last fact was contradicted by Mr Nicholls himself It was therefore necessarily to be inferred, that they went out for some purpose which they wished to conceal. In the evidence of Tetsall, it was to be observed, that Hunt, who had previously been in the habit of wearing long large whiskers, had shaved them all off on Monday It was for the consideration of the Jury whether this fact should have any weight, though undoubtedly the fancy of a man, in such a matter, might suddenly change. Rexworthy's evidence was given as to the fact of Thurtell and the deceased having been at his house, and, as to the identity of the body of Weare, his testimony is confirmed by the brother of the deceased and by other evidence. There can, I think, be no doubt about it. The other facts to which he gives evidence are I think not material Mrs. Maloney, the laundress, identified the wearing apparel and property of Mr. Weare. You will consider, Gentlemen, how it is to be accounted for that those clothes on the table which were the property of a gentleman in Lyon's-inn, at three o'clock in the afternoon, should get down at nine or ten o'clock at night to a place in the county of Hertford? How could it be possible that these things should be in possession of John Thurtell without throwing on him a strong suspicion of guilt? It has often been said by me, on other occasions, and by other Judges continually, that the early possession of property that has been stolen throws on the party so possessing it the necessity of showing how he obtained it. It is not enough, in such a case, for him to assert his innocence, he should produce evidence to show in what manner he obtained that property. I will, therefore, not suppose at all that Mr. Weare went out of town with Mr Thurtell, we know that he did go out of town, that he was never heard of, or rather never seen afterwards till he was found in a ditch, and that the property very soon after his having left town was seen 11 or 12 miles off, in the possession of another. The hackney coachman, who took Mr. Weare from Lyon's Inn, says that he met a gentleman in the New Road, whom he took up into the coach with Weare This gentleman was dressed in a long white great coat, but he cannot say that it was Thurtell. Whether it was Thurtell or not is not important. When Hunt went to hire the gig, the Learned Judge remarked, he informed the witness Shepherd that he was going to Dartford. This was a very material circumstance, as affecting Hunt. Why was it, if he knew nothing of what was going on, that he gave this false account of the direction that he was about to take? Why should he not have said that he was going into Hertfordshire, instead of endeavouring to throw them on an entirely wrong scent? The next witness, Stephen Marsh, stated a very important circumstance, and one very confirmatory of the testimony of Probert He says, that Hunt took a gig from Charing-cross about half-past three on Monday, and returned about half-past two o'clock in the morning—a very unseasonable hour; that the gig and horse were very dirty, and that there was a little blood at the bottom of the gig This agreed with the testimony of Probert, who said that in that interval the body was removed in that gig from the pond in Probert's garden to the pond where it was ultimately found. The evidence of Stephen Probatt, though not material in proof of the facts of the case, shewed the shocking and depraved mind of Hunt If the conduct attributed to Hunt consisted in mere idle declarations, I should pay as little attention to them as the prisoner's Counsel seems inclined to do; but the facts which I am about to mention are such as cannot be so lightly spoken of The Learned Judge then read from Probatt's evidence.

The prisoner, THURTELL said, My Lord, there is a fact in Field's evidence I wish to call your attention to He says that Hunt was at his house on the Tuesday.

Mr Justice PARK: Yes, Sir, but I am not going to read Field's evidence now, I have read it all before

THURTELL But I wish, my Lord, to point out a fact which escaped you; namely, that he saw Hunt there on the Tuesday alone

Mr. Justice PARK then read Field's evidence.

THURTELL I did not know, before my Counsel came down, that what Hunt said to the prisoners could be admitted in evidence. There was a whole yard full of them, to prove that he then told them that he planned the murder alone. It is with this view that I point attention to the fact mentioned by Field

Mr. Justice PARK You know that statements as to what witnesses could prove are of no use

THURTELL There is another fact that I wish to mention to your Lordship.—Freeman spoke of a yellow gig

Mr. Justice PARK: I am not come to that yet

THURTELL. No, my Lord, but I mention it now that I may not have to interrupt your Lordship again Freeman swore before the Magistrates that it was a yellow gig which he saw.—He also said it was a bay horse, which I omitted to state I wish your Lordship to look at the depositions before the Magistrates

Mr. Justice PARK looked at the depositions

THURTELL It is not the Coroner's depositions, my Lord, that I mean.

Mr. J PARK: No, Sir, it is not that I am looking at —(To the Jury)—I have asked the prisoner's Counsel what it is the prisoner means, as he is certainly entitled to any inference that can be drawn from the facts proved in evidence. It is stated by Field, that Hunt was at his house on the Tuesday alone, and the prisoner wishes it to be inferred that Hunt came there to throw the body into the pond alone. It is for you to consider what weight this inference is entitled to.

Mr Justice PARK then proceeded with the rest of the

evidence, and, in summing up the testimony of James Freeman, he said he had looked at the depositions before the Magistrates according to the suggestion of the prisoner, and found that not one word was said either about the colour of the gig or the horse

Mr ANDREWS suggested, we believe, that the wife of Freeman had spoken before the Magistrates of the colour of the gig and horse.

Mr Justice PARK· Freeman's wife has not been examined here It is of no use to rebut evidence that has not been called. I will not mention irregularities in such a case, they are not worthy of being mentioned, where a matter so important to individuals and society is at issue. But there is not a word of such a thing as you mention in the deposition of Freeman

The Learned Judge briefly stated the substance of the remaining evidence On the evidence of John Fleet being read by the Learned Judge, Thurtell observed: The coat taken from my lodgings in the Haymarket was a blue coat It is in the prison here. By omission, it was not proved

Mr. Justice PARK Gentlemen of the Jury, I have now gone through the whole of this evidence, and I am not conscious that I have omitted any fact which can bear on the case of the prisoners one way or the other. We shall have this satisfaction in the duty that we perform, that notwithstanding the attempts to prevent it, we shall discharge it with dispassionateness and care In behalf of the defence has been called Mr. Wadeson. a respectable solicitor, as every body knows, of the city of London He states, that he would not believe Probert on his oath unless he were confirmed by other testimony; and certainly, from what I have heard of him in this place, I must join with Mr. Wadeson, in that opinion In fact, in that character of Probert, Mr. Wadeson may be said to have told you all the law respecting accomplices. They are not to be believed on their oaths, except in as far as they are confirmed by other testimony. With respect to Hunt, you have heard that he is to apply for mercy to the Crown The prisoner, Thurtell, has made a long address to you, and it is for you to pay every attention due to his statement The prisoner Thurtell is to be distinguished from the prisoner Hunt in this, that he has called three witnesses to speak to his character—a respectable naval officer, Captain M'Kinley, a Mr. Haydon, and a Mr.

Walmsley. It must be observed of this testimony, and I speak it with concern, that it is in great part to character of an ancient date. If down to the present time Captain M'Kinley had known intimately the prisoner Thurtell—if he could have stated that his conduct was uniformly correct, and that he never had known him guilty of acts of inhumanity, such a character would undoubtedly have had considerable weight in a dubious case But when he tells us he has not known the prisoner since 1814; and when the prisoner, in his own statement, speaks of the difficulties and distresses which he has since that time encountered, and which too often have an influence on the character of him who suffers them, the value of that testimony cannot be considerable. Mr Haydon says, that he has known Thurtell down to the present time, he does not say how long he has known him, but he says he has not lost sight of him for the last three years, and that he has always thought him a liberal and open-hearted man Mr. Walmsley, says he has known him to the present time. What his knowledge was, and how the acquaintance originated, he does not state, but he always thought the prisoner a gentlemanly and honest man. I must observe to you, Gentlemen, that testimony as to character ought to prevail only in cases where fair and rational doubts are entertained as to other evidence—or I may explain my principle, by stating, that if this prisoner had been proved to us to have maintained the most respectable character, we should not sit here to try that good character, or to allow that good character to prevail against the evidence of facts And, on the other hand, neither should we try his bad character —for if he had been the worst character in the land, we should not be justified in making use of it to bear out unsatifactory evidence as to the crime with which he specially stands charged The prisoner, indeed, has reason to complain of the horrible calumnies, which he states have been propagated concerning him, and it is inconceivable, if such things there are---for I myself know nothing of them---how men of liberal education, who have had the advantage of living in a land where good morals and sound religion are cherished---should be guilty of such conduct towards a man placed in the situation of the prisoner at the bar. But you, Gentlemen, are not to try the prisoner on his bad character, you are not to try him on his good character—you are to try whether he be guilty of the crime with which he is charged. And if he were an angel, I might say still, if the evidence as to that crime were clear and satisfactory, it would be your duty to return a verdict accordingly. If, on the other hand, there be rational doubts, such as may occur to fair minds, and to men acting on their oaths, you should then give the prisoner the benefits of these doubts, and throw into the scale whatever testimony to his character has been adduced. But, Gentlemen, and I can say no more than this, after the careful examination of the evidence through which I have led you, you must consider the weight of the facts proved in that evidence. If, notwithstanding the darkness at the time the crime was committed—if, notwithstanding the secresy with which guilt seeks to shroud itself, the finger of God has pointed as plainly to the criminals as if they had committed their crime in the face of day, and before your eyes, it is your duty to your country, your duty to God, your duty to yourselves, to pronounce the verdict which must satisfy your consciences, notwithstanding any feeling you may have towards the individuals its consequences may effect. Gentlemen, consider of your verdict

The Jury having consulted, desired to withdraw.—An officer was sworn to attend the Jury in the usual form.

The prisoner Hunt then said (before the Jury had withdrawn), "Will your Lordship allow me to say a few words?"

Mr. Justice PARK. I am greatly distressed to have appeals made to me which the law and the constitution of England do not permit me to attend to, but your very Learned Counsel shall communicate with you, and he will state to me what it is you wish to say, if it be of weight, I will hear you.

Mr. THESSIGER then communicated with Hunt for a minute or two, and afterwards spoke on the Bench to Mr. Justice Park.

Mr. Justice PARK then addressed the Jury, "Gentlemen, I have nothing to say to you"

The Jury then retired from the Court at half-past three o'clock.

About ten minutes before four, the Jury returned into Court, and were called over by their names, to which they all answered.

The Clerk of the Arraigns then asked in the usual form, whether John Thurtell was Guilty or Not Guilty of the Murder of which he stood arraigned?

The Foreman of the Jury, in a low tone, GUILTY.

CLERK. How say you, is Joseph Hunt Guilty nor Not Guilty?

FOREMAN. GUILTY, as an Accessary.

CLERK. Then you say they are both Guilty as they are indicted?—Foreman. Yes

The Prisoners heard the verdict unmoved.

The Judge was preparing to pass sentence of death, when Mr. Chitty moved an arrest of judgment, on account of the trial having been held on a day directed by a positive statute to be kept holy: the festival of the Epiphany—and begged his Lordship would recollect a story of Mr. Dunning, who, when Lord Mansfield said to him, " I shall sit on Good Friday," said, " Then your Lordship will be the first Judge since Pontius Pilate, who did. However, after a spirited and ingenious argument, the Learned Judge refused the motion.

THE JUDGMENT.

The Officer of the Court then said—What have you, or either of you, to say why sentence of death should not pass on you?

THURTELL. My Lord, before you pass sentence, I pray you to take into your serious consideration what I say. I now, for the last time, assert that I am innocent. I entreat a short delay in the execution of the sentence you may pass, as I have friends now at a distance, with whom it is necessary that I should transact some business. It is for the sake of some friends that are dear to me, that I ask this indulgence (here the prisoner seemed affected, and shed a tear), not for myself, for I am this moment ready; my request, I hope your Lordship will take into consideration, and beyond Sunday next is all I ask.

Mr. Justice PARK. John Thurtell, and you, Joseph Hunt; after a very fair, and I trust, a most impartial trial, a Jury of your country have with, I think, the most perfect propriety, found you guilty. It cannot but give great compunction to every feeling mind, that a person, who from his conduct this day, has shewn that he was born with capacity for better things —who, according to his statement, received in his childhood religious impressions from a kind and careful mother—who in his youth served his country without reproach—should, notwithstanding, have been guilty of so foul a crime. For notwithstanding your repeated and confident asseverations of your innocence, I must declare, that such has been the force of the evidence against you, that I am, in my mind, as confident of your guilt as if my mortal eyes had seen the commission of the crime. And I trust that you will not lay that flattering unction to your soul, that the declarations of your innocence will avail you here, still less before the all-seeing eye, who searches all hearts, and not add to your misfortunes and your guilt by rushing into his presence with a lie in your mouth and perjury in your right hand. You best know what your conscience says to those declarations of innocence, but on the evidence on which we must act, it does most clearly appear that you have been guilty of one of the most foul, most bloody, and deliberate murders that has ever been perpetrated. That you should go with your victim into those haunts of gamblers which afford the incentives to the basest and the most furious passions—that you should propose to introduce him to the house of your friend—that you should lead him to make preparation for enjoyment and for social intercourse with you, and that in the moment of darkness, before he reached that house, you should betray and murder him, does seem the height of cruelty and crime. If he was the person in point of human conduct which he is described to be, consider how much your guilt is aggravated in sending him to account before his Maker without one short moment of preparation. I say not this to aggravate your sufferings—I say it only to awaken your mind to the sense of your awful condition, and to lead you to the only refuge that is now left for you. Short as is your time of preparation for your great change, I trust you will lose not a moment in applying to the Throne of Grace. Short as it may be, too, recollect that it was more than twenty times told the space given by you to the unhappy man whose blood you violently shed. And I trust, too, that even in the past month, which the postponement of your trial has afforded you, instead of having fixed your mind entirely on the means of defence against the just punishment, which you cannot escape here, you have employed yourself in a way which must have been, and which must be more profitable to you, in seeking to make your peace with that God with whom is mercy towards the worst of sinners. I understand that the Clergyman of this gaol is a most respectable man. He will shew you the way to salvation, he will shew you that grace may yet be given to a contrite heart. Seek, O! seek it earnestly, I beseech you, knock earnestly at that gate which is never shut to a repentant sinner. Pour yourselves out at the feet of your Redeemer in humbleness and truth, and to his grace and mercy I commit you, and, while you are seeking for it, you shall have my devout and constant prayers that your supplications may be heard. (The Learned Judge was deeply affected, and wept during this warm exhortation.) The sentence of the law which I have to pronounce upon you,

John Thurtell, according to the Statute, is this—that you, John Thurtell, be taken to the place from whence you came, and from thence that you be taken on Friday, the 9th instant, to a place of execution, and that you be hanged by the neck till you be dead, and that your body be taken down and given to the surgeons for dissection. As for you, Joseph Hunt, the sentence of the law is, that you be taken from hence to the place from whence you came, and from thence to a place of execution, and that you be hanged by the neck till you be dead; and may God of his infinite mercy have compassion on both your souls

During the delivery of the sentence, Hunt covered his face for a short time with his handkerchief. Thurtell was attentive, but did not change countenance, and immediately after, having slightly bowed to the Bench, leaned over the bar to speak to some one who was near him, which he did in his usual manner. Soon after he passed Hunt, who was on his right, and leaned over towards the box where our Reporter was, and said, " I wish to speak a word to one of the Gentlemen there, the Reporters." One of them accordingly leaned forward to listen to him, but his intended communication was interrupted by the Officers of the Court, who seemed apprehensive, from his having come into too close contact with Hunt. He quietly withdrew at the suggestion of Mr. Wilson, to whom he has always expressed the greatest regard.

The Court was then dissolved.

As soon as sentence was passed, the two prisoners shook hands, and then retired to the back part of the dock.

On their arrival at the gaol, they were conducted into the kitchen, where their irons were again put on. As is customary on capital convictions for murder, the persons of the prisoners were searched, in order that every thing which might be used as a weapon of destruction might be removed.

The fastening of Thurtell's irons being completed, he was told he was to be placed in a different cell to that which he had previously occupied. He made no observation, but shaking his head in a significant manner, prepared to submit. Before he went he put out his hand to Bishop, and begged to shake hands with him for the last time, Bishop instantly grasped his hand, and they parted. He was then removed to one of the condemned cells, where he was left, attended by two persons, who are to remain with him till taken forth for execution. Some suspicions are entertained that he may design to destroy his own life, but to prevent this every precaution will be taken. Hunt scarcely uttered a word, he submitted to be searched in silence, and heaved several heavy sighs. He was so much depressed, in fact, that he appeared incapable of entering into conversation. He, like Thurtell, was removed into a condemned cell, and was attended by two persons in the same manner. He was informed that Mr. Harmer, his solicitor, had set off to town, in order that he might draw up a memorial to the Crown in his favour, as quickly as possible.

We understand that the executioner from Newgate came down to Hertford by Norris's coach, in the morning, bringing with him the ropes necessary for his dreadful office. He came outside the coach, and was certainly not considered a very agreeable companion by those to whom his business was suggested.

The execution of Thurtell, it is understood, will take place in a gravel-pit. opposite the prison, which is the usual spot for such purposes in this county. A new drop has been prepared for the occasion.

Hertford, Eleven o'Clock.

When the Rev. Mr. Franklin saw Thurtell this evening, his spirits were completely gone. He found him sitting in the cell, bathed in tears, and evidently oppressed by great mental anguish Mr. Franklin asked him whether he felt contrition for the past; he answered in the affirmative, he then asked him whether he was ready to make his peace with God? to which he replied that he was; he felt, he said, that this world had closed upon him, and that he had but a very few hours to live; that he was perfectly ready to meet death in any shape, but that he could not contemplate so awful an exit, without recollecting those near and dear connexions to whom his death must be a source of affliction and shame. From the state in which the wretched man's mind then was, it was evident, that had he been pressed, he would have made an ample disclosure of all he knew connected with the horrible occurrence, for which he is to suffer. The Rev. Gentleman felt, that under such circumstances, however, it would be unfair to press him, and therefore abstained from putting any questions. He pressed upon him the necessity of devoting the few hours he had to live in preparing himself for death, and left him in a state of deep dejection—not, apparently, arising from any apprehensions of personal suffering, but from a conviction of the disgraceful situation in which he was placed. Mr. Franklin afterwards visited Hunt, who was crying bitterly, but as the fate of this prisoner may be considered in some degree, uncertain, his stay was not long.

It is undertood that there will be a condemned sermon to-morrow. The execution of Thurtell is fixed for Friday morning, at ten o'clock Hunt, of course, will not suffer with him. By the usage at assizes, he will not suffer for a fortnight. The alledged promise, by which Hunt was induced to make his confession, is to come under the consideration of the twelve judges.

Mr. Jay sent off an express to Norwich, to Thurtell's father, immediately after the return of the verdict this day.

Thomas Thurtell had an interview with his brother this evening, they were both greatly affected,

EXECUTION OF THURTELL.

AT ten o'clock on Thursday night Thurtell intimated an earnest wish that Hunt might pass the night in his apartment. Hunt was introduced, he was received by Thurtell with a strong manifestation of cordiality. Thurtell took him by the hand, and said " Joe, the past is forgotten. I stand on the brink of eternity, and we meet now only as friends. It may be your fate to lose your life as ignominously as myself, but I hope the Royal mercy will be extended to you, and that you will live to repent of your past errors. Although you have been my enemy, I freely forgive you. Hunt, who had entered the room with feelings bordering on apprehension that some unfortunate turn had taken place in his affairs, and that he was himself to suffer, was suddenly relieved by this address, and squeezing Thurtell's hand most vehemently, he burst into tears, he then sat down by the fire, and Thurtell and he continued to pray, and to read until one o'clock. Soon after one, he shewed symptoms of fatigue, and laying himself on the bed, uttered a fervent prayer to the Almighty, for strength to meet his approaching execution with the firmness of a man, and the resignation of a Christian. In a few moments afterwards he dropped into a profound sleep.

During Thursday afternoon persons of all ranks were seen driving into Hertford, by the desire of being present at the execution, and influenced by an expectation that some extraordinary declaration would be made by Thurtell in his dying moments. All the inns were completely filled. It would seem from the appearance of some, and the jaded state of their cattle, that they had come long distances; many hundreds of them had actually come from Worcester, the scene of the late contest between Spring and Langan.— Among these we noticed several distinguished leaders in the sporting circles, whose acquaintance with Thurtell rendered the approaching tragedy still more attractive. Many were incapable of procuring beds, while others would not submit to the extraordinary prices demanded. In this state of things, scarcely a public house was closed for the night, and parties remained engaged in drinking and gambling till the light of day burst upon them. As the morning approached, fresh arrivals added to the bustle which prevailed, the roads from London, Cambridge, St. Albans, and elsewhere, were covered with vehicles of every description.

In the course of Thursday, Thurtell saw *The Times* newspaper, in which mention was made of his resignation and contrition. He expressed great satisfaction at the statement, read it over twice and observed, that it would be seen by his father and his family, to whom it would afford the utmost gratification.

MORNING OF EXECUTION.

On Friday morning, at day-break, the road between the prison wall and the hedge, was completely choaked up with spectators; the hedges, and the fields beyond, were also thickly thronged by the multitude. As the day advanced London sent forth its immense swarms, who came pouring in on every side. Every road leading to Hertford was thronged with travellers.

At half-past six, Mr. Wilson, jun. entered the prisoner's room and found him on the bed, fast asleep, and snoring loudly. The prisoner Hunt was also in a deep slumber, sitting by the fire-side. Mr. Wilson, unwilling to disturb their repose, retired, and at seven o'clock returned again with his father. The wretched men were still asleep, unconscious of the scene which was so shortly to be acted, and in which one of them was to take so prominent a part. Mr. Wilson approached the bed of Thurtell, and found his face covered over with the rug, and so profound was his sleep at this moment, that he could not hear him breathe He immediately uncovered the prisoner's face, and called him by name. Thurtell started up, and for a moment seemed lost to his situation, not even knowing where he was. Mr. Wilson addressed him, and his recollection immediately returned.

During this conversation Hunt awoke, and casting a look of despair towards the bed, seemed to shudder within himself, and then became extremely dejected. Thurtell arose, and asked for some water to wash. Having bathed his face, his breakfast was brought in; it consisted of some tea and bread and butter, but he partook only of the former, and that but slightly.

At eight o'clock the Chaplain arrived—he shook hands with Thurtell, and addressed him in the most soothing language, expressing at the same time his gratification at finding the unhappy man in a frame of mind so firm and composed Mr. Wilson retired, taking with him the three attendants The Chaplain on being left alone with Thurtell and Hunt, called upon them to join him in prayer

At eleven o'clock, the mass of spectators had increased The road at each end was completely blocked up, so as to prevent the possibility of any person passing, and the coaches going to and coming from London, were obliged to take a circuitous route

At half-past eleven Thurtell and Hunt were conducted into the chapel. The Rev. Mr. Franklin then administered the sacrament to them. Thurtell read the appropriate prayers in a distinct and audible voice, and seemed fully impressed with the importance of this solemn rite. At its conclusion, Thurtell turned round to the prisoner Hunt, and grasped his hand repeatedly, and renewed, in the most forcible terms, the assurance of his perfect forgiveness of the past, and of his being about to die in peace and charity with all the world. The Chaplain and Mr. Nicholson retired from the chapel, leaving Mr. Wilson, and the prisoner Thurtell alone. Hunt had previously been reconducted to his cell, overpowered by his feelings. Mr. Wilson then turning to Thurtell, said, "Now Thurtell, as there is no eye to witness what is passing between us but that of God, you must not be surprised if I ask you a question." Thurtell turned round, and regarded him with a look of surprise. Mr. Wilson continued—"If you intend to make any confession, I think you cannot do it at a better period than the present." Thurtell paused for a few moments. Mr. Wilson then went on to say, "I ask you if you acknowledge the justice of your sentence." Thurtell immediately seized both Mr. Wilson's hands, and pressed them with great fervour within his own, and said, " I am quite satisfied. I forgive the world; I die in peace and charity with all mankind, and that is all I wish to go forth upon this occasion."

The Chaplain then returned to the prisoner, and offered him some further words of comfort, asking him, whether there was any thing he could do to ease his mind with respect to his family and friends. Thurtell replied that he was anxious the Rev. Gentleman would write to his father, and inform him of his extreme contrition, resignation, and penitence, which Mr. Franklin promised faithfully to do. The unfortunate man then uttered a short prayer, that the minds of his family might be strengthened under the deep affliction they must feel, and of which he had been the unhappy author.

At twelve o'clock precisely, Mr. Nicholson tapped at the door with his wand, as the signal that the hour of execution had arrived. Thurtell then seized Mr. Franklin's hands, and thanked him, not alone for all the personal kindnesses for which he was indebted to him, but for that Christian spirit with which he was about to depart this world. The chapel-door was then thrown open, and the prisoner went forth with a steady and assured step. He looked round with perfect calmness. The distance from the chapel-door to the door leading to the scaffold was not more than ten yards; and thither he was accompanied by the Chaplain. The Under Sheriff, Mr. Wilson, an assistant of Mr. Wilson's, and the Upper Turnkey. The Church-bell mournfully tolled as he advanced. On their arrival at the door, Thurtell again squeezed Mr. Franklin's hand, and again exclaimed "God bless you, Sir; God bless you." He then mounted the steps, preceeded by the Under Sheriff and the executioner, and followed by Mr. Wilson and the head Turnkey.

THE EXECUTION

The scaffold was surrounded by a body of the javelin-men, and some persons in an elevated situation, having intimated the approach of the prisoner, there was a sudden exclamation from the surrounding multitude, and almost all present took off their hats. Thurtell, on taking his station under the gallows, looked round with a countenance unchanged by the awfulness of his situation —His manner was firm and undaunted, at the same time that it betrayed no unbecoming levity After regarding the crowd for a moment, he appeared to recognize an individual beneath him, to whom he bowed in a friendly manner Previously to his mounting the scaffold, he had begged that as little delay as possible might take place in his execution after his appearance upon the platform

His hands were confined with handcuffs, instead of being tied with cord, as is usually the case on such occasions, and, at his own request, his arms were not pinioned. He wore a pair of black kid gloves. The irons, which were very heavy, and consisted of a succession of chain links, were still on his legs, and were held up in the middle by a Belcher handkerchief tied round his waist.

The moment he placed himself under the beam, the executioner commenced by taking off his cravat. He stood perfectly calm and unmoved, holding out his neck in order to facilitate the hangman's duty. A white cap was then put upon his head and drawn over his eyes, this cap was so thin, as still to afford the wretched man a view of those about him, and he continued to look round in various directions. At that moment, the clock sounded the last stroke of twelve. The rope was then placed round his neck, and while the executioner was attaching the other end to the beam above, Thurtell looked up, and turning to him, said, " give me fall enough " The hangman replied, " that he might be assured he should have plenty of fall, and that all would be right." Thurtell next turned to Mr Wilson, and repeated the same request, and that gentleman assured him, that his wishes had been fully attended to All being now in readiness, Mr Wilson drew close to the prisoner, and squeezing his hands, exclaimed, " Thurtell, God Almighty bless you," the prisoner pressing his hands in return, responded "God bless you, Sir "

Mr. Wilson then stood back upon some boards placed immediately behind the drop, and the executioner having previously retired, the Under Sheriff, with his wand, gave the last fatal signal the drop suddenly fell, and the unhappy man was in an instant launched into eternity. His sufferings were but momentary, for, with the exception of a few convulsive motions of his hands and legs, he seemed to be deprived of all sensation. Thus perished, in an untimely manner a man, who, but for untoward circumstances and the violence of his passions, might have been the pride of his family.

During the whole of this appalling ceremony there was not the slightest symptom of emotion discernible in his features, his demeanour was perfectly calm and tranquil, and he behaved like a man acquainted with the dreadful ordeal he was about to pass, but not unprepared to meet it Though his fortitude was thus conspicuous, it was evident, from the alteration in his appearance, that in the interval between his conviction and his execution, he must have suffered much. He looked careworn, his countenance had assumed

CPSIA information can be obtained at www.ICGtesting.com
Printed in the USA
LVOW110759230213

321408LV00004B/160/P

9 781274 893673